FIRST AID
MANUAL

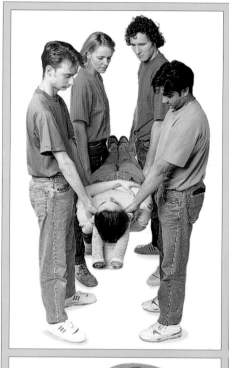

THE VOLUNTARY AID SOCIETIES

The Irish
Red Cross Society

The Order of
Malta Ambulance Corps

FIRST AID MANUAL

The Authorised Manual of
The Irish Red Cross Society
and
The Order of Malta Ambulance Corps

Dr Michael Webb CStJ FFOM DIH
Medical Director (Association and Resources),
St. John Ambulance

Mr Roy Scott JP MD FRCSGlas FRCSEd DL
Chief Medical Officer, St. Andrew's Ambulance Association

Sir Peter Beale KBE FRCP FFCM FFOM DTM&H
Chief Medical Adviser, British Red Cross

DORLING KINDERSLEY
LONDON • NEW YORK • SYDNEY • DEHLI • MUNICH • PARIS • JOHANNESBURG
www.dk.com

A DORLING KINDERSLEY BOOK
www.dk.com

Managing Editor	Jemima Dunne
Managing Art Editor	Philip Gilderdale
Senior Art Editor	Karen Ward
Project Editors	Annelise Evans, Dawn Bates
Art Editor	Mary-Elizabeth McNeill
Designer	Lucy Parissi
Production	Manjit Sihra
Photography	Steve Gorton

Text for Irish editon prepared with guidelines from the
The American Heart Association and The Irish Heart Foundation

This edition first published 1997
Updated edition published 2000

UK edition first published in Great Britain in 1997 by
Dorling Kindersley Limited, 9 Henrietta Street, Covent Garden,
London WC2E 8PS

A CIP catalogue record for this book is available from
the British Library

ISBN 0-906077-07-9

Reproduced in Singapore by Colourscan
Printed in Hong Kong by Wing King Tong Co. Ltd.

FOREWORD

The need to heighten awareness of first-aid principles faces new challenges with the dawn of the new Millennium. Changes in the Irish economy in recent years have meant many people face a faster-paced lifestyle, which brings its own attendant risks. More cars, more child-care places, more infrastructural projects, and a more mobile workforce – that trains and retrains continuously – all contribute to the increasing need for basic first-aid assistance.

Other changes in our society too have lead to an increased demand for first-aid training. These include the needs employers and employees for workplace first-aid programmes as well as the requirements of the growing sports sector, community-based employment schemes, schools, parents and carers. Other wider developments in Irish State policy make their own contributions to the calls for first-aid training. Policies concerning community resuscitation programmes, first responder schemes and empowering vulnerable groups, all combine to emphasise the growing value of first aid.

This revised text is the standard text on first aid in Ireland. The easy-to-read format with extensive high-quality step-by-step photography make it *the* choice as an aid to practical training as well as an ongoing reference manual. The design makes it easy for every reader to follow life-saving steps as well as understand the correct action for dealing with less serious conditions.

As first aid is chiefly the application of practical skills combined with some core knowledge it is best learned on a structured course. The Irish Red Cross runs first-aid courses for the general public as well as occupational first aid courses for the work place. To find out about these courses contact your local Red Cross Branch or National Head Office by telephone or via the Internet.

IRISH RED CROSS 2000

CONTENTS

4 RESUSCITATION

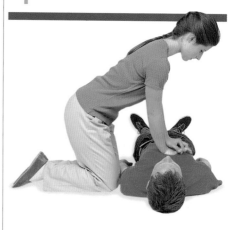

5 DISORDERS OF THE RESPIRATORY SYSTEM

12 FOREIGN BODIES

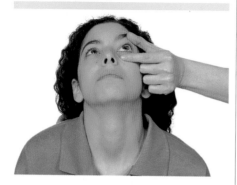

13 POISONING

14 BITES AND STINGS

15 EMERGENCY CHILDBIRTH

16 MISCELLANEOUS CONDITIONS

17 DRESSINGS AND BANDAGES

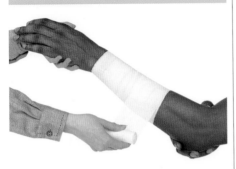

18 HANDLING AND TRANSPORT

19 EMERGENCY FIRST AID

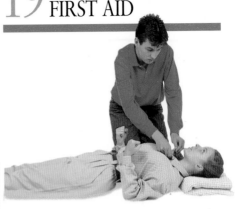

INTRODUCTION

This new edition of the *Manual* has been fully revised and expanded. All of the first-aid treatments are illustrated photographically to give you clear and comprehensive step-by-step guidance.

First-aid procedures are constantly being reviewed to ensure that the casualty is getting the best possible care. This edition provides you with the most up-to-date guidelines for all conditions and first-aid treatments, including the latest recommendations for resuscitation techniques.

To help you to understand why and how first-aid techniques work, greater emphasis has been placed on how we are structured (anatomy) and how we function (physiology). A clearer understanding of what is

normal should help you to decide what may be wrong or abnormal, and enable you to provide the correct treatment.

There is an expanded chapter on Emergency First Aid that gives you at-a-glance, life-saving action plans for all emergency situations. This quick-reference guide has been placed at the end of the Manual for easy access, but it is also provided as a separate booklet for you to keep in your first-aid kit or to carry with you at all times.

Wherever you are using it, at home, at work or as a basis for training, this indispensable Manual is the only guide to first aid that you will need to take you into the next millenium.

HOW TO USE THIS BOOK

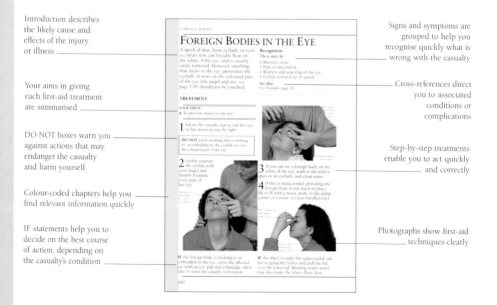

Introduction describes the likely cause and effects of the injury or illness

Your aims in giving each first-aid treatment are summarised

DO NOT boxes warn you against actions that may endanger the casualty and harm yourself

Colour-coded chapters help you find relevant information quickly

IF statements help you to decide on the best course of action, depending on the casualty's condition

Signs and symptoms are grouped to help you recognise quickly what is wrong with the casualty

Cross-references direct you to associated conditions or complications

Step-by-step treatments enable you to act quickly and correctly

Photographs show first-aid techniques clearly

WHAT IS FIRST AID?

1

First aid is the immediate assistance or treatment given to someone injured or suddenly taken ill before the arrival of an ambulance, doctor or other appropriately qualified person. The person offering this help to a casualty must act calmly and with confidence, and above all must be willing to offer assistance whenever the need arises.

Being a First Aider

Most people can, by following the guidance given in this book, give useful and effective first aid. However, first aid is a skill based on knowledge, training, and experience. The term "First Aider" is usually applied to someone who has completed a theoretical and practical instruction course, and passed a professionally supervised examination.

The standard First Aid Certificate, awarded by the Irish Red Cross Society, and the Order of Malta Ambulance Corps, is proof of all-round competence. A certificate is valid for only three years; to keep up to date, you must be re-examined after further training. Once qualified, you may volunteer for additional training to broaden the scope of your skills.

CONTENTS

AIMS OF FIRST AID

◆ To preserve life.
◆ To limit worsening of the condition.
◆ To promote recovery.

THE FIRST AIDER IS:

◆ Highly trained.
◆ Examined and regularly re-examined.
◆ Up-to-date in knowledge and skill.

BEING A FIRST AIDER

The first aid learned from a manual or course is not quite like reality. Most of us feel apprehensive when dealing with "the real thing". By facing up to these feelings, we are better able to cope with the unexpected.

Doing your part

First aid is not an exact science, and is thus open to human error. Even with appropriate treatment, and however hard you try, a casualty may not respond as hoped. Some conditions inevitably lead to death, even with the best medical care. If you do your best, your conscience can be clear.

Assessing risks

The golden rule is, "First do no harm", while applying the principle of "calculated risk". You should use the treatment that is most likely to be of benefit to a casualty, but do not use a doubtful treatment just for the sake of doing *something*.

The "Good Samaritan"

This principle supports those acting in an emergency (but not those who go beyond accepted boundaries). If you keep calm, and you follow the guidelines in this book, you need not fear any legal consequences.

PROTECTING THE CASUALTY

To avoid infecting a casualty when giving first aid, if possible you should:
♦ avoid direct contact with body fluids where possible;
♦ wash your hands;
♦ wear protective gloves.
IF gloves are unavailable, life-saving treatment must still be given.

YOUR RESPONSIBILITIES AS A FIRST AIDER

♦ To assess a situation quickly and safely, and summon appropriate help.
♦ To protect casualties and others at the scene from possible danger.
♦ To identify, as far as possible, the injury or nature of the illness affecting a casualty.
♦ To give each casualty early and appropriate treatment, treating the most serious conditions first.
♦ To arrange for the casualty's removal to hospital, into the care of a doctor, or to his or her home.

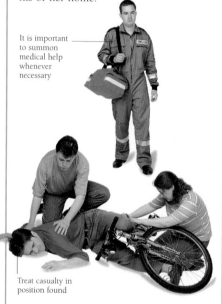

It is important to summon medical help whenever necessary

Treat casualty in position found

♦ To remain with a casualty until appropriate care is available.
♦ To report your observations to those taking over care of the casualty, and to give further assistance if required.
♦ To prevent cross-infection between yourself and the casualty (*see left and page 14*) as much as possible.
  More information concerning first-aid requirements at work and in public places can be found on page 250.

GIVING CARE WITH CONFIDENCE

Every casualty needs to feel secure and in safe hands. You can create an air of confidence and assurance by:
◆ being in control, both of yourself and the problem;
◆ acting calmly and logically;
◆ being gentle, but firm, with your hands, and speaking to the casualty kindly, but purposefully.

Building up trust

Talk to the casualty throughout your examination and treatment.
◆ Explain what you are going to do.
◆ Try to answer questions honestly to allay fears as best you can. If you do not know the answer, say so.

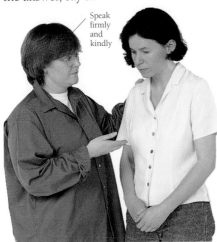

Speak firmly and kindly

◆ Continue to reassure the casualty even when your treatment is complete – find out about the next-of-kin, or anyone else who should be contacted about the incident. Ask if you can help to make arrangements so that any responsibilities the casualty may have, such as collecting a child from school, can be taken care of.
◆ Do not leave someone whom you believe to be dying. Continue to talk to the casualty, and hold his or her hand; never let the person feel alone.

Talking to relatives

The task of informing relatives of a death is usually the job of the garda or the doctor on duty. However, it may well be that you have to tell relatives or friends that someone has been taken ill, or has been involved in an accident.

Always check that you are speaking to the right person first. Then explain, as simply and honestly as you can, what has happened, and, if appropriate, where the casualty has been taken. Do not be vague or exaggerate; you may cause undue alarm. It is better to admit ignorance than to give misleading information.

Coping with children

Young children are extremely perceptive and will quickly detect any uncertainty on your part. Gain an injured or sick child's confidence by talking first to someone he or she trusts – a parent if possible. If the parent accepts you and believes you will help, this confidence will be conveyed to the child.

Always explain simply to a child what is happening and what you intend to do; do not talk over his or her head. You should not separate a child from his or her mother, father or other trusted person.

Reassure child by explaining what you are going to do

Looking After Yourself

It is important not to jeopardise your personal safety. Do not attempt heroic rescues in hazardous circumstances.

Coping with unpleasantness

The practice of first aid can be messy, smelly, and distasteful, and you may feel that you will not be able to cope with this. Such fears are common but usually groundless. First-aid training will bolster your self-reliance and confidence and will help you to control your emotions in a difficult situation.

Taking stock after an emergency

Assisting at an emergency is a stressful event, and you may suffer a "delayed reaction" some time afterwards. You may feel satisfaction or even elation, but it is common to be upset, particularly if the casualty was a stranger and you might not know the outcome of your efforts.

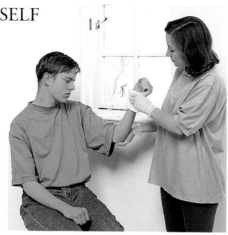

Never reproach yourself or bottle up your feelings. It often helps to talk over your experience with a first-aid trainer. Patient confidentiality must be maintained.

See also:
Stress, *page 27.*

PROTECTING YOURSELF AGAINST INFECTION

You may worry about picking up infections from casualties. Often, simple measures such as washing your hands and wearing gloves will protect both you and the casualty from cross-infection.

However, there is a risk that blood-borne viruses, such as hepatitis B or C and HIV (which can lead to AIDS – Acquired Immune Deficiency Syndrome), may be spread by blood-to-blood contact.

These viruses can be transmitted only if an infected person's blood makes contact with a break in the skin, such as a cut or abrasion containing blood or blood products, of another person. No evidence exists of hepatitis or HIV being passed on during mouth-to-mouth resuscitation.

To prevent cross-infection, you should:
 ◆ always carry protective gloves;
 ◆ cover your own sores or skin wounds with a waterproof plaster;
 ◆ wear a plastic apron when dealing with large quantities of a casualty's body fluids

and wear plastic glasses to protect your eyes against splashes;
 ◆ take care not to prick yourself with any needle found on or near the casualty, or to cut yourself on glass;
 ◆ if your eyes, nose or mouth or any wound on your skin is splashed by the casualty's blood, wash thoroughly with soap and water as soon as possible, and consult a doctor;
 ◆ use a mask or face shield (*see page 50*) for mouth-to-mouth ventilation if the casualty's mouth or nose is bleeding;
 ◆ dispose of blood and waste safely after treating the casualty (*see page 218*).

Seeking immunisation

First Aiders should seek medical advice on hepatitis B immunisation from their own doctors. If, after giving first aid, you are concerned that you have been in contact with infection of any sort, seek further medical advice.

ACTION AT AN EMERGENCY

2

Effective first aid usually begins before any direct contact with the casualty. You should approach any incident with firmness, authority, and control in order to reassure the casualty and any bystanders. This is particularly important if there are many casualties, when a calm, systematic attitude on your part can help to prevent further injuries and enhance the survival of the casualties.

The principles of emergency first aid

Clear rules exist to ensure safety in hazardous situations and this chapter will make you aware of these. You will also learn how and when to alert the emergency services, understand which branch is appropriate to different emergencies, and be able to brief them clearly on their arrival.

FIRST-AID PRIORITIES

Assess the situation

- Observe what has happened quickly and calmly.
- Look for dangers to yourself and to the casualty.
- Never put yourself at risk.

Make the area safe

- Protect the casualty from danger.
- Be aware of your limitations.

Assess all casualties and give emergency first aid

- Assess each casualty to determine treatment priorities, and treat those with life-threatening conditions first (*see pages 30 and 44-58*).

Get help

- Quickly ensure that any necessary specialist help has been summoned and is on its way.

CONTENTS

First Aid at an Emergency

Working to a clear plan during an emergency will help to ensure that you are effectively prioritising the many demands upon your attention.

Do not allow yourself to become distracted by non-vital activities. Always bear in mind the main steps of emergency action – *Assess, Make Safe, Give Emergency Aid,* and *Get Help.*

♦ Control your feelings.
♦ Take a moment to think.
♦ Do not place yourself in danger.
♦ Use your common-sense.
♦ Do not attempt too much alone.
♦ Be aware of potential dangers such as gas or petrol: use your eyes, ears, and nose to look for clues, for example the hiss of gas or smell of petrol.

Assess the Situation

Your approach should be brisk, but calm and controlled, so that you can quickly take in as much information as possible. Your priorities are to identify any risks to yourself, to the casualty, and to any bystanders, then to assess the resources available to you and the kind of help you may need. State that you have first-aid skills when offering your help. If there are no doctors, nurses, or more experienced people present, calmly take charge. First ask yourself these questions:

♦ is there any continuing danger?
♦ is anyone's life in immediate danger?
♦ are there bystanders who can help?
♦ do I need specialist help?

Make the Area Safe

The conditions that caused the accident may still be presenting further danger. Remember that you must put your own safety first. You cannot help others if you become a casualty yourself.

Often, very simple measures, such as turning off an electric switch, are enough to make the area safe. Sometimes more complicated procedures are required. Never put yourself and the casualty at further risk by attempting to do too much; be aware of your limitations.

Dealing with ongoing danger

If you cannot eliminate a life-threatening hazard, you must try to put some distance between it and the casualty, by attempting to remove the danger from the casualty if possible. As a last resort, remove the casualty from the danger (*see pages 235–49*). In many situations, you will need specialist help and equipment.

First switch off ignition, even if engine is not running

GIVE EMERGENCY AID

Once it is safe, quickly make an initial assessment of each casualty following the ABC of resuscitation (*see page 44–58*), so that any casualty needing emergency first aid is treated immediately.

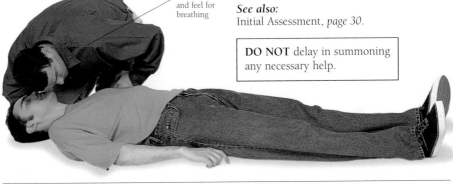

Look, listen, and feel for breathing

Establish whether each casualty:
- is conscious;
- has an open airway;
- is breathing;
- has a pulse.

Your findings dictate your priorities and when and how much help is needed.

See also:
Initial Assessment, *page 30.*

> **DO NOT** delay in summoning any necessary help.

GET HELP

You may be faced with a number of tasks: to maintain safety, to telephone for help (*see overleaf*), and to start first aid. Other people can be asked to:
- make the area safe;
- telephone for assistance;
- fetch first-aid equipment;
- control traffic and onlookers;
- control bleeding or support a limb;
- maintain the casualty's privacy;
- transport the casualty to a safe place.

The control of onlookers

The reaction of bystanders may cause you concern or even anger. Most of them will have no first-aid training and that could make them feel helpless or frightened. If they have witnessed or been involved in the incident, they too may be injured without realising it, and will certainly be distressed. If you need to ask a bystander to help, do so in a firm, but gentle manner.

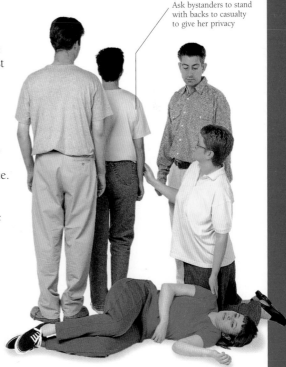

Ask bystanders to stand with backs to casualty to give her privacy

TELEPHONING FOR HELP

You can summon help by telephone from a number of sources.

- *Emergency services* (999 or 112): garda, fire, and ambulance services; mountain, cave and coastguard. 112 is also the European Union emergency number.
- *Utilities:* gas, electricity, and water.
- *Health services:* doctor, dentist, nurse or midwife.

If you have to leave a casualty alone, minimise risk to him or her by taking any vital action first (*see page 30*). Make your call short but accurate.

FINDING A TELEPHONE

Emergency calls are free, and can be made on any telephone, including most mobile and car phones. On motorways, emergency telephones can be found every mile; marker posts between them indicate the nearest box. These telephones simply need to be picked up to be answered.

Most large companies have special arrangements for calling for assistance. Make sure that you are familiar with them. If you ask someone else to make the call, ask them to come back and confirm that help is on the way.

MAKING THE CALL

On dialling 999 or 112, you will be asked which service you require, and will be put through to the appropriate control officer. Whenever there are casualties involved, ask for the ambulance service; the control officer can, if necessary, pass on messages to other emergency services.

When you get through to the control officer, give clear details of the accident or emergency (*see right*). If you are not sure of your precise location, do not panic – your call can be traced to any call box or motorway telephone. Do not put the telephone down until the control officer clears the line.

You may be required to stay by the telephone to "lead in" the emergency services. If you delegate this task, make sure that the person understands its importance and reports back to you.

CALLING THE EMERGENCY SERVICES

Think, and give clear, concise details

State your name and say that you are acting in your capacity as a First Aider.

The following details are essential

- Your telephone number.
- The exact location of the incident; a road name or number, if possible, and any junctions or other landmarks.
- The type and gravity of the incident, for example, "Traffic accident, two cars, road blocked, three people are trapped".
- The number, sex, and approximate ages of the casualties, and anything you know about their condition, for example, "Man, early fifties, suspected heart attack, cardiac arrest".
- Details of any hazards such as gas, hazardous substances (*see page 20*), power-line damage, or relevant weather conditions, for example fog or ice.

MULTIPLE CASUALTIES

In situations such as major traffic accidents, you may find yourself in the difficult position of having to deal with several casualties at the same time. You may be on your own, working with other first aiders, or with professionals. A methodical and calm approach will be crucial in the initial chaos. Always follow the ABC of resuscitation (*see page 44*) in order to establish treatment priority, and attend first to any unconscious casualty. Remember, you can only do your best in these circumstances.

MAJOR INCIDENTS

Major incidents involving a large number of casualties may place overwhelming demands on rescuers. The first task is to ensure that the emergency services are contacted immediately and given accurate information about the incident. The next priority is to assess the scene, and providing it is safe to do so, to start giving emergency first aid.

If other First Aiders come forward, give them as much information as possible. The most senior First Aider present should take charge of the team. When the emergency services arrive, the senior officer will take absolute control.

When a major accident occurs, the garda will establish rendezvous points and nominate officers for all rescuers to report to. It is vital not to disturb any evidence on site, especially following fatal accidents, as there may be a legal inquiry.

The role of the First Aider

At major public events, especially when there is a doctor on your team, you constitute the on-site medical team until hospital and other services arrive. When they do arrive, your role will diminish.

At any major incident, you must leave the scene if asked to do so by a member of the emergency services. However, you may be asked to help the medical teams by performing simple tasks, for example holding drips or supporting limbs. Always do as you are asked; your help will be greatly appreciated.

How you can help

◆ Identify the serious casualties and mark them for immediate treatment. Move casualties with minor injuries quickly from the site to allow access to serious cases; minor injuries can be treated when time allows. This process is called *triage*.
◆ Casualties who are obviously dead, e.g., decapitated, should be left, so that help can be given to those who need it.
◆ All those involved should be logged, and casualties labelled, so that accurate records can be made and maintained.
◆ Workers or residents at or near the site of a disaster should be alerted to security risks and any further hazards.

Emergency personnel will deal with serious injuries

You may be able to help casualties with minor injuries

ROAD ACCIDENTS

Road accidents range from a fall from a bicycle to a major incident with many casualties. Often, the accident site will present serious risks to safety, largely because of passing traffic. It is essential to make the area safe – to protect yourself, the casualty, and other road users.

MAKE THE ACCIDENT SITE SAFE

First ensure your own safety, and do not do anything that might create danger.
◆ Park safely, well clear of the accident site. Set your hazard lights flashing.
◆ Do not run across a busy motorway.
◆ At night, wear or carry something light or reflective, and use a torch.
Then take these general precautions.
◆ Send bystanders to warn other drivers.
◆ Set up warning triangles or lights 200 metres (250 yards) in each direction.
◆ Switch off the ignition of any damaged vehicle and, if you can, disconnect the battery. Switch off the fuel supply on diesel vehicles and motorcycles.
◆ Stabilise vehicles. If a vehicle is upright, apply the hand-brake and put it in gear, or put blocks at the wheels. If a vehicle is on its side, do not right it, but try to prevent it from rolling over.
◆ Look out for physical dangers. Is anyone smoking? Are there goods vehicles displaying Hazchem symbols? Are there damaged power lines or spilt fuel? If you see a radiation hazard sign, make sure that you alert the police immediately.

HAZARDOUS SUBSTANCES

Accidents may be complicated by the spillage of dangerous substances or the escape of toxic vapours. Never make a rescue attempt unless you are sure that you will not come into contact with a dangerous substance. Keep bystanders away from the scene, bearing in mind that poisonous fumes may be released and travel some distance. Stand upwind of the accident to ensure that any fumes are blown away from you.

Hazchem symbols

A Hazchem placard on a vehicle warns that it is carrying a hazardous substance. If in doubt about your safety, or the meaning of the sign, keep your distance, especially if there is any spillage, or if you see the letter "E" (*see below, left*). The information is coded and will be understood by the emergency services, so make a note of it and pass it on when telephoning for help.

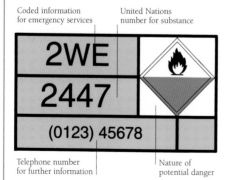

Coded information for emergency services

United Nations number for substance

Telephone number for further information

Nature of potential danger

Flammable substances

Poisonous substances

Oxidising agents

Radioactive substances

Corrosive substances

Compressed gases

CHECK THE CASUALTIES

Quickly assess all casualties, moving them only if they are in danger or you need to do so to apply life-saving treatment. Deal with life-threatening conditions first.

Search the area thoroughly, so that you do not overlook a casualty who may have been thrown clear in the accident or have wandered away while confused.

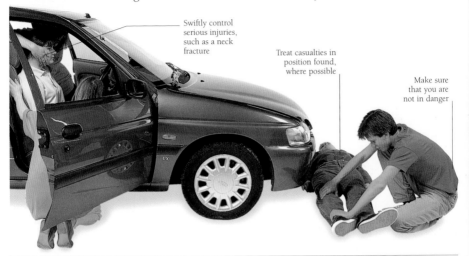

Swiftly control serious injuries, such as a neck fracture

Treat casualties in position found, where possible

Make sure that you are not in danger

FOR AN UNCONSCIOUS CASUALTY

1 Assume there is a neck injury until it has been proved otherwise. Support head and neck with your hands, so that the casualty can breathe freely. Apply a collar, if possible (*see page 144*).

> **DO NOT** move the casualty unless it is absolutely necessary.

2 Treat any life-threatening injuries if possible. Monitor and *record* breathing, pulse, and level of response every ten minutes.

IF it is essential to move the casualty you will need three people to help you: one to support the shoulders and chest, one for the hips and abdomen, and one for the legs. Support the casualty's head continuously and direct all movements.

See also:
Back Injuries, *page 142.*

FOR A CASUALTY TRAPPED UNDER A VEHICLE

1 Mark the exact position of the vehicle and the casualty first. The police will need this information.

2 Try to find help to lift or move the vehicle and, only if it is *absolutely necessary*, drag the casualty clear.

See also:
Crush Injuries, *page 96.*

FIRES

Rapid, clear thinking at a fire is vital. Fire spreads very quickly, so warn any people at risk, and alert the emergency services immediately. Panic also spreads quickly, so you must calm anyone who is likely to increase alarm.

If leaving a burning building, try to help everyone out of the building without putting yourself at risk. Shut all doors behind you. Look for fire exits and assembly points. You should know the evacuation procedure at your workplace. If visiting business premises, follow instructions given by staff.

If arriving at a fire or burns incident, STOP, OBSERVE, THINK, and DO NOT RUSH IN. There may be flammable or explosive substances, such as gas, or toxic fumes or a risk of electrocution. A minor fire can escalate in minutes to a serious blaze. If there is a risk to you, wait for the emergency services.

See also:
Burns and Scalds, *pages 155-66.*
Inhalation of Fumes, *page 70.*

> **DO NOT** use lifts in any circumstances.

LEAVING A BURNING BUILDING

1 Activate the first fire alarm you see.

2 Close each door behind you as you go.

3 Do not run, but walk quickly and calmly.

DEALING WITH A FIRE

A fire needs three components to start and maintain it: ignition (an electric spark or naked flame); a source of fuel (petrol, wood or fabric); and oxygen (air). Remove any one of these to break this "triangle of fire". For example:
◆ switch off a car's **ignition** or pull the fuel cut-off on large diesel vehicles;
◆ remove from the path of a fire any combustible materials, such as curtains or cardboard, that may **fuel** the flames;
◆ shut a door on a fire to cut off its **oxygen** supply; smother flames with a smoke blanket or other impervious substance.

The triangle of fire
Eliminating any of the components necessary for combustion will break the triangle and prevent fire.

> **DO NOT** attempt to fight a fire unless you have called the emergency services and made sure that you are not putting your own safety at risk.

CLOTHING ON FIRE

Always follow the same procedure for a casualty with burning clothing: STOP, DROP, AND ROLL. If possible, wrap the casualty before rolling them.

> **DO NOT** attempt to use flammable materials to smother flames.

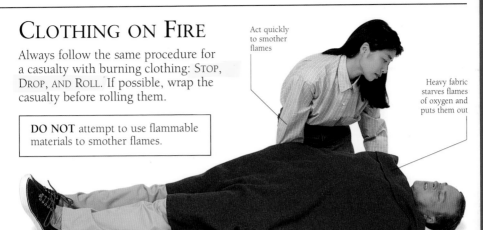

Act quickly to smother flames

Heavy fabric starves flames of oxygen and puts them out

What you can do

- STOP the casualty panicking or running around or outside; any movement or breeze will fan the flames.
- DROP the casualty to the ground.
- If possible, WRAP the casualty tightly in a coat, curtain, blanket (not the nylon or cellular type), rug, or other heavy fabric. The best fabric for this is wool.
- ROLL the casualty along the ground until the flames have been smothered.

IF water or another non-flammable liquid is readily available, lay the casualty down with burning side uppermost, and extinguish the flames by dousing him in plenty of the liquid.

IF your own clothes catch fire and help is not available, extinguish the flames by wrapping yourself up tightly in suitable material, and rolling along the ground.

SMOKE AND FUMES

Any fire in a confined space creates a highly dangerous atmosphere that is low in oxygen and may be contaminated by carbon monoxide and toxic fumes. Never enter a burning or fume-filled building, or open a door leading to a fire. Leave it to the emergency services.

What you can do

- If trapped in a burning building, go into a room with a window and shut the door. If you must pass through a smoke-filled room, keep low down: the air at floor level is the clearest.
- If you have to escape through a window, go out feet first and lower yourself to the full length of your arms before dropping to the ground.

Open window and call for help

Put blanket or coat against bottom of door to keep out smoke

Keep low: smoke in room may not be visible

ELECTRICAL INJURIES

When a person is electrocuted, the passage of electrical current through the body may stun the casualty, causing breathing and even the heart to stop. The current may cause burns both where it enters the body and where it leaves the body to go to "earth". Alternating current also causes muscle spasms that often prevent the casualty from letting go of an electric cable, so the casualty may still be "live" when you come on the scene.

LIGHTNING

A natural burst of electricity discharged from the atmosphere, lightning forms an intense trail of light and heat that seeks contact with the ground through the nearest tall feature in the landscape, and, possibly, anyone standing by it.

A lightning strike may set clothing on fire and knock the casualty down. Occasionally, it may cause instant death. Clear everyone from the site of a lightning strike as soon as possible.

HIGH-VOLTAGE CURRENT

Contact with high-voltage current, found in power lines and overhead high-tension (HT) cables, is usually immediately fatal. Severe burns always result. The sudden muscular spasm produced by the shock may propel the casualty some distance, causing injuries such as fractures.

High-voltage electricity may jump ("arc") up to 18 metres (20 yards). Materials such as dry wood or clothing will not protect you. The power must be cut off and isolated before you approach the casualty. This is crucial where railway overhead power lines are damaged.

ACTION

DO NOT approach the casualty until you are told by the ESB (Electricity Supply Board) that the power has been cut off and isolated. Stay at least 18 metres (20 yards) away, and keep any bystanders back.

1 ☎ *DIAL 999 OR 112 FOR THE EMERGENCY SERVICES.*

2 The casualty will probably be unconscious; once it is safe to do so, open the airway, check breathing and pulse, and be ready to resuscitate if necessary (*see pages 44–58*). Place him in the recovery position (*see page 48*).

3 Treat any burns (*see pages 155–66*) and associated injuries.

4 Take steps to minimise the effects of shock (*see page 78*).

LOW-VOLTAGE CURRENT

Domestic current, as used in homes, offices, workshops, and shops, can cause serious injury, and even death. Many injuries result from faulty switches, frayed flex, or defects within an appliance itself. Young children are especially at risk.

You must be aware of the hazards of water, which is a dangerously efficient conductor of electricity. Handling an otherwise safe appliance with wet hands, or when standing on a wet floor, greatly increases the risk of a shock.

ACTION

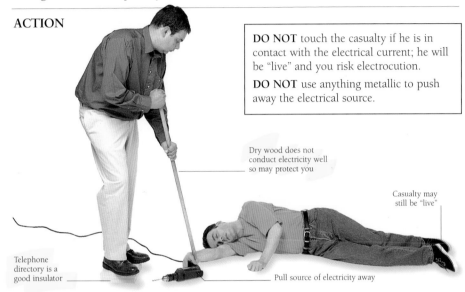

DO NOT touch the casualty if he is in contact with the electrical current; he will be "live" and you risk electrocution.

DO NOT use anything metallic to push away the electrical source.

Dry wood does not conduct electricity well so may protect you

Casualty may still be "live"

Telephone directory is a good insulator

Pull source of electricity away

Break the contact by switching off the current, at the mains or meter point if it can be reached easily. Otherwise, remove the plug or wrench the cable free.

IF you are unable to reach the cable, socket, or mains, follow this procedure.
♦ Stand on dry insulating material such as a wooden box, a rubber or plastic mat, a telephone directory or a thick pile of newspaper. Push the casualty's limbs away from the source with a broom, wooden chair or stool, or push the source away from the casualty, whichever is the easier.
♦ Without touching the casualty, loop rope around his feet or under the arms and pull him away from the source.
♦ If absolutely necessary, pull the casualty free by pulling at his loose, *dry* clothing. Do this only as a last resort.

IF the casualty is unconscious, open the airway, check breathing and pulse, and be ready to resuscitate if necessary (*see pages 44–58*). Place him in the recovery position (*see page 48*). Cool any burns with cold water (*see page 160*). ☎ *DIAL 999 OR 112 FOR AN AMBULANCE*.

IF the casualty seems to be unharmed, he should be advised to rest. Observe him closely and, if in doubt, call a doctor.

IF THE HEART STOPS

Apply the ABC of resuscitation (*see pages 44–58*) and carry out CPR. Although CPR is unlikely to restart a stopped heart, if it is applied correctly, it will keep the circulation going until expert help arrives.

RESCUE FROM DROWNING

Open water in and around Ireland is cold, even in summer. Temperatures in the sea range from 5°C (41°F) to 15°C (59°F); inland waters may be even colder. The cold increases the dangers to both the casualty and rescuer, as it may cause:

♦ uncontrollable gasping on entering the water, with the consequent risk of water inhalation;

♦ a sudden rise in blood pressure, which can precipitate a heart attack;
♦ sudden inability to swim;
♦ hypothermia – if immersion in the water is prolonged or the casualty is exposed to the wind.

See also:
Drowning, *page 68.*
Hypothermia, *pages 170–72.*

ACTION

YOUR AIMS ARE:
■ To get the casualty on to dry land with minimum danger to yourself.
■ To treat the casualty for drowning and hypothermia if necessary.
■ To arrange removal to hospital.

1 Choose the safest way to rescue the casualty. Remember to REACH AND THROW, DON'T GO into the water. Stay on land and reach out with your hand, a stick or branch, or throw a rope or a float.

IF you are a trained life-saver, or if the casualty is unconscious, you may have to swim to the casualty and tow him to dry land. It is safer to wade than to swim.

DO NOT enter the water yourself unless it is absolutely necessary.

IF the casualty is unconscious, carry her with her head lower than her chest once she is clear of the water, to minimise risk of vomiting.

Support chest and knees and keep torso higher than head

2 Shield the casualty from the wind if possible, to prevent the body from being chilled any further (this is known as the "wind chill" factor).

3 Treat the casualty for drowning (*see page 68*) and the effects of severe cold (*see page 172*).

4 Send the casualty to hospital, even if he or she seems to have recovered well or, if necessary, ☎ *DIAL 999 OR 112 FOR AN AMBULANCE.*

STRESS

Even for the most experienced First Aider, an emergency situation can be upsetting. It is natural to feel stressed whenever you are called upon to administer first aid, and to be very emotional once you have finished treating the casualty.

It is possible that the incident will affect you afterwards, so it is important to face up to how you feel and what has happened. In extreme cases, you may experience the more serious condition, Post-traumatic Stress Disorder (*see overleaf*).

COPING DURING AN EMERGENCY

Many First Aiders worry that they might not be able to cope in a real-life situation, but in fact your body has a natural mechanism that prompts you to act quickly in an emergency. In the "fight or flight" response (see right), your body is prepared for physical exertion. So the stress you will feel is your body's way of getting you through a difficult situation.

Calming down

Although the "fight or flight" response is beneficial, sometimes too great a rush of adrenaline may affect your ability to cope. Taking slow, deep breaths will help you to calm down, leaving you better able to remember your first-aid procedures.

"FIGHT OR FLIGHT" RESPONSE

When faced with any stressful situation, the body will automatically respond by releasing the hormones, adrenaline, noradrenaline, and cortisol, which prepare the body to "fight or flee". This response occurs in all animals as a reaction to a threatening or stressful situation, but in the human body the signs include:
- a pounding heart;
- deep, fast breathing;
- pupils widening to let in more light;
- increased sweating;
- alertness of mind;
- greater blood flow to the muscles;
- a rise in blood sugar level for energy.

FEELINGS AFTER THE INCIDENT

After you have treated the casualty, depending on the type of incident and the outcome, you might experience:
- satisfaction and pleasure – it is natural to feel good about yourself if the treatment has gone well;
- confusion and doubt – you might question your actions and feel you could have done more, especially if the outcome is unclear;
- anger and sadness – being upset is normal, especially in major incidents; releasing these feelings at the time will help you get over the event more quickly.

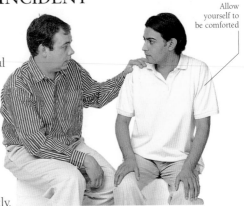

Allow yourself to be comforted

Delayed Reaction

Involvement in an incident can lead to stress once you have returned to your normal, everyday environment. The extent of the effect may depend on the level of your first-aid experience and the type of incident, and it is important to recognise the signs and deal with your feelings as soon as possible.

Symptoms and signs

Stress can lead to interference with a person's physical and mental well-being, and some people are more susceptible to it than others. It is quite normal to suffer from some stress after a traumatic event. Stress can manifest itself in very many different ways (*see below*), but these symptoms should pass in time.

Recognition

There may be:

- ◆ Tremor of the hands and stomach.
- ◆ Excessive sweating.
- ◆ Flashbacks of the incident.
- ◆ Nightmares or disturbed sleep.
- ◆ Tearfulness.
- ◆ Tension and irritability.
- ◆ A feeling of withdrawal and isolation.

DEALING WITH STRESS

If you experience stress after an incident, do not think that you are weak or over-reacting. It is important that you do not bottle up your feelings as this will cause you more stress. Your feelings can also be relieved by exercise or relaxation. In fact, doing any activity that you enjoy is a good way to distract yourself, and may help to relieve any lasting tension caused by the incident.

Talking to a friend
Face up to what has happened by confiding in a friend or relative. Ideally, speak to someone who also attended the incident: you may find they have the same feelings as you.

Dealing with stress alone
Try writing down your feelings and what happened, including all the positive actions you took. You can then use this as a talking point.

POST-TRAUMATIC STRESS DISORDER (PTSD)

If you have witnessed or experienced a serious threat to life or physical well-being, and suffer all of the following symptoms, you may have Post-traumatic Stress Disorder:
- ◆ reliving the event in some way;
- ◆ persistent avoidance of situations, people or situations associated with the event;
- ◆ persistent hyperactivity;
- ◆ symptoms that appear more than 30 days after the event, and last for a minimum of a month.

The condition can be made worse by reminders of the event, and it is important to see a doctor or counsellor for help.

THE PRACTICE OF FIRST AID

3

In most situations that require first aid, there will be no life-threatening danger. You will simply be assisting a conscious casualty, whose recovery from some minor injury or illness is not in doubt. In all cases, your aim is to work to a plan and discover what is wrong with the casualty, and to give prompt, correct treatment in a methodical way.

Assessing the situation

Before tending to a casualty, however, you must survey the whole scene. Your first responsibility is to make sure that the area is safe. Often hazards such as passing traffic can be dealt with simply, but where the danger is too great or too imminent, you may need to move the casualty even at the risk of aggravating the injury. Do this only if it is safe to approach the casualty: you cannot help others if you also become a casualty. Only when the casualty is safe can you begin to treat the illness or injury.

THE FIRST AIDER SHOULD:

Preserve life
◆ Pay strict attention to safety (*pages 16–26*).
◆ Follow the ABC of resuscitation (*pages 44–58*).
◆ Control any major bleeding (*pages 88 and 99*).

Limit the effects of the condition
◆ Make a diagnosis of the injury or illness, if possible, by means of a thorough examination.
◆ Give priority to seriously injured casualties.
◆ Treat multiple injuries in order of priority, dealing with life-threatening conditions first. Consider the possibility of "hidden" secondary conditions.

Promote the casualty's recovery
◆ Relieve any discomfort, pain or anxiety.
◆ Arrange for appropriate medical attention.

29

INITIAL ASSESSMENT

When you are sure that it is safe to do so, quickly perform a brief examination of the casualty. This initial assessment is to check for any life-threatening conditions that need urgent first aid to preserve life.

You must perform the checks shown below before making a full diagnosis, and, if necessary, you should be prepared to carry out the appropriate steps to resuscitate the casualty first.

If you suspect that there may be head or neck injuries involved, move the casualty very carefully and only if it is absolutely necessary.

Sending for help

If you think it is needed, send for help promptly (see page 18). Try to send someone else while you stay with the casualty, but ensure that they report back to you after making the call.

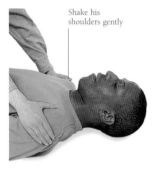

Shake his shoulders gently

1 Check for consciousness
If the casualty does not respond when spoken to, he may be unconscious. Try to elicit a response (see page 46). Be careful not to move the head or neck.

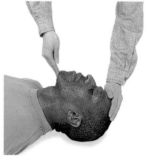

2 Open the airway
An unconscious casualty's airway may be obstructed – by a foreign body, for example. Open the airway by tilting the head back (see page 47).

3 Check for breathing
Once the casualty's airway is open, establish whether he is breathing by listening, looking, and feeling for signs (see page 47).

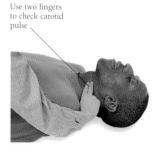

Use two fingers to check carotid pulse

4 Check for circulation
If the heart is beating, you should be able to feel a pulse in the neck (see page 52) or at the wrist (see page 77). Check for a baby's pulse on the inside of the upper arm (see page 57).

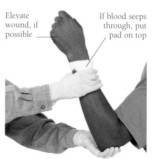

Elevate wound, if possible

If blood seeps through, put pad on top

5 Check for bleeding
Severe loss of blood reduces the circulation to the vital organs, and can cause serious shock. Control serious bleeding (see pages 88 and 99) as soon as breathing and pulse are established (see box, right).

WHAT TO DO NEXT

As soon as you have established the condition of the casualty, take appropriate action (see pages 44–58), based on whether he is:
- ◆ unconscious, not breathing, and without a pulse;
- ◆ unconscious, not breathing, with a pulse;
- ◆ unconscious, breathing, with a pulse;
- ◆ conscious, breathing, with a pulse.

MAKING A DIAGNOSIS

Once you have completed your initial assessment and made sure that the casualty is out of immediate danger, you need to make a diagnosis; this often requires a thorough physical examination (*see page 34*).

The diagnosis is made on the basis of the *history* and *clues* to any medical condition, and *symptoms* and *signs* (*see overleaf*). Circumstances will determine how detailed your examination will be. In wet, cold conditions, when an ambulance is on its way, only serious injuries need attention – the priority is to keep the casualty warm and dry. If a conscious casualty can describe the symptoms, concentrate on treating those.

In this book, the probable history, symptoms, and signs of specific illnesses and injuries are grouped under the heading *Recognition*.

HISTORY

This is the full story of how the incident happened, how the injury was sustained, or how the illness began and continued, including any previous conditions. Question the casualty, but if he or she is unconscious, talk to any onlookers. Witnesses can give useful information, but they can be unreliable, particularly if they are upset. Try to form a full picture of what took place. Take into account:

♦ when the casualty last had something to eat or drink;
♦ whether the casualty has any illness or is taking any medication;
♦ the amount of force involved and how it was applied to the body;
♦ the environment – was the casualty in a hot and stuffy, or cold, room or exposed to wind or rain;
♦ the casualty's age and state of health: a young, fit adult who trips may sprain a wrist, but an elderly lady who does the same is more likely to have broken her arm or her hip;
♦ establish who the casualty is, and where he or she lives.

Make a note of this information, including the time of injury and your examination.

EXTERNAL CLUES

If the casualty is unable to co-operate or is unconscious, look through pockets and bags for clues (beware of syringes if you suspect drug abuse). There may be an appointment card for a hospital or clinic or a card indicating a history of allergy, diabetes or epilepsy. Horse-riders or cyclists may carry such a card in a riding hat or helmet.

Medication carried by the casualty may give valuable clues about the emergency. Medical warning items ("Medic-Alert" or an "SOS Talisman") may be worn as a locket, bracelet, medallion, or on a key ring; some contain medical information. Take care of any such item and return it to the casualty.

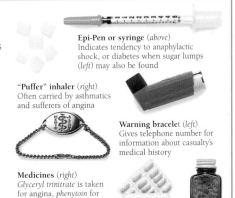

Epi-Pen or syringe (*above*)
Indicates tendency to anaphylactic shock, or diabetes when sugar lumps (*left*) may also be found

"Puffer" inhaler (*right*)
Often carried by asthmatics and sufferers of angina

Warning bracelet (*left*)
Gives telephone number for information about casualty's medical history

Medicines (*right*)
Glyceryl trinitrate is taken for angina, *phenytoin* for epilepsy; indigestion tablets may indicate stomach ulcer

Symptoms and Signs

Every injury and illness manifests itself in distinctive ways that may help your diagnosis. These indications are divided into two groups: symptoms and signs. Some will be obvious, but others may be missed unless you examine the casualty thoroughly from head to toe (*see page 34*). A conscious casualty should be examined, wherever possible, in the position found, or with any obvious injury comfortably supported; an unconscious

casualty's airway must first be opened and secured (*see page 47*). Do not remove clothing unnecessarily and do not leave the casualty exposed to cold conditions any longer than required.

Use your senses – look, listen, feel, and smell. Be quick and alert, but be thorough, and do not make unjustified assumptions. You should handle the casualty gently, but your touch must be firm enough to ensure that you feel any swelling or irregularity or detect a tender spot. Ask a conscious casualty to describe any sensations your touch causes.

Watch casualty's face for expressions of pain or anxiety throughout examination

Always examine from head to toe

Feel along and compare both sides of body at same time

ASSESSING SYMPTOMS

Symptoms are sensations that the casualty experiences, and may be able to describe, if she is conscious. Ask if she has any abnormal sensations, if there is any pain, where it is felt, what type of pain it is, and how movement affects it. If the pain did not follow an injury, find out how and where it began. Severe pain in one place can mask a more serious, but less painful, injury in another.

Ask if there are any other symptoms such as nausea, giddiness, heat, cold, weakness, or thirst. All symptoms should be assessed and confirmed, wherever appropriate, by an examination for signs of injury or illness.

Question casualty gently about her symptoms

LOOKING FOR SIGNS

Signs are details of a casualty's condition that you can see, feel, hear or smell. Many are obvious, but others may be discovered only during a thorough examination (*see overleaf*). Assess the casualty's level of response. If he or she is unconscious or unable to speak clearly, you may have to make a diagnosis purely on the circumstances of the incident, information obtained from onlookers, and the signs you find.

Apply your senses

Look for bleeding, discolouration or deformity. Feel the strength and rhythm of the pulse and listen to the breathing.

Gently feel parts of the body that are painful, noting tenderness or variation in the alignment of a bone. Note if the casualty is unable to perform any normal function, such as moving a limb. Use your sense of smell to search for clues.

Look for visible signs of injury

Always support injured part

Feel for signs of injury

SYMPTOMS AND SIGNS OF INJURY OR ILLNESS	
The casualty may tell you of these symptoms	• Pain • Anxiety • Heat • Cold • Loss of normal movement • Loss of sensation • Abnormal sensation • Thirst • Nausea • Tingling • Faintness • Stiffness • Momentary unconsciousness • Weakness • Memory loss • Dizziness • Sensation of broken bone
You may see these signs	• Anxiety and painful expression • Unusual chest movement • Burns • Sweating • Wounds • Bleeding from orifices • Response to touch • Response to speech • Bruising • Abnormal skin colour • Muscle spasm • Swelling • Deformity • Foreign bodies • Needle marks • Vomit • Incontinence • Containers and other circumstantial evidence
You may feel these signs	• Dampness • Abnormal body temperature • Tenderness to touch or pressure • Swelling • Deformity • Irregularity • Grating bone ends
You may hear these signs	• Noisy or distressed breathing • Groaning • Sucking sounds (chest injury) • Response to touch • Response to speech • Grating bone (*crepitus*)
You may smell these signs; remember to smell the casualty's breath	• Acetone • Alcohol • Burning • Gas or fumes • Solvents or glue • Incontinence • Cannabis

EXAMINING A CASUALTY

A detailed examination of the casualty should be undertaken only after taking any vital action needed (*see page 30*). You may need to move or remove clothing (*see page 35*), but ensure that, at every stage of your examination, you do not move the casualty more than is absolutely necessary. Always start at the head and work down; the "top-to-toe" routine is both easily remembered and thorough.

HEAD-TO-TOE SURVEY

1 Run your hands carefully over the scalp to feel for bleeding, swelling or depression, that may indicate a possible fracture. Be careful not to move any casualty who you think may have injured her neck, especially if she is unconscious.

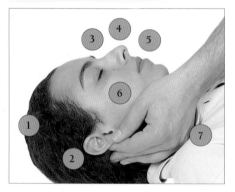

2 Speak clearly to the casualty in both ears to see if she responds or if she can hear. Look for blood or clear fluid (or a mixture of both) coming from either ear. These may be signs of damage inside the skull.

3 Examine both eyes, noting if they are open, the size of the pupils, whether they are equal in size, and whether they react to light (each pupil should shrink when light falls on it). Look for any foreign body, blood, or bruising in the whites of the eyes.

4 Check the nose for the same signs as in the ears. Look for blood or clear fluid (or a mixture of both) coming from either nostril. Any of these might indicate damage inside the skull.

5 Record the rate, depth, and nature (easy or difficult, noisy or quiet) of breathing. Note any odour on the breath. Look and feel inside the mouth for anything that might endanger the airway. If dentures are intact and fit firmly, leave them in place. Look for any wound in the mouth or irregularity in the line of the teeth. Examine the lips for burns.

6 Note the colour, temperature, and state of the skin: is it pale, flushed or grey-blue (*cyanosis*); is it hot or cold, dry or damp? For example, pale, cold, sweaty skin suggests shock; a flushed, hot face suggests heatstroke or fever. A blue tinge indicates lack of oxygen; you should look for this especially in the lips, ears, and face.

7 Loosen clothing around the neck, and look for any warning medallion, or hole in the windpipe left by a surgical operation (*see Stoma, page 51*). Run your fingers gently along the spine from the base of the skull downwards as far as possible, without disturbing the casualty's position, checking for irregularity, swelling or tenderness.

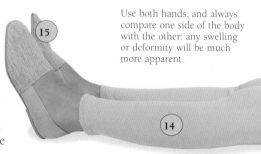

Use both hands, and always compare one side of the body with the other: any swelling or deformity will be much more apparent.

8 Ask the casualty to breathe deeply, and note whether the chest expands evenly, easily, and equally on the two sides. Gently feel the ribcage for any deformity, irregularity, tenderness or a grating sensation on breathing. Observe whether breathing causes the casualty any pain or discomfort. Look for signs of bleeding from any wounds.

9 Gently feel along both the collar bones and the shoulders for any deformity, irregularity or tenderness.

10 Check the movements of elbows, wrists, and fingers by asking the casualty to bend and straighten the arm at the joints. Check that the casualty can feel normally with her fingers and there are no abnormal sensations in the limbs.

Note the colour in the fingers, whether they are pale or grey-blue, as this indicates a problem with the circulation. Look for any needle marks on the forearms, or a warning bracelet. Take the pulse at the wrist (*see page 77*) or neck (*see page 52*).

11 If there is any sign of impairment of movement or loss of sensation in the limbs, *do not* move the casualty to examine the spine. Otherwise, gently pass your hand under the hollow of the back and feel along the spine without disturbing the casualty, checking for swelling and tenderness.

12 Gently feel the front of the abdomen for evidence of bleeding, and to identify any rigidity or tenderness of the muscular wall.

13 Feel both sides of the hips, and gently move the pelvis to look for signs of fracture. Note any incontinence or bleeding from orifices.

14 Ask the casualty to raise each leg in turn, and to move her ankles and knees. Look and feel for bleeding, swelling, deformity or tenderness.

15 Check movement and feeling in all the toes. Look at their colour: grey-blue skin may indicate a circulatory disorder or cold injury.

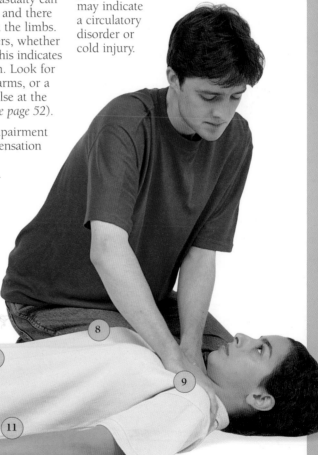

REMOVING CLOTHING

You may have to remove clothing to make a thorough examination, to obtain an accurate diagnosis, or to give the casualty appropriate treatment. This should be done with the minimum of disturbance to the casualty. Only remove as much clothing as is strictly necessary; try to maintain privacy for the casualty and prevent exposure to cold conditions as far as possible. Do not damage clothing unless it is absolutely necessary and, where you can, cut along the seams or sleeves.

REMOVING FOOTWEAR

Undo or cut any laces

Support the ankle and carefully remove the shoe. Long boots may need to be slit down the back seam with a sharp knife.

REMOVING SOCKS

Cut alongside your finger

If socks cannot be pulled off gently, lift each one away from the leg with your fingers and cut the sock with scissors.

REMOVING TROUSERS

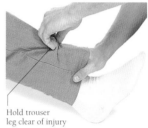

Hold trouser leg clear of injury

Gently pull up the trouser leg to expose the calf and knee, or pull trousers down from the waist to reveal the thigh.

REMOVING A SWEATER

1 Carefully remove the casualty's uninjured arm from its sleeve.

Roll up garment and slip over head

Ask casualty to support injured arm

2 Ease the garment over the casualty's head, without disturbing the injured arm, if possible.

3 Support the injured arm and slip off the other sleeve of the garment.

REMOVING A COAT OR SHIRT

1 Unbutton the garment, and pull it off the casualty's shoulders.

2 Remove the uninjured arm from its sleeve first, and pull the garment round to the injured side.

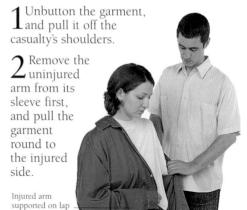

Injured arm supported on lap

3 Support the injured arm and ease the garment off the arm, keeping the arm straight if possible.

REMOVING PROTECTIVE HELMETS

A protective helmet, such as a riding hat or a motorcyclist's crash helmet, is best left on, and should be removed only if absolutely necessary (for example, a full-face helmet that encloses the head and face may prevent you from performing artificial ventilation). Any helmet should always, if possible, be removed by the casualty. Ideally, two people are required to remove a helmet so that the casualty's head and neck are constantly supported.

The casualty's head should also be carefully aligned with the spine in the neutral position (*see page 147*) if it is necessary to remove the helmet.

FOR AN OPEN-FACE HELMET OR RIDING HAT

> **DO NOT** remove the helmet unless it is absolutely necessary.

1 Unfasten the buckle, or cut through the chinstrap.

2 If the helmet or hat has sides, grip it from above, and force the sides of the helmet apart to take pressure off the casualty's head. Gently lift the helmet upwards and backwards to remove it.

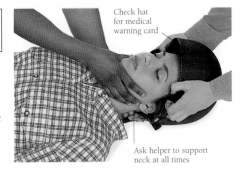

Check hat for medical warning card

Ask helper to support neck at all times

FOR A FULL-FACE HELMET

> **DO NOT** remove the helmet unless it is absolutely necessary.

2 Ask a helper, working from above, to tilt the helmet backwards (try not to move the head at all) and gently lift the front clear of the casualty's chin.

Support neck at all times

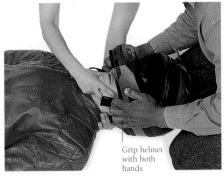

Grip helmet with both hands

1 Undo or cut the straps. Working from the base of the helmet, ease the fingers of both your hands underneath the rim. Support the neck with one hand and hold the lower jaw firmly.

3 Continue to support the neck and jaw. Ask your helper to tilt the helmet forwards slightly so that it will pass over the base of the skull, and then to lift it straight off the casualty's head.

TREATMENT AND AFTERCARE

Treat each condition methodically and calmly in order of priority. Reassure the casualty, and listen to what he or she has to say. Do not keep questioning the casualty, do not let people crowd round, and avoid moving him or her unnecessarily.

Treatment priorities

- Follow the ABC of resuscitation.
- Maintain a clear airway and breathing; place the casualty in the recovery position (*see page 48*).
- Control bleeding.
- Treat large wounds and burns.
- Immobilise bone and joint injuries.
- Give appropriate treatment for other injuries and conditions.
- Check airway, breathing, and pulse (*see pages 47 and 52*) regularly and deal with any problem immediately.

Arranging appropriate aftercare

Ascertain whether the casualty needs medical treatment and, if so, what is needed. If you require help, send someone else if possible, in the event that the casualty's condition alters or worsens. Stay with the casualty until help arrives. According to your assessment of the casualty, you may:

- call a doctor for advice;
- call an ambulance or arrange transport to hospital;
- pass care of the casualty to a doctor, nurse or ambulance crew;
- take the casualty to a nearby house or shelter to await medical help;
- allow the casualty to go home, accompanied if possible – ask if someone will be at home to meet him or her, or, if you can, arrange this;
- advise the casualty to see a doctor.

DO NOT allow home a casualty who has been unconscious (other than a faint), had severe breathing difficulty or signs of shock. Stay with him or her until help arrives.

DO NOT give anything by mouth to an unconscious casualty who may have internal injuries or need hospital care.

CARE OF PERSONAL BELONGINGS

If you have to search a casualty's belongings for identification or clues to his condition (*see page 31*), make sure that you do so in front of a reliable witness. Take care of any clothing or property, and ensure that it accompanies the casualty to hospital, or is handed over to the garda. Make sure that someone accepts responsibility for contacting the casualty's family.

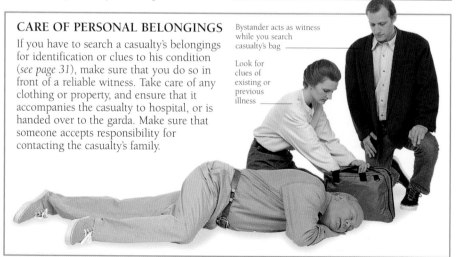

Bystander acts as witness while you search casualty's bag

Look for clues of existing or previous illness

Passing on Information

Having summoned medical aid, try to make notes on the incident and the condition of the casualty so that you can pass on all the information you have gathered. The observation chart overleaf, which is recommended for use by the Voluntary Aid Societies, will enable you to note your observations of the casualty's condition, such as pulse, breathing, and level of response, clearly and at intervals of ten minutes. If the casualty is in a critical condition, record these observations more frequently.

Make a brief written report to accompany your observations. A record of the timing of events is particularly valuable to medical personnel. Note carefully, for example, the length of a period of unconsciousness, the duration of a fit, the time of any changes in the casualty's condition, and the time of any intervention or treatment.

If possible, stay with the casualty until help arrives, or accompany him or her to the hospital, so that you can hand over your notes personally.

Making a report

Your report should include:
- the casualty's name and address;
- history of the accident or illness;
- a brief description of any injuries;
- any unusual behaviour;
- any treatment given, and when;
- breathing, pulse, and level of response.

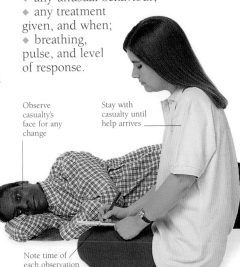

Observe casualty's face for any change

Stay with casualty until help arrives

Note time of each observation recorded

THE USE OF MEDICATION

Medication within first aid is largely confined to relieving general aches and pains, and is generally limited to helping a casualty to take paracetamol, as described in the relevant sections of this book.

A wide range of medications may be bought over the counter without a doctor's prescription, and you may know and have used many of them. However, when treating a casualty, you must not buy or borrow medication to administer it yourself, even if the casualty has forgotten his or her own medication or you have the type they may normally expect to use.

If you administer or advise any medication other than those stipulated in this manual when giving first aid, the casualty may be put at risk, and you could find yourself facing legal or civil action as a consequence.

If the necessary medication is not available, seek expert medical treatment. The only exception to this principle occurs where there are clear protocols laid down by an employer or voluntary organisation. Such protocols allow trained staff or members to administer medication in specific circumstances, such as antidotes to industrial poisons (*see page 187*).

Whenever medication is taken, it is essential to ensure that:
- it is appropriate for the condition;
- it is not out of date;
- it is taken as advised;
- any precautions are strictly followed;
- the recommended dose is not exceeded whatever the circumstances;
- a detailed record is kept of all medication administered.

OBSERVATION CHART

The information from this chart will be very valuable when decisions are taken about further treatment:
* use a photocopy of it to record your observations while waiting for help;

* tick the appropriate boxes;
* update them at ten-minute intervals;
* send the completed chart, and any notes, with the casualty when he or she leaves your care.

DATE . . . .   CASUALTY'S NAME . . . .

Time of observation (10-minute intervals)		10	20	30	40	50	60
Eyes Observe for reaction while testing other responses.	Open spontaneously						
	Open to speech						
	Open to painful stimulus						
	No response						
Movement Apply painful stimulus: pinch ear lobe or skin on back of hand.	Obeys commands						
	Responds to painful stimulus						
	No response						
Speech When testing responses, speak clearly and directly, close to casualty's ear.	Responds sensibly to questions						
	Seems confused						
	Uses inappropriate words						
	Incomprehensible sounds						
	No response						
Pulse (beats per minute) Take pulse at wrist (*see page 77*) or at neck on adult (*page 52*); at inner arm on baby (*page 57*). Note rate, and whether beats are weak (**w**) or strong (**s**), regular (**reg**) or irregular (**irreg**).	Over 110						
	101-110						
	91-100						
	81-90						
	71-80						
	61-70						
	Below 61						
Breathing (breaths per minute) Note rate, and whether breathing is quiet (**q**) or noisy (**n**), easy (**e**) or difficult (**diff**).	Over 40						
	31-40						
	21-30						
	11-20						
	Below 11						

RESUSCITATION

4

For life to continue, the body requires an adequate supply of oxygen to enter the lungs and be transferred to all cells in the body through the bloodstream. In particular, if the brain, the organ that controls all bodily functions, does not have a constant supply of oxygen it will begin to fail after three or four minutes. Without oxygen, the casualty will lose consciousness, the heartbeat and breathing will cease, and death will result.

The ABC of life

Three elements are involved in getting oxygen to the brain. The air passage, or *Airway*, must be open so that oxygen can enter the body; *Breathing* must take place so that oxygen can enter the bloodstream via the lungs; and the blood must travel around the body (the *Circulation*), taking the oxygen to all the tissues and organs, including the brain.

Resuscitation techniques

The priority in treating any casualty is to establish and maintain effective breathing and circulation. This chapter tells you what you can do to assist a casualty whose breathing or heart has stopped. The sequence of techniques used to sustain life in the absence of spontaneous breathing and a heartbeat is known as *Cardio-pulmonary Resuscitation (CPR)*.

FIRST-AID PRIORITIES

♦ Keep the brain supplied with oxygen by following the ABC of resuscitation: open the *Airway*, and maintain *Breathing* and *Circulation*.

♦ Obtain professional medical help urgently.

CONTENTS

BREATHING AND CIRCULATION

Oxygen is essential to support life. The process of breathing enables air, which contains oxygen, to be taken into the air sacs (*alveoli*) in the lungs (*see page 60*).

In the lungs, oxygen is absorbed by the blood and the waste product of breathing, carbon dioxide, is released. The blood is pumped to the lungs from the heart through *pulmonary arteries* to be oxygenated, and then returned to the heart through *pulmonary veins* to be circulated to the rest of the body.

Arteries carry the oxygenated blood from the left side of the heart around the body; veins bring deoxygenated blood back from the body to the right side of the heart (*see page 76*).

The composition of air

Air is a mixture of gases, of which 79% is nitrogen and 21% is oxygen. Only 5% of the oxygen is used up by respiration, so that when we exhale the air still contains approximately 16% oxygen, in addition to a small amount of carbon dioxide.

This means that the amount of oxygen that we breathe out is sufficient to oxygenate another person, when it is forced into his or her lungs during artificial ventilation (*see opposite, below*).

See also:
The Circulatory System, *page 76.*
The Respiratory System, *page 60.*
The Resuscitation Sequence, *page 45.*

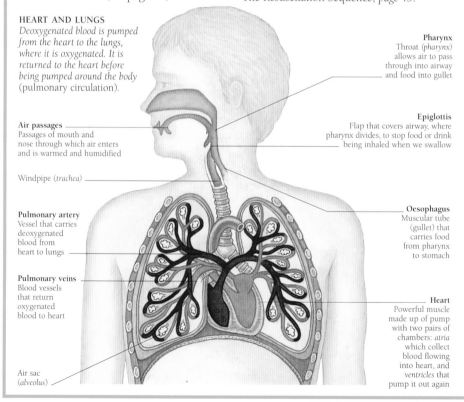

HEART AND LUNGS
Deoxygenated blood is pumped from the heart to the lungs, where it is oxygenated. It is returned to the heart before being pumped around the body (pulmonary circulation).

Air passages
Passages of mouth and nose through which air enters and is warmed and humidified

Windpipe (*trachea*)

Pulmonary artery
Vessel that carries deoxygenated blood from heart to lungs

Pulmonary veins
Blood vessels that return oxygenated blood to heart

Air sac (*alveolus*)

Pharynx
Throat (*pharynx*) allows air to pass through into airway and food into gullet

Epiglottis
Flap that covers airway, where pharynx divides, to stop food or drink being inhaled when we swallow

Oesophagus
Muscular tube (gullet) that carries food from pharynx to stomach

Heart
Powerful muscle made up of pump with two pairs of chambers: *atria* which collect blood flowing into heart, and *ventricles* that pump it out again

HOW THE HEART BEATS

The walls of the heart are made up of specialised muscle fibres. The contraction of these fibres is synchronised by an "electrical" current produced by a node (*sino-atrial node*), situated in the wall of one of the upper chambers of the heart.

When this impulse fails, the heart muscle cannot function properly, blood stops circulating and the brain is deprived of oxygen. The heartbeat can often be regulated with a defibrillator (*see page 84*). This delivers an electric shock to the heart, jolting it into a normal rhythm of about 60–80 beats per minute.

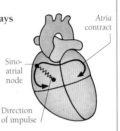

The electrical pathways
Impulses travel from the sino-atrial node to the upper chambers (atria), causing them to contract. The impulses then travel on to contract the lower chambers (ventricles).

Atria contract

Sino-atrial node

Direction of impulse

WHAT CAN GO WRONG

◆ Damage to the tracts of tissue that conduct electrical impulses through the heart can cause abrupt slowing or complete stoppage of the heartbeat.
◆ Fast electrical activity in the ventricles causes all co-ordinated pumping action to be lost (*ventricular fibrillation*).

◆ Any process that severely affects the function of the brain's respiratory centre, such as a stroke (*see page 119*) or poisoning (*see pages 183–90*) can lead to a total cessation of breathing (respiratory failure). This results in complete absence of oxygen (*anoxia*) in the body.

RESTORING BREATHING AND CIRCULATION

The blood is oxygenated by breathing and is circulated around the body by the beating of the heart. If the body's natural mechanisms of breathing and heartbeat break down, it is essential to resuscitate the casualty by taking over the ventilation and circulation, through artificial ventilation and chest compressions respectively. This restores the supply of oxygen to the brain.

Artificial ventilation (see page 50)
When breathing stops, blowing air into the lungs can give enough oxygen to keep a person alive. In mouth-to-mouth ventilation, pinch the nose so that air cannot escape. The heart must be beating to circulate the oxygenated blood. If it is not beating, give chest compressions (see below).

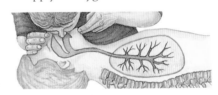

Chest compressions (see page 52)
If the heart stops beating, blood does not circulate and the brain is starved of oxygen, so the heart needs mechanical help. By pressing down rhythmically, at about 100 compressions per minute, on the lower half of the chest, blood is driven from the heart. When pressure is released, the chest returns to its normal position, and blood refills the heart. To oxygenate blood, this must be done with artificial ventilation.

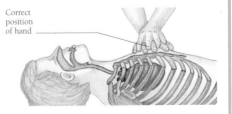

Correct position of hand

PRINCIPLES OF RESUSCITATION

For life to be sustained, a constant supply of oxygen must be maintained and delivered to the brain and other vital organs by the circulating blood. The "pump" that maintains this circulation is the heart. If the heart stops (cardiac arrest), urgent action must be taken if death is to be prevented.

In certain cases, the use of a machine called a "defibrillator" (*see page 84*), which is carried in most ambulances, can start the heart beating again, so you should inform the medical services if you suspect cardiac arrest.

The casualty is most likely to survive if:
- help is summoned immediately;
- the flow of oxygenated blood is restored to the brain by artificial ventilation and chest compressions (cardio-pulmonary resuscitation CPR);
- a defibrillator is used promptly;
- the casualty quickly receives specialised treatment at a hospital.

Although CPR is unlikely to restart a stopped heart, it is essential to carry it out. If applied correctly, it will ensure that the blood supply to the brain is maintained until expert help arrives. In some areas, GP's are equipped to provide Cardiac Care.

Cardiac arrest – the chain of survival
The casualty's chances of survival are greatest when all the following steps are taken.

Early access	Early CPR	Early defibrillation	Early advanced care
Help is summoned immediately so that a defibrillator can be brought to the casualty.	Resuscitation techniques are used to maintain circulation until help arrives.	A controlled electric shock is given, which jolts the heart into a normal rhythm.	Specialised treatment stabilises the casualty's condition quickly and efficiently.

THE ABC OF RESUSCITATION

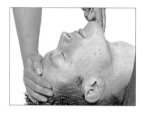  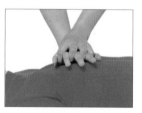

*A is for **AIRWAY***

Tilting the casualty's head back and lifting the chin will "open the airway". The tilted position lifts the casualty's tongue from the back of the throat so that it does not block the air passage (*see page 47*).

*B is for **BREATHING***

If a casualty is not breathing, you can breathe for him, and thus oxygenate the blood, by giving "artificial ventilation": blowing your own expired air into the casualty's lungs (*see page 50*).

*C is for **CIRCULATION***

If the heart stops, you can apply "chest compressions" to force blood through the heart and around the body. You must combine these with artificial ventilation so that the blood is oxygenated (*see page 52*).

THE RESUSCITATION SEQUENCE

When dealing with a collapsed casualty, following the sequence below will enable you to check the casualty's breathing and circulation, as well as show you how to resuscitate if it is necessary.

CHECK CASUALTY'S RESPONSE
Try to get a response by asking questions or gently shaking him (*see overleaf*).
☎ *DIAL 999 OR 112 FOR AN AMBULANCE*

OPEN THE *AIRWAY*; CHECK BREATHING
Tilt the head back to open the airway (*see page 47*). Check for breathing (*see page 47*).

IF the casualty is breathing, place him in the recovery position (*see page 48*).

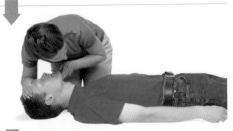

BREATHE FOR THE CASUALTY
Look into the mouth and remove any *obvious* obstruction (*see page 51*). If the casualty is not breathing, keep the head tilted back, pinch the nostrils closed, and give two breaths of mouth-to-mouth ventilation (*see page 50*).

CHECK FOR *CIRCULATION*
Check the pulse for ten seconds. If you can feel a pulse, continue artificial ventilation. If there is no pulse or no other sign of recovery (*see page 52*), begin CPR.

COMMENCE CPR
Alternate 15 chest compressions to two breaths of artificial ventilation. Repeat this sequence as necessary (*see page 52*).

WHEN TO CALL AN AMBULANCE
◆ **IF** you have a helper, always send him or her to call for an ambulance immediately.
◆ **IF** you are alone, breathing is absent, and the condition is due to injury or drowning, continue with the resuscitation sequence for one minute, and then call an ambulance. For any other adult casualty, call for an ambulance, after noting that the casualty is unresponsive, and then continue with the resuscitation sequence until help arrives.

RESUSCITATION TECHNIQUES

To assess and treat a casualty who has collapsed, use the resuscitation techniques outlined on the following pages. If breathing and pulse return at any point, place the casualty in the recovery position (*see page 48*).

THE RESUSCITATION SEQUENCE				
CHECK RESPONSE	OPEN AIRWAY AND CHECK BREATHING	BREATHE FOR THE CASUALTY	CHECK FOR CIRCULATION	COMMENCE CPR

CHECKING RESPONSE

On discovering a collapsed casualty, you should first establish whether he is conscious or unconscious.

Ask a simple question such as "What has happened?" or give a command such as "Open your eyes!". Speak loudly and clearly, close to the casualty's ear.

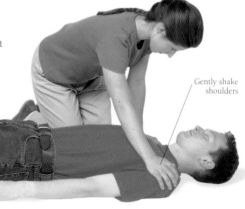

Gently shake shoulders

IF the casualty does not respond, try gently shaking his shoulders.
* A fully unconscious casualty will make no response at all.
* The casualty may respond to pain; try gently pinching the skin.
* A casualty who is only partially conscious may mumble, groan or make slight movements.

ALWAYS assume there are head or neck injuries; handle the head carefully and shake the shoulders very gently.

IF a collapsed casualty does respond to you, keep a check on him until he recovers or help arrives, as he may drift in and out of consciousness.

THE AVPU CODE
There are different degrees of impaired awareness. You should assess the casualty quickly by using the AVPU code:
A - Alert
V - responds to Voice
P - responds to Pain
U - Unresponsive.

Check points
Eyes: do they remain closed?
Speech: does the casualty respond to the questions you ask?
Movement: does the casualty obey commands? Does he respond to a painful stimulus, such as pinching?

OPENING THE AIRWAY

An unconscious casualty's airway may become narrowed or blocked. This makes breathing difficult and noisy, or completely impossible.

The main reason for this is that muscular control in the throat is lost, which allows the tongue to fall back and block the airway. Lifting the chin and tilting the head back lifts the tongue away from the entrance to the air passage, allowing the casualty to breathe.

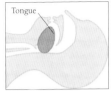

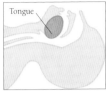

Blocked airway
Unconsciousness relaxes the muscles, the tongue falls back and blocks the throat, preventing breathing.

Open airway
Head tilt and chin lift enable the tongue to be lifted from the back of the throat, leaving the airway clear.

TO OPEN THE AIRWAY

Placing two fingers under the point of the casualty's chin, lift the jaw.
At the same time, place your other hand on the casualty's forehead, and gently tilt the head well back.

IF you think that there are head or neck injuries, handle the head very carefully to avoid injuring the casualty further. Tilt the head back very slightly – just far enough to open the casualty's airway.

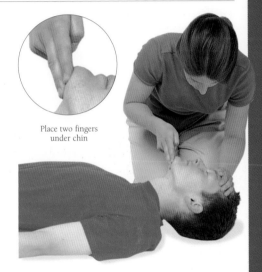

Place two fingers under chin

CHECKING BREATHING

Kneel beside the casualty, and put your face close to his mouth. Look, listen, and feel for breathing.
◆ Look along the chest to see if the chest rises, indicating breathing.
◆ Listen for sounds of breathing.
◆ Feel for breath on your cheek.
Do these checks for up to five seconds before deciding that breathing is absent.

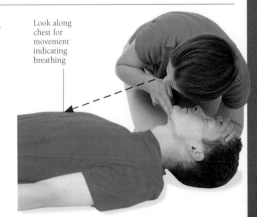

Look along chest for movement indicating breathing

THE RECOVERY POSITION

An unconscious casualty should be placed in the recovery position. This position prevents the tongue from blocking the airway and, because the head is slightly lower than the rest of the body, it allows liquids to drain from the mouth and reduces the risk of the casualty inhaling stomach contents.

The head, neck, and back are kept aligned, while the bent limbs keep the body propped in a comfortable and secure position. If you are forced to leave an unconscious casualty unattended, he or she can safely be left in the recovery position while you get help.

The technique for turning the casualty shown below assumes that he is found lying on his back. Not all the steps will be necessary if a casualty is found lying on his side or front.

See also:
Spinal Recovery Position, *page 146.*

METHOD

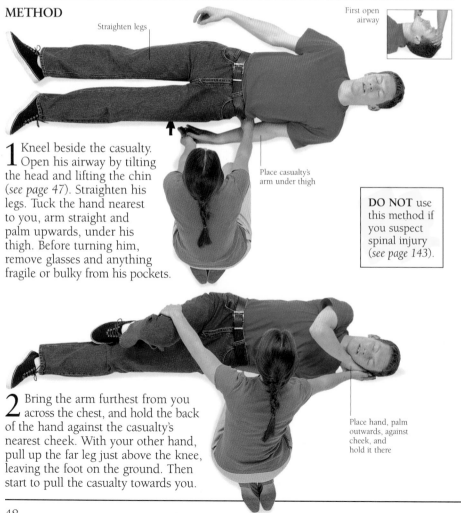

Straighten legs

First open airway

Place casualty's arm under thigh

1 Kneel beside the casualty. Open his airway by tilting the head and lifting the chin (*see page 47*). Straighten his legs. Tuck the hand nearest to you, arm straight and palm upwards, under his thigh. Before turning him, remove glasses and anything fragile or bulky from his pockets.

> **DO NOT** use this method if you suspect spinal injury (*see page 143*).

2 Bring the arm furthest from you across the chest, and hold the back of the hand against the casualty's nearest cheek. With your other hand, pull up the far leg just above the knee, leaving the foot on the ground. Then start to pull the casualty towards you.

Place hand, palm outwards, against cheek, and hold it there

Pull bent leg towards you until knee rests on the ground

Tilt chin to drain mouth

Roll casualty on to your knees

3 Keeping the casualty's hand pressed against his cheek, roll the casualty towards you and on to his side.

4 Use your knees to support the casualty so that he is prevented from rolling too far forwards.

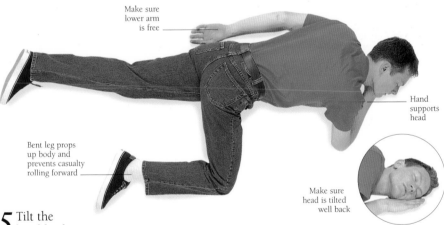

Make sure lower arm is free

Hand supports head

Bent leg props up body and prevents casualty rolling forward

Make sure head is tilted well back

5 Tilt the head back to ensure the airway remains open. If necessary, adjust the hand under the cheek.

6 Adjust the upper leg, if necessary, so that both the hip and the knee are bent at right angles.

7 Adjust the lower arm so that the casualty is not lying on it. Make sure that his hand is still positioned with the palm facing upwards.

8 ☎ *DIAL 999 OR 112 FOR AN AMBULANCE*. Monitor and *record* breathing and pulse every ten minutes.

MODIFYING THE RECOVERY POSITION FOR INJURIES

You may have to modify the recovery position for certain injuries. For example, a casualty with a spinal injury needs extra support at the head and neck, and the head and trunk need to be aligned at all times (*see page 143*). If limbs are injured and cannot be bent, placing rolled blankets around the casualty, or getting extra helpers to support him, can stop him from toppling forwards.

THE RESUSCITATION SEQUENCE

CHECK RESPONSE OPEN AIRWAY AND CHECK BREATHING **BREATHE FOR THE CASUALTY** CHECK FOR CIRCULATION COMMENCE CPR

BREATHING FOR THE CASUALTY

The body, especially the brain, requires oxygen to keep the cells alive. The air that you breathe out still contains about 16% of oxygen, so it can save life if it is blown into the casualty's lungs (artificial ventilation). If the pulse is absent, artificial ventilation must be combined with chest compressions (cardio-pulmonary resuscitation or CPR, *see page 52),* otherwise the oxygen will not reach the body's vital organs.

USING FACE SHIELDS

Artificial ventilation carries little or no risk of the transfer of infection. However, First Aiders may receive training in the use of face shields for hygienic purposes. If you are trained to use a shield, carry one at all times – but if you do not have one with you, you should never hesitate to give a casualty mouth-to-mouth ventilation.

GIVING MOUTH-TO-MOUTH VENTILATION

1 With the casualty lying flat on his back, remove any *obvious* obstruction, including broken or displaced dentures, from the mouth. Leave well-fitting dentures in place.

2 Open the airway by tilting the head and using two fingers to lift the chin *(see page 47).*

3 Close the casualty's nose by pinching it with your index finger and thumb. Take a full breath, and place your lips around his mouth, making a good seal.

4 Blow into the casualty's mouth until you see the chest rise. Take about two seconds for full inflation.

5 Remove your lips and allow the chest to fall fully, which takes about four seconds. Repeat this once and then assess for signs of circulation *(see page 47).*

IF the pulse is absent *(see page 52)* and there are no other signs of recovery, such as return of skin colour, or any movement, such as swallowing, coughing, or breathing, begin cardio-pulmonary resuscitation (CPR, *see page 52)* immediately.

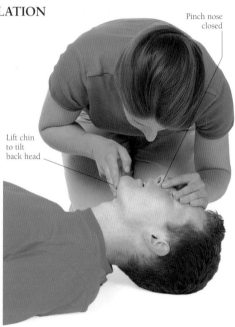

Pinch nose closed

Lift chin to tilt back head

IF the pulse is present, continue ventilations and check the pulse after every ten breaths.

IF breathing returns, place the casualty in the recovery position *(see page 48).*

IF THE CHEST DOES NOT RISE

If after attempting two artificial ventilations the chest does not rise, check that:
- the head is tilted sufficiently far back;
- you have closed the nostrils completely;
- you have a firm seal around the casualty's mouth;
- the airway is not obstructed by vomit, blood or a foreign body.

CLEARING AN OBSTRUCTION

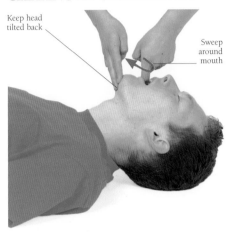

Keep head tilted back

Sweep around mouth

1 If you can see any *obvious* obstruction inside the mouth, use your finger to hook it out carefully.

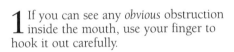

DO NOT use your fingers to feel blindly down the throat.

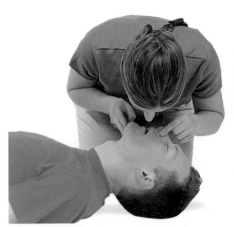

2 Attempt two further breaths. If, after carrying out the rechecks shown above, the chest still does not rise, follow procedure for obstructed airway (*see page 63-5*). If chest rises, check for circulation (*see overleaf*). If circulation present, continue ventilations, see opposite.

OTHER FORMS OF ARTIFICIAL VENTILATION

In some situations, such as rescue from water, or where mouth injuries make a good seal impossible, you may choose to use the mouth-to-nose method of artificial ventilation. While it is usually easy to blow air into the casualty's nose and down into the lungs, it is not so easy for the air to escape; the soft parts of the nose may flop back to act like a valve.

To give mouth-to-nose ventilation
With the casualty's mouth closed, form a tight seal with your lips around the nose, and blow. Open the casualty's mouth to let the breath out.

Mouth-to-stoma ventilation
A laryngectomee is someone whose voice box (*larynx*) has been surgically removed, leaving a permanent opening (*stoma*) in the front of the neck through which breathing takes place.

Artificial ventilation must be given through the stoma. If the chest fails to rise and air escapes from the casualty's mouth, he or she may be a "partial neck breather". In this situation, it is necessary to close off the mouth and nose with your thumb and fingers while giving mouth-to-stoma ventilation.

THE RESUSCITATION SEQUENCE				
CHECK RESPONSE	OPEN AIRWAY AND CHECK BREATHING	BREATHE FOR THE CASUALTY	**CHECK FOR CIRCULATION**	**COMMENCE CPR**

CHECK FOR CIRCULATION

Check the pulse for ten seconds. During this time, look for other signs of recovery, such as return of colour to the skin, any movement such as breathing, swallowing, and coughing. **IF** you cannot find the pulse or there are no other signs of circulation, begin chest compressions immediately.

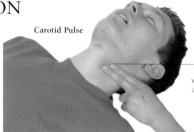

Carotid Pulse

Hollow between windpipe and large neck muscle

CARDIO-PULMONARY RESUSCITATION (CPR)

If there is no pulse, this means that the heart has stopped beating and you will have to provide an artificial circulation (*see page 43*) by means of chest compressions.

To be of any use, chest compressions must always be combined with artificial ventilation. This process is known as cardio-pulmonary resuscitation, or CPR for short. If both you and your helper have been trained to administer CPR, you can do so together.

Calling an ambulance

♦ *If you have a helper*, send him or her to call an ambulance.

♦ *If you are alone* and the condition is due to injury or drowning, continue with the resuscitation sequence for one minute (*see page 45*), then call an ambulance. For any other adult casualty, call an ambulance, then begin the resuscitation sequence (*see page 45*).

GIVING CHEST COMPRESSIONS

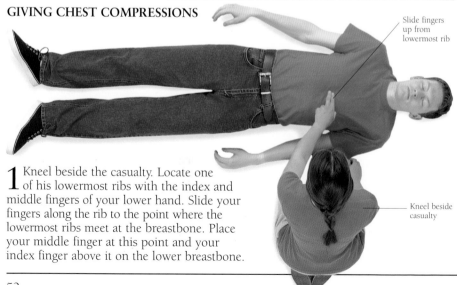

Slide fingers up from lowermost rib

Kneel beside casualty

1 Kneel beside the casualty. Locate one of his lowermost ribs with the index and middle fingers of your lower hand. Slide your fingers along the rib to the point where the lowermost ribs meet at the breastbone. Place your middle finger at this point and your index finger above it on the lower breastbone.

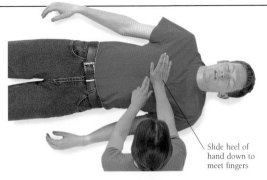

Slide heel of hand down to meet fingers

2 Place the heel of your other hand on the breastbone, and slide it down until it reaches your index finger. This is the point at which you should apply pressure.

Keep fingers clear of chest

3 Place the heel of your first hand on top of the other hand, and interlock your fingers.

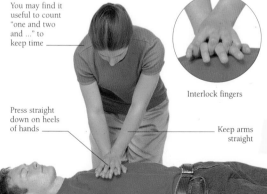

You may find it useful to count "one and two and ..." to keep time

Interlock fingers

Press straight down on heels of hands

Keep arms straight

HOW CHEST COMPRESSION WORKS

Pushing vertically down on the breastbone squeezes the heart against the backbone, expelling blood from the heart's chambers and forcing it into the tissues. As pressure is released, the chest rises, and replacement blood is "sucked" in to refill the heart; this blood is then forced out of the heart by the next compression.

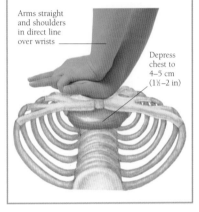

Arms straight and shoulders in direct line over wrists

Depress chest to 4–5 cm (1½–2 in)

4 Leaning well over the casualty, with your arms straight, press vertically down and depress the breastbone approximately 4–5 cm (1½–2 in). Release the pressure without removing your hands.

5 Compress the chest 15 times, aiming for a rate of about 100 compressions per minute. Then give two breaths of artificial ventilation (*see page 50*). Continue this cycle of alternating 15 chest compressions with two breaths of artificial ventilation until help arrives.

53

RESUSCITATION FOR CHILDREN

Respiratory failure is the main cause of cardiac arrest in a child. The resuscitation techniques used depend on the child's age and size (*see page 58*). If he is aged eight or over, use the adult sequence (*see page 45*).

CHECK CASUALTY'S RESPONSE
Try to get a response by talking to the child or gently shaking her (*see opposite*). Tap a baby on the sole of the foot.

OPEN THE *AIRWAY*; CHECK BREATHING
Tilt the head back to open the airway – only tilt a baby's head very slightly. Check for breathing (*see page 56*).

IF the child is breathing, place her in the recovery position (*see page 56*).

BREATHE FOR THE CASUALTY
Look into the mouth and clear any *obvious* obstruction. For a child, keep the head tilted back, pinch the nose, and give two breaths of mouth-to-mouth ventilation (*see page 57*). For a baby, keep the head tilted back slightly and breathe into the mouth and nose (*see page 57*). Don't over-extend a baby's neck.

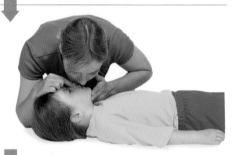

CHECK FOR *CIRCULATION*
Check the pulse for ten seconds. If there is a pulse, continue with artificial ventilation (*see page 57*). If you cannot feel a pulse and there are no signs of recovery (*see page 57*), commence CPR.

COMMENCE CPR
Alternate five chest compressions with one breath of artificial ventilation (*see page 58*) for one minute (approximately 20 cycles), before calling an ambulance.

WHEN TO CALL AN AMBULANCE

IF you have a helper, he should call an ambulance while you treat the casualty.
IF you are alone, for an infant give one minute of CPR if pulse is absent, or one minute of ventilations if the pulse is present, before calling an ambulance.

THE RESUSCITATION SEQUENCE

| CHECK RESPONSE | OPEN AIRWAY AND CHECK BREATHING | BREATHE FOR THE CASUALTY | CHECK FOR CIRCULATION | COMMENCE CPR |

CHECKING RESPONSE

BABY (UNDER ONE) AND CHILD (AGED 1–8)

Try to stimulate a baby or child to establish whether she is unconscious. Talk to a baby or tap her on the sole of her foot. Talk to a child or gently shake her. An unconscious baby or child will make no response.

Try asking her questions

Gently shake shoulders

OPENING THE AIRWAY

BABY (UNDER ONE)

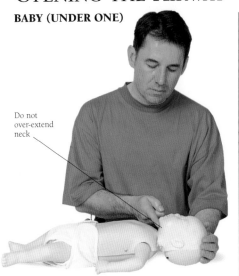

Do not over-extend neck

1 Use one finger to lift the chin. Place the other hand on the baby's head and tilt it back slightly.

CHILD (AGED 1–8)

Place two fingers under chin

1 Use two fingers to lift the chin. Place the other hand on the child's forehead and tilt the head back.

THE RESUSCITATION SEQUENCE				
CHECK RESPONSE	OPEN AIRWAY AND CHECK BREATHING	**BREATHE FOR THE CASUALTY**	**CHECK FOR CIRCULATION**	COMMENCE CPR

CHECKING BREATHING

FOR BOTH BABY (UNDER ONE) AND CHILD (AGED 1–8)

1 Listen for sounds of breathing; feel for breath on your cheek; and look along the chest for movement.

2 Check for five seconds before deciding that breathing is absent.

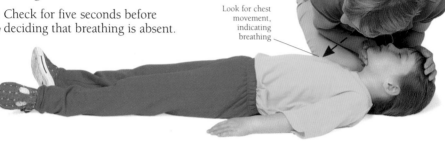

Lean right down over casualty

Look for chest movement, indicating breathing

THE RECOVERY POSITION

BABY (UNDER ONE)

IF breathing and pulse are present, or return at any point during the resuscitation sequence, put the baby into the recovery position.

Technique for a baby
The recovery position technique for a baby is to cradle him in your arms with his head tilted downwards. This prevents him from choking on his tongue or from inhaling vomit.

CHILD (AGED 1–8)

IF breathing and pulse are present, or return at any point during the resuscitation sequence, place the child into the recovery position to stop her choking on her tongue or from inhaling vomit.

Bend leg to prop up body

Ensure head is tilted back

Technique for a child
Place a child into the recovery position in the same way you would an adult (see page 48). The airway should be opened before you begin turning the child, and then rechecked once the turn is complete, to ensure that the child is able to breathe.

BREATHING FOR THE CASUALTY

BABY (UNDER ONE YEAR)

1 Carefully remove any *obvious* obstruction from the mouth. Seal your lips tightly around the baby's mouth and nose and breathe into the lungs.

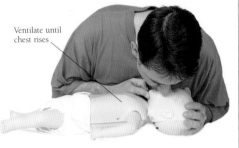

Ventilate until chest rises

2 Give two breaths of mouth-to-mouth ventilation, aiming at one complete breath every three seconds. Check the brachial pulse (*see below*) and look for other signs of recovery, such as coughing, swallowing or breathing.

CHILD (AGED 1–8)

1 Carefully remove any *obvious* obstruction from the mouth. Pinch the child's nostrils closed. Seal your lips around her mouth and breathe into the lungs until the chest rises.

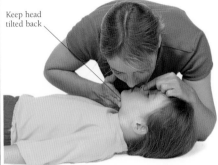

Keep head tilted back

2 Give two slow breaths, allowing about one to two seconds per breath. Check pulse and look for signs of circulation.

FOR BOTH BABY (UNDER ONE) AND CHILD (AGED 1–8)

IF there is no pulse or other sign of recovery (*see below*), give CPR by alternating five chest compressions (*see page 58*) with one breath of artificial ventilation for one minute before calling an ambulance.

IF the pulse is present, continue artificial ventilation for one minute before calling an ambulance.
IF breathing starts, stop artificial ventilation and place the baby or child into the recovery position (*see opposite*).

CHECKING FOR CIRCULATION

Spend ten seconds checking the pulse. While you are doing this, look for other signs of recovery, such as return of colour to the skin, and any signs of movement, for example breathing, swallowing or coughing.

CHECKING THE PULSE

BABY
Feel with two fingers for the brachial pulse on the upper inside of the arm (*see right*).

CHILD
Using two fingers, check the carotid pulse as for an adult (*see page 52*).

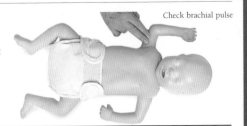

Check brachial pulse

CARDIO-PULMONARY RESUSCITATION (CPR)

If a child appears lifeless and you cannot detect a pulse, or if the pulse of an infant of less than one year is less than 60 beats per minute, you must begin cardio-pulmonary resuscitation (CPR). The technique used depends on the child's age and size. The table below outlines the technique for each age group.

GUIDELINES FOR CPR ON CHILDREN

Should you have doubts about which technique to use, follow this general rule: if you have to move from the chest to reach the head for mouth-to-mouth ventilation, the child is big enough for you to perform adult resuscitation (see page 45).

Age	Chest compressions	Artificial ventilations
Under one	5 (with two fingers)	1 (on mouth and nose)
1–8	5 (with one hand)	1 (on mouth only)
Over 8 (treat as for an adult)	15 (with two hands)	2 (on mouth only)

BABY (UNDER ONE YEAR)

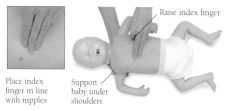

Place index finger in line with nipples

Support baby under shoulders

Raise index finger

1 Place the baby on her back on a flat surface. Place two fingers on the baby's lower breastbone, one finger's width below the nipple line. Press down to a depth of 1.25–2.5cm (½–1in) at a rate of 100 per minute.

Cover baby's mouth and nose

2 Give one gentle puff of artificial ventilation (see page 57).

3 Alternate five chest compressions to one breath of ventilation for one minute before calling an ambulance. Continue CPR while waiting for help.

CHILD (AGED 1–8)

1 Position your hand as you would for an adult (see page 52), but use the heel of one hand only to press down 2.5–3.75cm (1–1½in). Do this five times at a rate of 100 per minute.

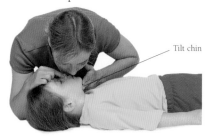

Tilt chin

2 Give one gentle breath of mouth-to-mouth ventilation, by breathing into the child's mouth (see page 57).

3 Alternate five chest compressions to one breath of mouth-to-mouth ventilation for one minute before calling an ambulance. Continue while waiting.

DISORDERS OF THE RESPIRATORY SYSTEM 5

Oxygen is essential to support life. The action of breathing enables air containing oxygen to be taken into the lungs, so that the oxygen can be transferred to the blood and circulated throughout the body. The action of breathing and the process of gas exchange in the lungs are together commonly described as "respiration", and the organs, tissues, and structures that enable us to breathe as the "respiratory system" (*see overleaf*).

What can go wrong

Respiration can be impaired in various ways: by obstruction of the airway, for example as in choking or drowning; by preventing normal exchange of gases in the lungs, such as in fume or smoke inhalation; or by conditions affecting the function of the lungs, for instance as with a collapsed lung, or the mechanism of breathing, as in asthma. Disorders affecting respiration always require urgent first aid and may be life-threatening.

CONTENTS

FIRST-AID PRIORITIES

◆ Recognise respiratory distress.

◆ Restore and maintain the casualty's breathing and, if necessary, apply the ABC of resuscitation, and be prepared to resuscitate if necessary.

◆ Identify and remove the cause of the problem, and provide fresh air.

◆ Obtain appropriate medical aid. Any casualty who has experienced severe difficulties with the airway or breathing *must* be seen at hospital, even if first aid seems to have been successful.

THE RESPIRATORY SYSTEM

This system comprises the mouth, nose, windpipe (*trachea*), lungs, and pulmonary blood vessels. Respiration involves the process of breathing and the exchange of gases (oxygen and carbon dioxide) in the lungs (*see below*) and in cells through-out the body (*see page 76*).

We breathe in air in order to take oxygen into the lungs, and we breathe out to expel the waste gas carbon dioxide, a by-product of respiration. When we breathe, air is drawn through the nose and mouth into the airway and the lungs.

In the lungs, oxygen is taken from air sacs (*alveoli*) into tiny blood vessels (*pulmonary capillaries*). At the same time, carbon dioxide is released from the capillaries into the alveoli and expelled as we breathe out.

THE LUNGS
These two large, spongy organs, together with the circulatory system, perform the vital function of gas exchange in order to distribute oxygen around the body. An average man's lungs can hold about six litres of air; a woman's, four litres.

Ribs

Muscle

Blood capillaries

Bronchi
These branch from base of windpipe, then divide and sub-divide to form a network in each lung

Pleural membrane
Two layers of membrane, separated by lubricating fluid, that surround and protect each lung

Nasal cavity

Mouth cavity

Trachea
Pipe that channels air into lungs

Food pipe

Alveoli
Millions of tiny, elastic air sacs where exchange of oxygen and carbon dioxide takes place

Bronchioles
Tiny air passages that branch off from bronchi and eventually open into alveoli

Deoxygenated blood

Oxygenated blood

Alveolus

Diaphragm
Sheet of dome-shaped muscle, separating chest and abdominal cavities

Gas exchange in the alveoli
A network of tiny blood capillaries surrounds each alveolus. The thin walls of both structures allow oxygen to diffuse into the blood, and carbon dioxide from it.

THE PROCESS OF BREATHING

Breathing is controlled by the brain through the autonomic nervous system (*see page 108*), a system that also helps to monitor the levels of oxygen and carbon dioxide in the blood.

The average adult normally breathes about 16 times per minute; children breathe about 20–30 times per minute. The rate can be altered (usually increased) by the respiratory centre in the brain as a response to abnormal levels of oxygen or carbon dioxide, stress, exercise, injury or illness. The body can also change the depth and the rate of breathing voluntarily.

The breathing process consists of breathing in (*inspiration*), breathing out (*expiration*), and a pause. There is always some air left in the lungs so that oxygen is constantly available to the blood.

Breathing in
The muscles contract to expand the chest cavity and the lungs fill the space. The alveoli (see below left) open up and suck in air via the windpipe.

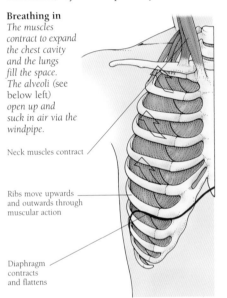

Neck muscles contract

Ribs move upwards and outwards through muscular action

Diaphragm contracts and flattens

Breathing out
The muscles relax and the elastic chest wall returns to its resting position. This forces out air from the lungs.

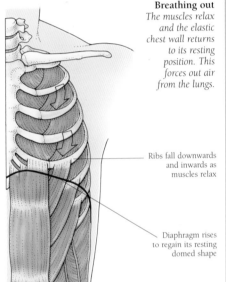

Ribs fall downwards and inwards as muscles relax

Diaphragm rises to regain its resting domed shape

WHAT CAN GO WRONG

◆ Chronic disease of the lungs, such as *emphysema*, which affects the alveoli, can cause shortness of breath and eventually respiratory failure.
◆ Allergic reactions may be confined to the respiratory tract, as in hay fever, when inflamed nasal membranes lead to congestion, sneezing, and watery eyes.
◆ Infections cause inflammation of the windpipe (*see Croup, page 74*), bronchi (*bronchitis*), and lung tissue (*pneumonia*), causing coughing and phlegm production.
◆ Infections and other conditions can affect the two layers of pleural membrane (*pleurisy*), making breathing painful.
◆ Other conditions that lead to breathing difficulties include hyperventilation (*see page 72*), pneumothorax (*see page 94*), asthma (*see page 73*), and anaphylactic shock (*see page 81*).

DISORDERS OF RESPIRATION

Any disturbance of the respiratory process is potentially fatal, since it may lead to suffocation (see opposite); a condition caused not only by smothering, but also by any condition that stops oxygen being taken up from the lungs by the blood.

The depletion of oxygen in the body is known as *hypoxia*. In this state, the tissues begin to deteriorate rapidly – brain cells will start to die if their oxygen supply is interrupted for as little as three minutes.

Symptoms of low blood oxygen

♦ Rapid, distressed breathing and gasping for breath.
♦ Confusion, and aggression, leading to unconsciousness.
♦ Usually, grey-blue skin (*cyanosis*).
♦ Breathing or the heart may stop if hypoxia is not swiftly reversed.

GIVING OXYGEN

Oxygen should only be administered by a person trained in its use. Light, portable oxygen equipment is now widely available, and advanced First Aiders receive relevant training. Oxygen can be used to supplement artificial ventilation (*see page 50*) or to enrich inhaled air for casualties who can breathe, for example those who have inhaled smoke or fumes (*see page 70*).

Using oxygen apparatus safely

When giving oxygen to a casualty, always observe the following rules.

♦ Do not smoke or allow any naked flames anywhere near oxygen.

♦ Do not use any oils or greases on the control knobs or valves.

♦ Keep the equipment in good order.

♦ Make sure that the apparatus is thoroughly checked over and recharged with oxygen after every use.

CONDITIONS CAUSING LOW BLOOD OXYGEN (HYPOXIA)	
Condition	*Causes*
Insufficient oxygen in inspired air	• Suffocation by smoke or gas • Changes in atmospheric pressure, for example at high altitude or in a depressurised aircraft
Airway obstruction	• Suffocation by an external obstruction, such as a pillow or water (drowning) • Blockage or swelling in the air passages • Compression of the windpipe, for example caused by hanging or strangulation
Conditions affecting the chest wall	• Crushing, for example by a fall of earth or sand or pressure from a crowd • Chest wall injury with multiple rib fractures or constricting burns
Impaired lung function	• Lung injury • Collapsed lung • Lung infections, such as pneumonia
Damage to the brain or nerves that control respiration	• A head injury, or stroke, that damages the breathing centre in the brain • Some forms of poisoning • Paralysis of nerves controlling the muscles of breathing, as in spinal cord injury
Impaired oxygen uptake by the tissues	• Suffocation by carbon monoxide or cyanide poisoning

AIRWAY OBSTRUCTION

The airway may be obstructed by food, vomit, or some other foreign material, by swelling of the throat after injury, by muscle spasms in drowning, a heavy weight on the chest or, in an unconscious casualty, by the tongue. A child may inhale a foreign body that can then block the lower air passages, or swell within the lung, possibly resulting in a collapsed lung (*see page 94*) or in pneumonia.

General signs and symptoms

- Noisy, laboured breathing.
- Grey-blue skin (*cyanosis*).
- Flaring of the nostrils.
- Reversed movement of the chest while breathing: the chest wall will suck in as the casualty breathes in.
- Drawing in of the chest wall between the ribs and of the soft spaces above the collar bones and breastbone.

SUFFOCATION

The medical term for this condition is *asphyxia*. Suffocation is often thought to result from a physical barrier to the airway, and associated with smothering.

In fact, suffocation occurs when life is threatened because the breath is deficient in oxygen. Suffocation can therefore result not just from an airway obstruction, but also from contamination of the air with, for example, fumes or carbon monoxide that interfere with the ability of the blood to absorb oxygen.

See also:
Inhalation of Fumes, *page 70.*

See also:
Burns to the Airway, *page 162.*
Drowning, *pages 26 and 68.*
Inhaled Foreign Bodies, *page 182.*
Opening the Airway, *page 47.*
Unconsciousness, *page 110.*

TREATMENT

YOUR AIMS ARE:
- To restore a supply of fresh air to the casualty's lungs.
- To seek medical aid.

Remove any obstruction to the casualty's breathing, such as debris restricting chest movement or anything over the mouth and nose. If needed, move her into fresh air.

IF the casualty is unconscious, open the airway, check breathing and pulse, and be ready to resuscitate (*see pages 44–58*). ☎ *DIAL 999 OR 112 FOR AN AMBULANCE.* Place her in the recovery position (*see page 48*).

IF the casualty is conscious, reassure her, but keep her under observation. Call a doctor, even if she seems to have recovered completely.

Place cheek close to mouth to feel for breath

Listen for breaths and watch to see if chest rises

CHOKING

A foreign object that is stuck at the back of the throat may either block the throat or induce muscular spasm. This is choking. Adults may choke on food that has been hurriedly swallowed. Young children and babies are curious and like putting objects in their mouth. Choking requires *prompt action* from the First Aider; be prepared to resuscitate if the casualty stops breathing. If there is only a partial airway obstruction and the casualty is still able to speak or breathe, do not carry out the rescue procedure as you may worsen their condition.

Call for help and encourage the casualty to attempt to cough up the foreign object and remain calm until help arrives. Complete airway obstruction means the casualty cannot breathe, speak, or cough.

There may be:

◆ Congested face initially.
◆ Grey-blue skin (*cyanosis*) later.
◆ Distressed signs from the casualty, who may point to the throat, or grasp the neck.

See pages 66–7 for Choking Baby *or* Child

TREATMENT

YOUR AIMS ARE:

■ To remove the obstruction and so restore normal breathing.
■ To arrange urgent removal to hospital if necessary.

FOR A CONSCIOUS ADULT

1 Ask the casualty to cough. If she cannot cough up the foreign object, proceed to step 2 and perform abdominal thrusts.

Watch to see if obstructing object falls out of her mouth

2 Put your arms around her trunk. Place your fist, thumb inward, against the abdomen between the navel and tip of the breastbone.

Link hands and pull sharply inwards and upwards

3 Grasp your fist with other hand and pull sharply inwards and upwards against the casualty's diaphragm. This should help to expel the object; check to see if it falls out of her mouth.

4 Be persistent; continue abdominal thrusts until the obstruction is relieved or advanced help is available.

5 Call for help. ☎ *DIAL 999 OR 112 FOR AN AMBULANCE.*

IF the casualty becomes unconscious, lay her face up on the floor, and treat as described opposite.

FOR AN UNCONSCIOUS ADULT

1 Unconsciousness may relieve any muscle spasm in the throat of a choking casualty clearing the obstruction. If the casualty is still not breathing, assess him following the ABC of resuscitation (*see pages 44–53*).
☎ *DIAL 999 OR 112 FOR AN AMBULANCE.*
Begin mouth to mouth (*see page 50*). If unsuccessful, proceed to step 2.

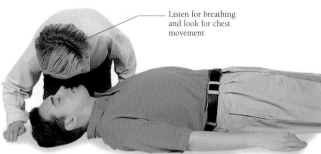

Listen for breathing and look for chest movement

2 Reposition the head to open the airway using the head-tilt, chin-lift method and attempt to give him breaths of mouth to mouth ventilation again.

IF, at any stage, the casualty begins to breathe normally, place him in the recovery position (*see page 48*). Monitor and *record* breathing, pulse, and level of response every ten minutes.

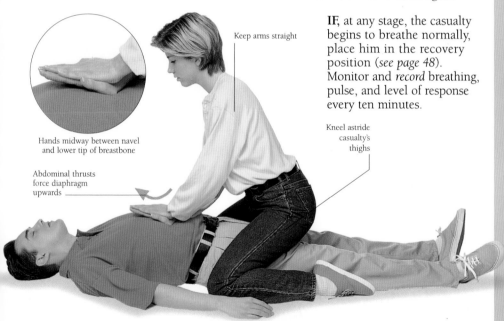

Keep arms straight

Hands midway between navel and lower tip of breastbone

Abdominal thrusts force diaphragm upwards

Kneel astride casualty's thighs

3 If the casualty's airway is still obstructed, kneel carefully astride or alongside him. Place the heel of one of your hands above his navel, and cover it with your other hand. Press sharply inwards and upwards. Do this up to five times, and then look for signs of breathing again.

4 Keep the casualty face up. Perform a tongue-jaw lift followed by a finger sweep to remove any obvious foreign object. Attempt to give more breaths of mouth to mouth. Repeat steps 2–4 until medical help arrives or the obstruction to the airway is relieved and the casualty begins to breath again normally.

CHOKING (CONTINUED)

FOR A CONSCIOUS BABY (0–12 months)

IF at any stage the baby becomes unconscious, follow the ABC of resuscitation (*see pages 54-8*).

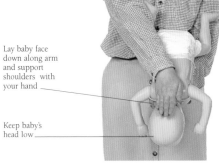

Lay baby face down along arm and support shoulders with your hand

Keep baby's head low

1 Lay the baby along your forearm. Give five sharp slaps on his back.

2 Check the baby's mouth; remove any *obvious* obstruction with one finger.

> **DO NOT** feel blindly down the throat.

3 If this fails, turn the baby over, head lower than trunk. Give five chest thrusts as for CPR, but at a slower rate.

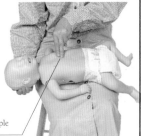

Push downwards one finger's breadth below nipple line with your fingertips

4 Check the baby's mouth again and remove any *obvious* obstruction.

> **DO NOT** use abdominal thrusts on a baby.

5 Repeat 1–4 three times, then if the baby is still not breathing, or if at any stage he becomes unconscious,
☎ *DIAL 999 OR 112 FOR AMBULANCE.*
Repeat steps 1–4 again until help arrives.

FOR A CONSCIOUS CHILD (1–8 years)

1 Stand or kneel behind child. Make a fist with one hand and place it thumb inwards midway between the tip of the breastbone and his navel.

Place thumb side of fist midway between tip of breastbone and navel

2 Grasp your fist with your other hand and press into the abdomen with a sharp inward thrust (abdominal thrust), at a rate of about one every three seconds.

3 Check child's mouth to see if the obstruction has been cleared. Remove any *obvious* obstruction.

4 Continue abdominal thrusts for one minute or until obstruction clears, or the child becomes unconscious.

5 If the obstruction has not cleared after one minute, call for help.
☎ *DIAL 999 OR 112 FOR AMBULANCE*

IF the child loses consciousness, treat as opposite until the ambulance arrives or the child begins to breathe normally.

FOR AN UNCONSCIOUS CHILD (1–8 years)

☎ *DIAL 999 OR 112 FOR AN AMBULANCE*
If possible, ask a helper, to make the call.

1 Lay the child on his back on the floor, and assess him following the ABC of resuscitation (*see page 54-58*). Check his mouth, unconsciousness may relieve muscle spasm in the throat. Try ventilations (*see page 57*), if unsuccessful, go to step 2.

Tilt head to open airway

Look, listen, and feel for breathing. Attempt to ventilate

2 Reposition the child's head to ensure that the airway is open, seal the mouth and nose again and attempt two further breaths of artificial ventilation. Assess the child (*see below right*). If you still cannot ventilate, proceed to step 3.

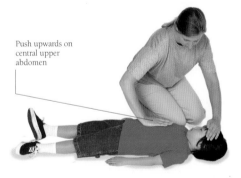

Push upwards on central upper abdomen

3 Place the heel of your hand on the child's abdomen in the midline slightly above the navel and well below the tip of the breastbone. Give up to five quick upward thrusts (abdominal thrusts). Assess the treatment (*see right*).

4 Repeat the cycle until the ambulance arrives. If at any stage the child begins to breathe, place him in the recovery position (*see page 56*).

ABDOMINAL THRUSTS

For children over the age of 8, perform abdominal thrusts with two hands as for an adult (*see page 64*). In smaller children, kneel beside or astride the child's body (*see left*), and only use one hand to perform the abdominal thrusts.

ASSESSING TREATMENT

Carry out the following checks every time you complete steps 2, 3, or 4 before going on to the next one.

◆ Check the mouth and remove any *obvious* obstruction with one finger.

DO NOT use your fingers to feel blindly down the throat.

◆ If the child begins to breathe, place her in the recovery position (*see page 56*).

◆ If the child is still not breathing, attempt to give two breaths of mouth-to-mouth ventilation (*see page 57*).

◆ If her chest does not rise when you try to ventilate, proceed to the next step.

DROWNING

Death by drowning normally occurs when air cannot get into the lungs. This usually happens because a small amount of water enters the lungs, but drowning may also be caused by throat spasm.

The water that often gushes out of a rescued casualty's mouth is from the stomach, and should drain naturally. Attempts to force water from the stomach may result in the stomach contents being inhaled. A near-drowning casualty should always receive medical attention. Any water entering the lungs causes irritation and, even if the casualty seems to recover at the time, the air passages may begin to swell (secondary drowning) some hours later. A near-drowning casualty may also need to be treated for hypothermia.

See also:
Hypothermia, *page 170.*
Rescue from Drowning, *page 26.*

TREATMENT

YOUR AIMS ARE:
- To restore adequate breathing.
- To keep the casualty warm.
- To arrange removal to hospital.

DO NOT use the abdominal thrust unless the casualty's airway is obstructed and artificial ventilation has failed.

1 If carrying the casualty from the water to safety, keep her head lower than the rest of the body to allow water to drain from the mouth.

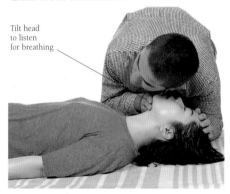

Tilt head to listen for breathing

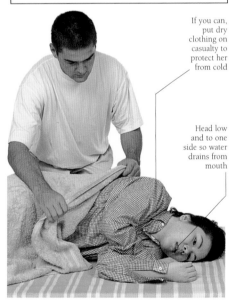

If you can, put dry clothing on casualty to protect her from cold

Head low and to one side so water drains from mouth

2 Lay her down on her back on a coat or rug. Open the airway, check breathing and pulse, and be prepared to resuscitate if necessary (*see pages 44–58*).

IF resuscitating, be aware that water in the casualty's lungs and the effects of immersion in cold water, can greatly increase his or her resistance to artificial ventilation and chest compression.

3 Treat the casualty for hypothermia: remove wet clothing and protect her from cold. Place her in the recovery position (*see page 48*). If she regains full consciousness, give her hot drinks.

4 ☎ *DIAL 999 OR 112 FOR AN AMBULANCE.*

HANGING, STRANGLING, AND THROTTLING

If pressure is exerted on the outside of the neck, the airway is squeezed and the flow of air to the lungs is cut off. The three main causes of such pressure are:

◆ *hanging*, suspension of the body by a noose around the neck;
◆ *strangling*, constriction around the neck;
◆ *throttling*, squeezing the throat.

Hanging and strangulation may occur accidentally, for example, by a tie or clothing caught in machinery. Hanging may also cause a broken neck, so the casualty must be handled carefully.

Recognition

There may be:

◆ A constricting article around the neck.
◆ Marks around the casualty's neck where a constriction has been removed.
◆ Rapid, distressed breathing; impaired consciousness; grey-blue skin (*cyanosis*).
◆ Congestion of the face, with prominent veins and, possibly, tiny red spots on the face or on the whites of the eyes.

See also:
Spinal Injury, *page 143.*

TREATMENT

YOUR AIMS ARE:

■ To restore adequate breathing.
■ To arrange removal to hospital.

DO NOT move the casualty unnecessarily in case of spinal injury.

DO NOT destroy or interfere with any material, such as knotted rope, that police may need as evidence.

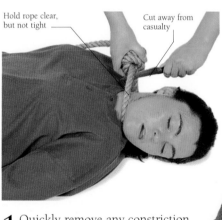

Hold rope clear, but not tight

Cut away from casualty

1 Quickly remove any constriction from around the casualty's neck. Support the body while you do so if it is still hanging.

2 Lay the casualty on the floor. Open the airway (*see page 47*), and check breathing and pulse.

IF she is not breathing, be prepared to resuscitate (*see pages 44–58*).

Tilt head only gently if neck injury is likely

Hand tucked under cheek

IF she is breathing, place her in the recovery position (*see page 48*).

3 ☎ *DIAL 999 OR 112 FOR AN AMBULANCE.*

INHALATION OF FUMES

The inhalation of smoke, gases, or toxic vapours can be lethal, so you should not make a rescue attempt if it puts your own life at risk. Smoke or fumes that have accumulated in a confined space may quickly overcome anyone who is not wearing protective equipment. A burning building presents additional hazards – not only the fire itself, but also, possibly, falling masonry or timber.

Smoke inhalation

Any person who has been enclosed in a confined space during a fire should be assumed to have inhaled smoke. Smoke from burning plastics, foam padding, and synthetic wall coverings will probably contain poisonous fumes. Casualties also should be examined for other injuries sustained as a result of the fire.

Carbon monoxide

This highly dangerous gas prevents the blood from carrying oxygen. A large amount in the air can very quickly prove fatal. Lengthy exposure to a small amount of gas – for example, a slow leak from a faulty gas heater – may also cause severe, possibly fatal, poisoning. Take care if you suspect a leak of carbon monoxide – it has no taste or smell.

See also:
Burns to the Airway, *page 162.*
Fires, *page 22.*
Unconsciousness, *page 110.*

THE EFFECTS OF FUME INHALATION		
Gas	*Source*	*Effects*
Carbon monoxide	Exhaust fumes of motor vehicles; smoke from most fires; back-draughts from blocked chimney flues; emissions from defective gas or paraffin heaters	• Chronic exposure may produce headache, confusion, aggression, nausea, vomiting, and incontinence • Acute poisoning may produce a dusky skin with a faint red tinge, rapid, distressed breathing, and impaired consciousness leading rapidly to unconsciousness
Smoke	Fires: smoke is a bigger killer than fire itself. Smoke is low in oxygen (which is used up by the burning of the fire) and may contain toxic fumes from burning materials	• Irritation of the air passages causing spasm and swelling, resulting in rapid, noisy, distressed breathing, with coughing and wheezing • Unconsciousness • Burning in or around the nose or mouth • Soot around the mouth and nose
Carbon dioxide	Tends to accumulate and become dangerously concentrated in deep enclosed spaces, such as coal pits, wells, and underground tanks	• Breathlessness • Headache • Depleted oxygen in the blood, leading rapidly to confusion and unconsciousness
Solvents and fuels	Glues; cleaning fluids; lighter fuels; camping gas and propane-fuelled stoves. Abusers may use a plastic bag to concentrate the vapour (especially with glues)	• Headache • Vomiting • Stupor and unconsciousness • Death can be caused by asphyxiation by a plastic bag (if an abuser), choking on vomit, or cardiac arrest • Some fuels when discharged from containers are very cold, and can, if inhaled, lead to cardiac arrest

TREATMENT

YOUR AIMS ARE:
- To restore adequate breathing.
- To obtain urgent medical attention and call the emergency services.

1 ☎ *DIAL 999 OR 112 FOR AN AMBULANCE*, asking for both fire and ambulance emergency services.

IF entering a garage filled with carbon monoxide, open the doors wide and let the gas escape before entering.

IF casualty's clothing is still burning, extinguish the flames (*see page 23*).

Keep your back as straight as possible

Squat behind casualty and drag her to safety

Hook your arms under casualty's folded arms and hold her wrists

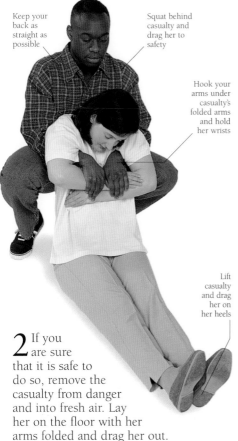

Lift casualty and drag her on her heels

2 If you are sure that it is safe to do so, remove the casualty from danger and into fresh air. Lay her on the floor with her arms folded and drag her out.

DO NOT enter a gas- or smoke-filled room without proper safety equipment.

Listen for breathing and look to see if chest rises

IF the casualty is unconscious, open the airway, check breathing and pulse, and be ready to resuscitate if needed (*see pages 44–58*). Place her in the recovery position (*see page 48*).

Make sure mask covers nose and mouth

3 Give oxygen if it is available, and you have been trained in its use. Treat any burns (*see pages 155–66*) or other injuries.

4 Stay with the casualty until medical help arrives. Monitor and *record* her breathing, pulse, and level of response every ten minutes.

BREATHING DIFFICULTIES

These may be caused by chronic illness, by respiratory system infections such as croup, and by allergic reactions, either respiratory or generalised. Laboured breathing can also occur in medical conditions that are not directly connected with the respiratory system. Sudden attacks of breathlessness may result from asthma or psychological stress (*hyperventilation*). Prompt first aid can do much to help a casualty's breathing, and ease distress.

See also:
Anaphylactic Shock, *page 81.*

COLLAPSED LUNG

If air enters the space between a lung and the chest wall, it may interfere with breathing and cause the lung to collapse (*pneumothorax*). This can occur because of a lung weakness or chest injury. Sometimes the pressure affects the action of the sound lung and heart (*tension pneumothorax*). This condition is life-threatening and a medical emergency.

If you suspect a collapsed lung, help the casualty into the position in which he or she can breathe most easily, and call an ambulance without delay.

See also:
Penetrating Chest Wounds, *page 94.*

HYPERVENTILATION

Excessive breathing (hyperventilation) is commonly a manifestation of acute anxiety and may accompany hysteria or a panic attack. It may be seen in susceptible individuals who have recently had a fright or a shock.

Excessive breathing increases oxygen intake and causes chemical changes that produce the symptoms of the condition. As breathing returns to normal, the casualty will gradually recover.

Recognition

◆ Unnaturally fast, deep breathing.

There may also be:

◆ Attention-seeking behaviour.
◆ Dizziness, faintness, trembling, or marked tingling in the hands.
◆ Cramps in the hands and feet.

See also:
Hysteria, *page 212.*

TREATMENT

YOUR AIM IS:
■ To remove the casualty from any cause of distress and calm him down.

1 When speaking to the casualty, be firm, but kind.

2 If possible, lead the casualty away to a quiet place, where he may be better able to regain control of his breathing.

3 Advise him to see his own doctor, to treat any underlying state of anxiety.

IF tingling or cramps persist, let him re-breathe his own expired air from a *paper* bag.

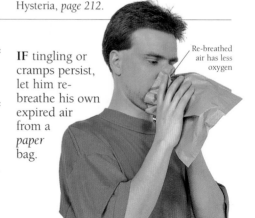

Re-breathed air has less oxygen

ASTHMA

This is a distressing condition in which the muscles of the air passages go into spasm and the linings of the airways swell. This results in narrowing of the airways, making breathing difficult.

Sometimes there is a recognised trigger for an asthmatic attack, such as an allergy, a cold, a particular drug, or cigarette smoke. At other times, no obvious trigger can be identified. Many sufferers are prone to sudden attacks at night.

Asthmatics usually deal with their own attacks. Many carry "relieving" inhalers, which have blue caps. They may carry other inhalers that they take regularly to prevent attacks; these usually have brown or white caps. The drugs in inhalers open the air passages, easing breathing. Plastic diffusers, or "spacers", can be fitted to help children breathe in the medication.

Recognition

◆ Difficulty in breathing, with a very prolonged breathing-out phase.

There may also be:

◆ Wheezing as the casualty breathes out.
◆ Distress and anxiety.
◆ Difficulty in speaking and whispering.
◆ Grey-blue skin (*cyanosis*).
◆ Dry, tickly cough.
◆ In a severe attack, the casualty may be exhausted. Rarely, he or she may become unconscious and stop breathing.

TREATMENT

YOUR AIMS ARE:
■ To ease breathing.
■ To seek medical aid if necessary.

> **DO NOT** make the casualty lie down.
> **DO NOT** try to use a preventer inhaler to help an asthma attack.

1 Keep calm and reassure the casualty. Asthma can be frightening but a reliever inhaler usually works within a few minutes.

Fit a spacer to a child's inhaler, if she has one

2 Place her in a comfortable position which is often sitting down. Ask her to breathe slowly and deeply. Give oxygen if you have been trained in its use.

IF the attack eases within 5–10 minutes, ask the casualty to take another dose from the inhaler. Urgent medical help is not vital, but she should inform her doctor of the attack.

IF this is the first attack, or if it is severe, and
◆ the inhaler has no effect after 5–10 minutes;
◆ the casualty is getting worse;
◆ breathlessness makes talking difficult;
◆ she is getting exhausted;
☎ *DIAL 999 OR 112 FOR AN AMBULANCE.* Help her to take her inhaler every 5–10 minutes. Monitor and *record* her breathing and pulse every ten minutes.

IF the casualty stops breathing or loses consciousness, open the airway, check breathing and pulse, and be ready to resuscitate if necessary. ☎ *DIAL 999 OR 112 FOR AN AMBULANCE.*

CROUP

An attack of severe breathing difficulty in very young children is known as croup. It is caused by inflammation in the windpipe and larynx. Croup can be alarming, but usually passes without lasting harm. It usually occurs at night and may recur before the child settles.

If the attack of croup persists or is very severe, and is accompanied by fever, call an ambulance. There is a small risk that the child may be suffering from a rare, croup-like condition called *epiglottitis*.

In this condition, a small flap-like structure in the throat, the epiglottis (*see page 42*) becomes infected and swollen, sometimes so much so that it blocks the airway completely. The child then requires urgent medical attention.

Recognition

♦ Distressed breathing in a young child.

There may also be:

♦ A short, barking cough.
♦ A crowing or whistling noise, especially on breathing in (*stridor*).
♦ Blue-grey skin (*cyanosis*).
♦ In severe cases, the child will be using muscles around the nose, neck, and upper arms in trying to breathe.

Suspect epiglottitis if:

♦ An older child is sitting bolt upright, evidently in severe respiratory distress.
♦ The child has a high temperature.

TREATMENT

YOUR AIMS ARE:
■ To comfort and support the child.
■ To seek medical advice.

1 Sit the child up, supporting her back and reassure her.

2 Create a steamy atmosphere: take the child into the bathroom and run the hot tap or shower, or into the kitchen and boil some water. Sit her down and encourage her to breathe in the steam to ease her breathing. *Take care* to keep the child clear of the running hot water.

> **DO NOT** try to examine the child's throat. This can produce spasm that may block the airway.
>
> **DO NOT** panic, you will alarm the child, and worsen the attack.

3 Call your doctor or, if severe, ☎ *DIAL 999 OR 112 FOR AN AMBULANCE.*

Similar signs and symptoms occur when a child inhales a foreign body. Suspect this if it occurs when eating or playing with small objects and the child does not have a high temperature (*see page 66*).

DISORDERS OF THE CIRCULATION

6

The heart and network of blood vessels, that are together known as the circulatory (or *cardiovascular*) system, work constantly to keep all parts of the body supplied with blood, which carries vital oxygen and nutrients.

The circulatory system can fail for two main reasons: severe bleeding and fluid loss may cause the volume of circulating blood to fall, and deprive the vital organs, primarily the brain, heart, and lungs, of oxygen; and secondly, age or disease can cause the body's circulatory system to break down.

First-aid techniques

The techniques described in this chapter demonstrate how to improve the blood supply to the heart and brain. In minor incidents, for example when a casualty faints, appropriate first aid should ensure recovery; in serious cases such as heart attack, your role may be vital in preserving life until medical aid arrives.

FIRST-AID PRIORITIES

◆ Position the casualty to improve the blood supply to the vital organs.

◆ Take any additional measures to improve the circulation and breathing – for example, loosening any tight clothing.

◆ Comfort and reassure the casualty; fear and panic will put extra strain on the heart.

◆ Obtain appropriate medical assistance. Always advise a casualty to inform his or her doctor of, for example, an angina attack or unexplained faint; never hesitate to call an ambulance if you suspect a more serious emergency.

THE CIRCULATORY SYSTEM

The heart and blood vessels form the circulatory system. Blood flows around the body constantly, pumped by the rhythmic contraction and relaxation, or beat, of the heart muscle. Blood runs in a network of blood vessels divided into three types: arteries, veins, and capillaries. The force exerted by the blood flow through the main arteries is called blood pressure. This force varies with the strength of the heartbeat, the elasticity of the arterial walls, and the volume and thickness of the blood. The circulating blood brings oxygen and nutrients to the tissues and carries waste products away.

HOW BLOOD CIRCULATES

Oxygenated blood is pumped out of the heart around the body. Blood that has given up its oxygen to body tissues flows back to the heart.

Aorta
Largest artery of body

Arteries
Strong, muscular, elastic walls enable arteries to expand with each surge of blood away from heart and towards tissues

Veins
Action of muscles around these thin-walled vessels squeezes blood through them, and one-way valves keep it flowing back towards heart

Gas exchange in the tissues

A network of fine blood vessels (*capillaries*) within the body tissues forms a link between the arteries and veins. The capillaries have thin walls and a slower blood flow to allow oxygen and nutrients to pass from the blood to the tissues, and waste products to be removed.

Capillaries | Small artery | Small vein
            | (*arteriole*) | (*venule*)

Blood flow through the heart

With each beat of the heart (*see page 43*), deoxygenated blood from the veins enters the right collecting chamber (*atrium*) and flows into the right pumping chamber (*ventricle*). Then the thick-walled ventricle contracts to force the blood via the pulmonary artery to the lungs (*see page 60*).

At the same time, oxygenated blood returns from the lungs, via the pulmonary veins, into the left atrium. It then passes into the left ventricle, to be pumped out to the body through the *aorta*.

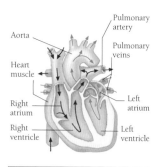

Aorta

Heart muscle

Right atrium

Right ventricle

Pulmonary artery

Pulmonary veins

Left atrium

Left ventricle

KEY

→ Direction of blood flow
▢ Oxygenated blood
▪ Deoxygenated blood

COMPOSITION OF THE BLOOD

There are about six litres (10 pints), or 1 pint per stone (0.5 litre per 6.4 kilos), of blood in the average adult body. It consists of roughly 60% clear yellow fluid (*plasma*) in which are suspended the red and white blood cells and platelets that make up the other 40%.

White blood cell

Plasma

Red blood cell

Platelet

The blood cells
Red blood cells contain haemoglobin, *a red pigment that enables them to carry oxygen. White cells defend the body against infection. Platelets help blood to clot (see page 86).*

WHAT CAN GO WRONG

◆ Oxygen levels in the blood may fall if the haemoglobin (*see left*) in the red blood cells is reduced (*anaemia*), or if there is not enough oxygen in the lungs (*see page 62*). Anaemia makes skin look pale (*pallor*); blood low in oxygen gives a grey-blue tinge to skin (*cyanosis*).

◆ Continuously high blood pressure, produced by conditions like hardening of the arteries (*arteriosclerosis*), may cause a blood vessel to burst, resulting in internal bleeding (*see page 99*).

◆ Poor circulation, hardened arteries, or narrowed blood vessels can cause a blood clot (*thrombosis*) to form. A clot may travel within the circulatory system to lodge elsewhere (*embolism*), and can endanger vital organs such as the lungs.

◆ A fall in blood pressure (as in severe bleeding) reduces blood supply, and hence oxygen, reaching vital organs (Shock, *see overleaf*).

THE PULSE

Each beat of the heart creates a wave of pressure (the pulse) that passes along the arteries. It can normally be felt where an artery passes close to the surface of the body. In adults, the pulse rate is usually between 60 and 80 beats per minute. It is faster in children and may be slower in very fit adults.

The pulse rate may increase with exertion, fear, fever, blood loss, and some illnesses. Certain heart disorders, fainting, and an increase in pressure inside the skull may slow the pulse.

Feeling for a pulse

The pulse can be recorded at the wrist (known as the *radial* pulse) or, in an emergency, at the neck (*carotid* pulse, *see page 52*). In babies, the *brachial* pulse (*see page 57*), on the inside of the upper arm, may be easier to find.

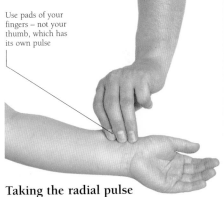

Use pads of your fingers – not your thumb, which has its own pulse

Taking the radial pulse

Place three fingers in the hollow immediately above the wrist creases at the base of the thumb, and press lightly. Check and *record*:

◆ the rate (beats per minute);
◆ the strength (strong or weak);
◆ the rhythm (regular or irregular).

SHOCK

The circulatory system distributes blood round the body, so that oxygen and nutrients can pass through and "perfuse" the tissues. When the system fails, circulatory (hyporolaemic) shock will develop. If this is not treated swiftly, vital organs may fail, which can lead to death. The condition can be made worse by fear and pain.

Where there is a risk of shock developing, reassuring the casualty and making him comfortable may be sufficient to prevent the condition from deteriorating. Do not confuse circulatory shock with *psychogenic shock*. This occurs when, for example, a person suffers deep emotional stress.

What causes circulatory shock?

Shock can develop if the heart fails to pump blood through the circulatory system (a common cause is a heart attack), or if the blood vessels dilate, as in severe infection or anaphylactic shock, reducing the blood pressure.

Shock may also occur if the blood supply to the body's vital organs is reduced through blood loss or loss of other bodily fluids through burns, severe diarrhoea, or vomiting. The body responds to fluid loss initially by diverting the blood supply from the surface to the vital organs. Shock develops if fluid loss is not stopped.

Recognition

At first, the release of adrenaline causes:

◆ A rapid pulse.
◆ Pale, grey-blue skin, especially inside the lips. A fingernail or earlobe, if pressed, will not regain its colour immediately.
◆ Sweating, and cold, clammy skin.

As shock develops, there may be:

◆ Weakness and giddiness.
◆ Nausea, and possibly vomiting.
◆ Thirst.
◆ Rapid, shallow breathing.
◆ A weak, "thready" pulse. When the pulse at the wrist disappears, about half the blood volume will have been lost.

As the brain's oxygen supply weakens:

◆ The casualty may become restless, anxious, and even aggressive.
◆ The casualty may yawn and gasp for air (known as "air hunger").
◆ The casualty will become unconscious.
◆ Finally, the heart will stop.

See also:
Severe Burns and Scalds, *page 160.*
Severe External Bleeding, *page 88.*
Unconsciousness, *page 110.*

THE BODY'S REACTION TO BLOOD LOSS	
Approximate volume	*Effect on the body*
0.5 litre (1 pint)	Little or no effect; this is the quantity normally taken in a blood-donor session.
2 litres (3½ pints)	Hormones such as adrenaline are released, quickening the pulse, and inducing sweating. Small blood vessels in non-vital areas, such as the skin, shut down to divert blood and the oxygen it carries to the vital organs. Shock becomes evident.
3 litres (5 pints)	As blood or fluid loss approaches this level (half the normal volume of the average adult), the pulse at the wrist may become undetectable. The casualty will usually lose consciousness; breathing and the heart may fail.

TREATMENT

YOUR AIMS ARE:
- To recognise shock.
- To treat any obvious cause.
- To improve the blood supply to the brain, heart, and lungs.
- To arrange removal to hospital.

> **DO NOT** let the casualty smoke, eat, drink, or move unnecessarily. If she complains of thirst, moisten her lips with a little water.
>
> **DO NOT** leave the casualty unattended.

1 Treat any cause of shock you identify (such as external bleeding).

2 Lay the casualty down on a blanket to protect her from the cold ground, keeping her head low. Constantly reassure the casualty.

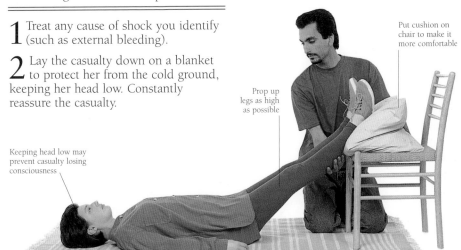

Put cushion on chair to make it more comfortable

Prop up legs as high as possible

Keeping head low may prevent casualty losing consciousness

3 Raise and support her legs to improve the blood supply to the vital organs. Take care if you suspect a fracture.

> **DO NOT** warm casualty with direct heat.
> **DO NOT** lower legs too rapidly, as this may cause a rapid reduction in blood pressure.

4 Loosen tight clothing, such as braces or belts, to reduce constriction at the neck, chest, and waist.

Check breathing, pulse, and level of response at regular intervals

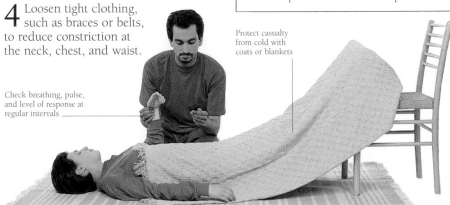

Protect casualty from cold with coats or blankets

5 Keep the casualty warm by covering her with coats or blankets. ☎ *DIAL 999 OR 112 FOR AN AMBULANCE.*

6 Check and *record* breathing, pulse, and level of response. Be prepared to resuscitate if necessary (*see pages 44–58*).

FAINTING

A faint (also known as *syncope*) is a brief loss of consciousness that is caused by a temporary reduction of blood flow to the brain. Unlike shock (*see page 78*), the pulse becomes very slow, although it soon picks up and returns to normal. Recovery from a faint is usually rapid and complete.

A faint may be a reaction to pain or fright, or the result of emotional upset, exhaustion, or lack of food. It is more common, however, after long periods of physical inactivity, such as standing still, especially in a warm atmosphere. The inactivity causes blood to pool in the lower part of the body, reducing the amount of oxygen available to the brain.

Recognition

◆ A brief loss of consciousness causing the casualty to fall to the floor.
◆ A slow pulse.
◆ Pale, cold skin and sweating.

See also:
Unconsciousness,
page 110.

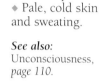

TREATMENT

YOUR AIMS ARE:
■ To improve blood flow to the brain.
■ To reassure the casualty as she recovers, and make her comfortable.

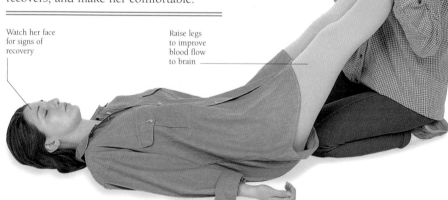

Support her ankles on your shoulders

Watch her face for signs of recovery

Raise legs to improve blood flow to brain

1 Lay the casualty down, and raise and support her legs.

2 Make sure that she has plenty of fresh air; open a window if necessary.

3 As she recovers, reassure her and help her sit up gradually.

4 Look for and treat any injury that has been sustained through falling.

IF she does not regain consciousness quickly, open the airway, check breathing and pulse, and be ready to resuscitate if necessary (*see pages 44–58*). Place her in the recovery position (*see page 48*).
☎ *DIAL 999 OR 112 FOR AN AMBULANCE.*

IF she feels faint again, raise and support her legs until she recovers fully.

ANAPHYLACTIC SHOCK

This is the name given to a major allergic reaction within the body. It is a serious potentially fatal condition that may develop in susceptible individuals within a few seconds or a few minutes of, for example,
+ the injection of a specific drug;
+ the sting of a certain insect;
+ the ingestion of a particular food, such as peanuts.

In the allergic reaction, chemical substances are released into the blood which dilate blood vessels and constrict air passages. Blood pressure falls dramatically and breathing is impeded. The face and neck can swell, increasing the risk of suffocation. The amount of oxygen reaching the vital organs (heart, brain, and lungs) is severely reduced. A casualty with anaphylactic shock urgently needs oxygen and acute medical treatment. First aid is limited to assisting breathing and minimising shock until specialised help arrives.

Recognition
There may be:

+ Anxiety.
+ Widespread red, blotchy skin eruption.
+ Swelling of the face and neck.
+ Puffiness around the eyes.
+ Impaired breathing, ranging from a tight chest to severe difficulty; the casualty may wheeze and gasp for air.
+ A rapid pulse.

See also:
Allergy, *page 213.*

TREATMENT

YOUR AIM IS:

■ To arrange urgent removal to hospital.

1 ☎ *DIAL 999 OR 112 FOR AN AMBULANCE.* Give any information you have on the casualty's condition.

2 Help a conscious casualty sit up in the position that most relieves any breathing difficulty.

Sitting position should help her breathing

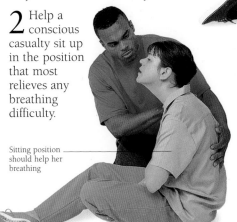

Check breathing and pulse every few minutes

Insulate casualty from cold with blanket or coat

IF she becomes unconscious, open the airway, check breathing and pulse, and be prepared to resuscitate if necessary (*see pages 44–58*). Place her in the recovery position (*see page 48*).

Some people are fully aware of their hypersensitivity, so check for a syringe of adrenaline (Epi-Pen, *see page 31*). If necessary, allow the casualty or a family member to use it.

DISORDERS OF THE HEART

The heart is a specialised pump. Its muscle, the *myocardium*, "beats" throughout our lives in a smooth, continuous, and co-ordinated way, controlled by an electrical impulse (*see* How the heart beats, *page 43*). The heart muscle has its own blood supply, provided by the coronary arteries (so-called because they encircle the heart like a crown).

Like all other arteries in the body, the coronary arteries are susceptible to narrowing and blockage, which can impede or even prevent the oxygen from reaching the heart muscle. In severe cases, or if the electrical impulse is disrupted, the heart may stop (*cardiac arrest*).

See also:
Blood flow through the heart, *page 76*.

ANGINA PECTORIS

The name means a pain of the chest, and describes the pain that a person experiences when narrowed coronary arteries are unable to deliver sufficient blood to the heart muscle to meet the demands of exertion or, sometimes, of excitement. An attack forces the casualty to rest; the pain should then soon ease.

Recognition
There may be:

◆ Gripping central chest pain, spreading often to the jaw and down the left arm.
◆ Shortness of breath.
◆ Weakness, often sudden and extreme.
◆ Sweating, nausea, and anxiety.

TREATMENT

YOUR AIMS ARE:
■ To ease strain on the heart by ensuring that the casualty rests.
■ To obtain medical help if necessary.

1 Help the casualty to sit down. Make her comfortable and reassure her.

2 If the casualty has medicine for angina, such as tablets or a "puffer" aerosol, let her administer it herself. If necessary, help her to take it.

3 Encourage the casualty to rest and keep any bystanders away. The attack should ease within a few minutes.

IF the pain persists or returns, suspect a heart attack. ☎ *DIAL 999 OR 112 FOR AN AMBULANCE.* Monitor and *record* her breathing and pulse rates every ten minutes, and be ready to resuscitate if necessary (*see pages 44–58*).

Casualty with known condition may have "puffer" to ease attack

HEART ATTACK

A heart attack most commonly occurs when the blood supply to part of the heart muscle is suddenly obstructed – for example, by a clot in one of the coronary arteries (*coronary thrombosis*). The main risk of a heart attack is that the heart will stop. The effect of the heart attack depends largely on how much of the heart muscle is affected; many casualties will recover completely.

Drugs that aid recovery include special medicines called *thrombolytics*, which act to dissolve the clot, and aspirin, which "thins" the blood.

See also:
Cardiac Arrest, *page 84.*

Recognition

There may be:

◆ Persistent, vice-like central chest pain, spreading often to the jaw and down the left arm. Unlike *angina pectoris (see opposite)*, the pain does not ease once the casualty is at rest, and indeed may occur at rest.
◆ Breathlessness, and discomfort high in the abdomen, often feeling similar to severe indigestion.
◆ Sudden faintness or giddiness.
◆ A sense of impending doom.
◆ "Ashen" skin, and blueness at the lips.
◆ A rapid, weak, or irregular pulse.
◆ Collapse, often without any warning.

TREATMENT

YOUR AIMS ARE:

■ To minimise the work of the heart.
■ To summon urgent medical help and arrange removal to hospital.

1 Make the casualty as comfortable as possible to ease the strain on his heart. A half-sitting position, with the casualty's head and shoulders well supported and his knees bent, is often best.

Help him into comfortable position

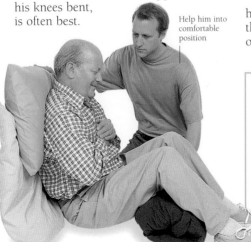

2 ☎ *DIAL 999 OR 112 FOR AN AMBULANCE.* State that you suspect a heart attack.

3 Constantly monitor and *record* the casualty's breathing and pulse rates, and be prepared to resuscitate if necessary (*see pages 44–58*).

4 If the casualty has medicine for angina, such as tablets or a "puffer" aerosol, help him to take it. If the pain persists, and the casualty is fully conscious, give him one tablet of ordinary aspirin to *chew.*

ACUTE HEART FAILURE

Heart failure is a condition in which the heart muscle is strained and fatigued – for example, following a coronary thrombosis – and becomes increasingly inefficient. Acute attacks often occur at night. They may appear similar to an asthma attack (*see page 73*), with severe breathlessness, often, but not always, accompanied by other signs and symptoms of heart attack. Follow the treatment for Heart Attack.

CARDIAC ARREST

The term "cardiac arrest" describes any sudden stoppage of the heart. There are many reasons for an arrest, including heart attack (*see page 83*), severe blood loss (*see page 88*), suffocation (*see page 63*), electric shock (*see page 24*), anaphylactic shock (*see page 81*), drug overdose (*see page 122*), and hypothermia (*see page 170*). Cardiac arrest is characterised by the absence of pulse and breathing. You must commence resuscitation immediately because, without oxygen supplied by the blood, the heart muscle and brain cells will deteriorate rapidly. The ABC of resuscitation is fully described in the chapter on Resuscitation (*see pages 44–58*).

Recognition
- Absence of pulse.
- Absence of breathing.

TREATMENT

YOUR AIMS ARE:
- To arrange urgent removal to hospital.
- To keep the heart muscle and brain supplied with oxygen until help arrives.

Check the level of consciousness, and breathing and pulse rates. ☎ *DIAL 999 OR 112 FOR AN AMBULANCE.*

IF breathing and pulse are absent, begin CPR (*see pages 52 and 58*).

VENTRICULAR FIBRILLATION

This most common cause of cardiac arrest is an electric storm originating in a chamber of the heart (*ventricle*) that has been damaged or deprived of oxygen. The electrical impulse of the heart becomes chaotic, and the heart muscle fails to contract in harmony.

The use of defibrillators
Ventricular fibrillation is often reversed by the early application of a controlled electric shock from a defibrillator machine, which is now carried by most ambulances. Your task as the First Aider is to keep the brain supplied with oxygen by cardiopulmonary resuscitation (*see pages 50–58*) until a defibrillator can be brought to the casualty and used by a *trained operator*.

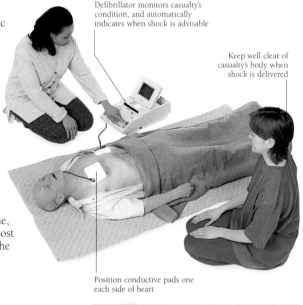

Defibrillator monitors casualty's condition, and automatically indicates when shock is advisable

Keep well clear of casualty's body when shock is delivered

Position conductive pads one each side of heart

NEVER deliver a shock to a casualty who has a pulse.

WOUNDS AND BLEEDING

7

Any abnormal break in the skin or the body surfaces is known as a wound. *Open* wounds allow blood and other fluids to be lost from the body and germs to enter. If the bleeding is purely internal, the wound is *closed*. This is most easily recognised by bruising, which indicates damage to blood vessels just beneath the skin.

Wounds can be quite daunting, particularly if there is a lot of bleeding, but prompt action is needed to reduce blood loss and shock.

Understanding treatment procedures

This chapter tells you how the body's defenses to blood loss function and shows you the effect of the various types of wound and bleeding. The nature of the wounding force determines the type of wound and influences its treatment. Recommended treatments for all types of wounds – major, internal, and minor – are covered here. It is also important that you take steps to guard against cross-infection while treating a wound (*see also page 14*).

FIRST-AID PRIORITIES

◆ Control blood loss by applying pressure over the wound and raising the injured part.

◆ Take steps to minimise shock, which can result from severe blood loss.

◆ Cover any open wound with a dressing, to protect it from infection and promote natural healing.

◆ Pay scrupulous attention to hygiene, so that there is no spread of infection between the casualty and yourself.

CONTENTS

BLOOD CLOTTING

Blood is carried around the body by vessels known as arteries, veins, and capillaries (*see* The circulatory system, *page 76*). When a blood vessel is torn or severed, blood loss and shock (*see page 78*) make blood pressure fall and the vessel contracts at the injury site.

Injured tissue cells at the site of a wound and specialised blood cells (*platelets*) trigger a series of reactions to produce the chemical *thrombin*. This reacts with a blood protein (*fibrinogen*) to create *fibrin* filaments that mesh together to form a clot.

The clot releases a pale fluid (*serum*) containing antibodies and specialised cells that begin the process of repair. Later, the clot dries into a crust (*scab*) that seals and protects the wound until the healing process is complete.

WHAT CAN GO WRONG

In some medical conditions, anti-coagulants are used to stop clots forming in blood vessels. Other conditions such as *haemophilia* (which usually affects only males), *purpura*, and *leukaemia* prevent normal blood-clotting; they can cause internal bleeding under the skin or into joints or from the linings of internal organs.

Components of blood
● Red cells
○ White cells
● Platelets

○ Plasma - dissolved proteins, such as fibrinogen
   - salts, sugars, fats
   - minerals, vitamins
   - water

☐ *Agents active in the clotting of blood*

HOW BLOOD CLOTS AT A WOUND

Platelets   Red blood cell   Fibrin   Skin   White blood   Clot   Scab   Scar tissue
                                                                  cell

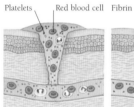 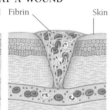 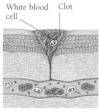 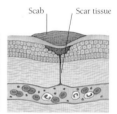

1 Blood *platelets* come into contact with the damaged vessel wall, become sticky, and clump at the injury site.

2 The platelets and damaged cells react with a blood protein to create a mesh of *fibrin* filaments.

3 The fibrin mesh traps more blood cells at the injury site to form a jelly-like clot within ten minutes.

4 The fibrin contracts and the clot rapidly shrinks, releasing *serum* that causes the area to swell, and leaves a scar.

BLOOD TRANSFUSIONS

If a person loses a litre (2 pints) or more of blood, they may need to be given a blood transfusion. Before this is done, a person's blood group must be determined. All red blood cells contain chemicals known as *antigens*. An individual's blood is classified according to whether it contains antigen A, B, both (AB), or neither (O). The Rhesus factor may also be present in (*Rhesus positive*), or absent from (*Rhesus negative*), the blood. A body only accepts blood with similar antigens.

Therefore, all patients' and donors' blood is cross-matched to ensure its compatibility before a transfusion. It is crucial that you get a casualty to hospital as soon as possible to allow time for accurate cross-matching.

TYPES OF WOUND

Incised wound
A clean cut from a sharp edge, such as broken glass, causes an incision. The blood vessels at the wound edges are cut straight across, so there may be profuse bleeding. Incised limb wounds may sever underlying structures such as tendons.

Laceration
Crushing or ripping forces result in rough tears or lacerations. They may bleed less profusely than clean-cut wounds, but there is likely to be more tissue damage and bruising. They are also often contaminated by germs; the risk of infection is high.

Abrasion (graze)
This is a superficial wound in which the top layers of skin are scraped off, leaving a raw, tender area. Abrasions are often caused by a sliding fall or a friction burn. They can contain embedded foreign particles that may result in infection.

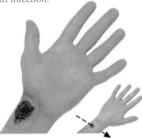

Entry wound

Contusion (bruise)
A blunt blow or punch can rupture capillaries beneath the skin. Blood then leaks into the tissues, causing bruising. The skin occasionally splits. Severe contusion may indicate deeper, hidden damage, such as fracture or internal injury.

Puncture wound
Standing on a nail or being stabbed, for example, will result in a puncture wound with a small entry site, but a deep track of internal damage. As germs and dirt can be carried far into the body, the infection risk is high.

Gunshot wound
A bullet or other missile may drive into or through the body, causing serious internal injury, and sucking in contaminants from the air. The entry wound may be small and neat; any exit wound may be large and ragged.

TYPES OF BLEEDING

Bleeding (also known as *haemorrhage*) is classified by the type of blood vessel that is damaged: artery, vein, or capillary (*see* page 76). Arterial bleeding is very serious and can be dramatic. Venous bleeding from a major vein can also be serious.

Arterial bleeding
Richly oxygenated blood is bright red and, under pressure from the heart, spurts from a wound in time with the heartbeat. A severed main artery may jet blood several feet high, and rapidly reduce the volume of circulating blood.

Venous bleeding
Venous blood, having given up its oxygen, is dark red. It is under less pressure than arterial blood, but as vein walls are capable of great distension, blood can "pool" within them. Blood from a severed major vein may gush profusely.

Capillary bleeding
This type of bleeding, or oozing, occurs at the site of all wounds. Capillary bleeding may at first be brisk, but blood loss is usually slight. A blunt blow may rupture capillaries under the skin, causing bleeding into the tissues (bruise).

SEVERE EXTERNAL BLEEDING

Massive external bleeding is dramatic and distressing, and may distract you from first-aid priorities; remember the ABC of resuscitation (*see page 44*). Bleeding at the face or neck can impede the airway. Rarely is blood loss so great that the heart stops. Bear in mind that shock is likely to develop; the casualty may lose consciousness.

See also:
Shock, *page 78.*
Unconsciousness, *page 110.*

PROTECTING YOURSELF

If possible use disposable gloves, and wash your hands well in soap and water before, and after, treatment. If you have any sores or open wounds, cover them with a waterproof adhesive dressing
(*see also page 14*).

TREATMENT

YOUR AIMS ARE:
- To control the bleeding.
- To prevent and minimise the effects of shock.
- To minimise the risk of infection.
- To arrange urgent removal of the casualty to hospital.

1 Remove or cut clothing to expose the wound. Watch out for sharp objects, such as glass, that may injure you.

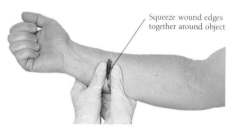

Squeeze wound edges together around object

IF you cannot apply direct pressure, for example, if an object is protruding, press down firmly on either side.

Press for ten minutes to give blood time to clot

2 Apply direct pressure over the wound with your fingers or palm, preferably over a sterile dressing or clean pad – but do not waste time hunting for a dressing.

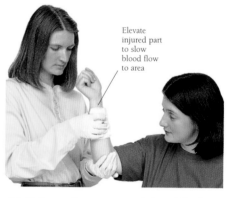

Elevate injured part to slow blood flow to area

3 Raise and support an injured limb above the level of the casualty's heart. Handle the limb very gently if the injury involves a fracture (*see page 130*).

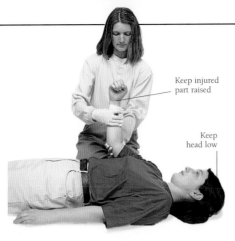

Keep injured part raised

Keep head low

4 Lay the casualty down. This will reduce blood flow to the site of injury, and minimise shock.

5 Leaving any original pad in place, apply a sterile dressing. Bandage it in place firmly, but not so tightly as to impede the circulation (*see page 223*). If bleeding seeps through the dressing, bandage another firmly over the top.

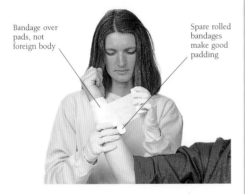

Bandage over pads, not foreign body

Spare rolled bandages make good padding

IF there is a protruding foreign body, build up padding on either side of the object until high enough to bandage over the object without pressing on it.

6 Secure and support the injured part with bandaging (*see page 131*).

7 ☎ *DIAL 999 OR 112 FOR AN AMBULANCE.* Treat for shock. Check dressing for seepage. Check circulation beyond the bandage (*see page 223*).

INDIRECT PRESSURE

Direct pressure at the bleeding point can be impossible to apply, or may be insufficient to staunch bleeding from a limb. In these cases, "indirect pressure" may be applied to a pressure point above the bleeding artery, where the main artery runs close to a bone.

First identify the artery by feeling for pulsation (*see below*) and then apply pressure until the blood supply to the limb is greatly reduced. This pressure must not be applied for longer than ten minutes, except for a femoral artery.

DO NOT apply a tourniquet; it can worsen the bleeding, and may result in tissue damage or even gangrene.

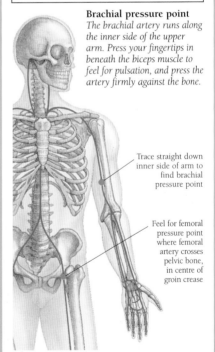

Brachial pressure point
The brachial artery runs along the inner side of the upper arm. Press your fingertips in beneath the biceps muscle to feel for pulsation, and press the artery firmly against the bone.

Trace straight down inner side of arm to find brachial pressure point

Feel for femoral pressure point where femoral artery crosses pelvic bone, in centre of groin crease

Femoral pressure point
Lay the casualty down with the knee bent to locate the groin or trouser fold, feel for the artery, then press firmly with your thumbs.

BLEEDING AT SPECIAL SITES

There are a number of wounds that require slight variations on the general rules of direct and indirect pressure if they are to be successfully treated. Blood loss from wounds at these special sites may be copious, and the casualty must be observed carefully for signs of shock.

SCALP AND HEAD WOUNDS

The scalp has a rich blood supply, and when it is damaged, the skin splits, producing a gaping wound. Bleeding may be profuse, and will often make the injury appear worse than it is. However, a scalp wound may be part of a more serious underlying injury, such as a skull fracture; examine the casualty very carefully, particularly if he or she is elderly, or when it is possible that a serious head injury is masked by alcohol or drug intoxication. If in doubt, follow the treatment for head injury.

See also:
Head Injuries, *page 113.*
Shock, *page 78.*

TREATMENT

YOUR AIMS ARE:
- To control blood loss.
- To arrange transport to hospital.

1 Wearing disposable gloves, if possible, replace any displaced skin flaps.

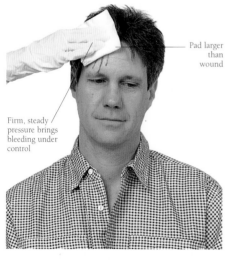

Pad larger than wound

Firm, steady pressure brings bleeding under control

2 Apply firm direct pressure over a sterile dressing or clean pad.

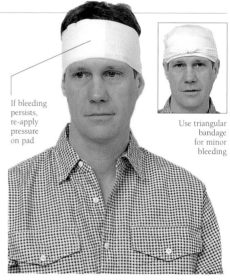

If bleeding persists, re-apply pressure on pad

Use triangular bandage for minor bleeding

3 Secure the dressing with a roller bandage. Lay the casualty down with head and shoulders slightly raised.

IF he becomes unconscious, open the airway, check breathing and pulse, and be ready to resuscitate if needed (*see pages 44–58*). Place in the recovery position.

4 Take or send the casualty to hospital in the final treatment position.

WOUNDS TO THE PALM

The palm is richly supplied with blood, and a wound may bleed profusely. A deep wound may sever tendons and nerves, and result in loss of feeling in the fingers. If a foreign body prevents fist-clenching, treat as described on page 105.

TREATMENT

YOUR AIMS ARE:
- To control blood loss.
- To arrange transport to hospital.

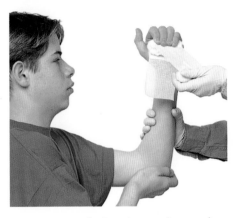

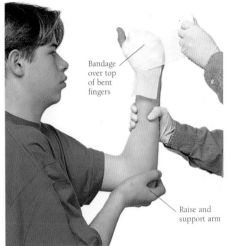

Bandage over top of bent fingers

Raise and support arm

1 Press a sterile dressing or clean pad firmly into the palm and ask the casualty to clench his fist over it. If he finds it difficult to press hard, he may grasp the fist with his uninjured hand.

2 Bandage the casualty's fingers so that they are clenched over the pad. Tie the knot over his fingers.

3 Support the casualty's arm in an elevation sling (*see page 233*), and arrange to take or send him to hospital.

WOUNDS AT JOINT CREASES

Major blood vessels cross the inside of the elbow and knee and, if severed, will bleed copiously. Remember that the technique described below will, by compressing the artery, impede the blood supply to the lower part of the limb.

TREATMENT

YOUR AIMS ARE:
- To control blood loss.
- To arrange transport to hospital.

1 Press a clean pad over the injury. Bend the joint as firmly as possible.

2 With the joint firmly bent to press on the pad, raise the limb. If possible, lay the casualty down to reduce shock.

3 Take or send the casualty to hospital in the treatment position. Release the pressure briefly every ten minutes to restore normal blood flow.

BLEEDING VARICOSE VEINS

Veins contain one-way valves that keep the blood flowing towards the heart. If these deteriorate, blood collects behind them and causes distension, most often in the legs. The "varicose" vein has taut, thin walls and is often raised, stretching the skin to give a characteristic "knobbly" appearance. It can be burst by gentle knocks and will bleed profusely. Shock may develop if bleeding is not controlled.

See also:
Shock, *page 78*

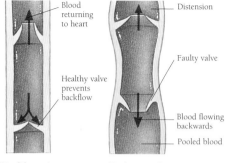

Blood returning to heart

Distension

Faulty valve

Healthy valve prevents backflow

Blood flowing backwards

Pooled blood

Healthy vein   **Varicose vein**

TREATMENT

YOUR AIMS ARE:
- To bring blood loss under control.
- To arrange urgent removal to hospital.
- To minimise shock.

1 Lay the casualty on her back and raise the injured leg as high as possible. This may reduce or stop the bleeding.

2 Expose the site of the bleeding and apply firm, direct pressure over a sterile dressing or clean pad with a securing bandage or with your fingers, until bleeding is controlled.

Keep leg high

Support leg on shoulder while bandaging

4 Put a large, soft pad over the dressing; bandage it firmly enough to exert even pressure, but not so tightly that the circulation is impeded (*see page 223*).

3 Remove garments such as garters or elastic-topped stockings that may be impeding blood flow back to the heart.

5 ☎ *DIAL 999 OR 112 FOR AN AMBULANCE.* Keep the leg raised and supported until the ambulance arrives.

MAJOR WOUNDS

Many wounds can cause serious internal injury without severe external bleeding. This applies particularly to wounds to the trunk; a stab wound to the abdomen, for example, may produce only a small, neat entry wound, yet cause massive internal damage that needs urgent treatment.

ABDOMINAL WOUNDS

The severity of an abdominal wound may be evident in external bleeding and protruding abdominal contents. More commonly, there is hidden internal injury and bleeding. A stab wound, gunshot, or crushing injury to the abdomen may puncture, lacerate, or rupture organs and blood vessels deep within the body. The risk of infection and of shock is high.

See also:
Internal Bleeding, *page 99.*
Shock, *page 78.*

TREATMENT

YOUR AIMS ARE:
- To minimise the risk of infection.
- To minimise shock.
- To arrange urgent removal to hospital.

1 Lay the casualty down on a firm surface. Loosen any tight clothing.

If wound cuts *across* abdomen, raise and support casualty's knees to ease strain on injury

IF the wound is *vertical*, do not raise the knees.

Undo belt

2 Put a large dressing over the wound, and secure it lightly in place with a bandage, or some adhesive tape.

IF blood seeps through the dressing, add another dressing or pad on top.

IF the casualty coughs or vomits, press firmly on the dressing to prevent the contents of the abdomen from pushing through the wound and being exposed.

IF part of the intestine is protruding, do not touch it, but cover with a plastic bag or kitchen film to prevent it from drying out. Alternatively, use a sterile dressing.

3 ☎ *DIAL 999 OR 112 FOR AN AMBULANCE.* Treat the casualty for shock. Stay with him and check his condition every few minutes.

IF the casualty becomes unconscious, open the airway, check breathing and pulse, and be ready to resuscitate if needed (*see pages 44–58*). Put him in the recovery position, supporting the abdomen.

PENETRATING CHEST WOUNDS

The heart and lungs, and the major blood vessels around them, lie within the chest (*thorax*), protected by the breastbone and the 12 pairs of ribs – the ribcage (*see page 124*). The ribcage also extends far enough downwards to protect the upper abdominal organs.

A penetrating chest wound can cause severe internal damage within both the chest and upper abdomen. The lungs are particularly vulnerable to injury, either directly, or because the wound perforates the membranes (*pleura*) that protect each lung. Air can then enter between the membranes, exerting pressure on the lung that can cause it to collapse, a condition known as *pneumothorax*.

Sometimes pressure builds up to such an extent that it affects the uninjured lung as well. Such damage causes the casualty to develop increasing breathlessness, or *dyspnoea*. The pressure may also stop the heart refilling properly with blood, impairing the circulation, and causing shock; this is a *tension pneumothorax*.

Recognition

- Difficult and painful breathing, possibly rapid, shallow, and uneven.
- An acute sense of alarm.

There may also be:

- Signs of shock.
- Coughed-up frothy, red blood.
- Grey-blue colouring (*cyanosis*) at the mouth, nailbeds, and skin.
- A crackling feeling of the skin around the site of the wound, caused by air collecting in the tissues.
- Blood bubbling out of the wound.
- The sound of air being sucked into the chest as the casualty breathes in.

See also:
Shock, *page 78.*

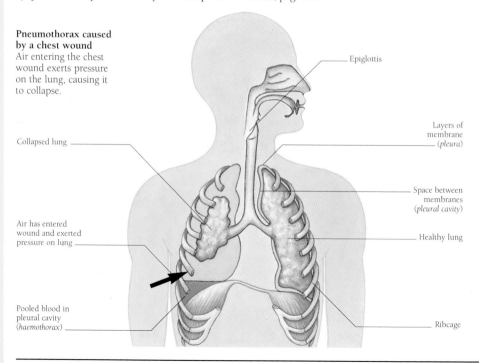

Pneumothorax caused by a chest wound
Air entering the chest wound exerts pressure on the lung, causing it to collapse.

Epiglottis

Collapsed lung

Air has entered wound and exerted pressure on lung

Pooled blood in pleural cavity (*haemothorax*)

Layers of membrane (*pleura*)

Space between membranes (*pleural cavity*)

Healthy lung

Ribcage

TREATMENT

YOUR AIMS ARE:
- To seal the wound and maintain breathing.
- To minimise shock.
- To arrange urgent removal to hospital.

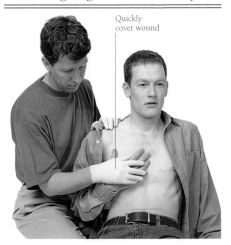

Quickly cover wound

1 Immediately use the palm of your gloved hand, or the casualty's hand, if he is conscious, to cover the wound.

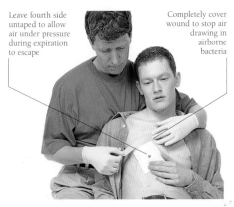

Leave fourth side untaped to allow air under pressure during expiration to escape

Completely cover wound to stop air drawing in airborne bacteria

2 Place a sterile dressing or clean pad over the wound and surrounding area. Cover with a plastic bag, foil, or kitchen film. Secure firmly with adhesive tape on three sides, or with bandaging, so that the dressing is taut.

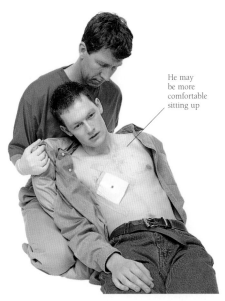

He may be more comfortable sitting up

3 Provide firm support for a conscious casualty, in the position he finds most comfortable. Encourage him to lean towards the injured side.

4 ☎ *DIAL 999 OR 112 FOR AN AMBULANCE.* Treat the casualty for shock if necessary.

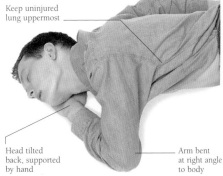

Keep uninjured lung uppermost

Head tilted back, supported by hand

Arm bent at right angle to body

IF he becomes unconscious, open the airway, check breathing and pulse, and be ready to resuscitate if necessary (*see pages 44–58*). Place him in the recovery position (*see page 48*), lying with the uninjured side uppermost. This will help the healthy lung to work effectively.

CRUSH INJURIES

These are commonly caused by traffic accidents and incidents during building work, and by train crashes, explosions, earthquakes, or mining accidents.

Local injuries may include fractures, swelling, blistering, and internal bleeding. The crushing force may also impair the circulation, causing numbness at or below the site of injury; there may be no detectable pulse in a crushed limb.

The dangers of prolonged crushing

If the casualty is trapped for any length of time, two serious complications may endanger him. Firstly, prolonged crushing may cause extensive damage to tissue, especially to muscles. Once the pressure is removed, shock may develop rapidly as tissue fluid leaks into the injured area.

Secondly, and more dangerously, toxic substances will build up in damaged muscle tissue around a crush injury. If released suddenly into the circulation, these toxins may cause kidney failure. This process, called "crush syndrome", is extremely serious and can be fatal.

See also:
Fractures, *pages 130–31.*
Internal Bleeding, *page 99.*
Shock, *page 78.*

TREATMENT

YOUR AIMS ARE:
■ To obtain specialist medical aid urgently, meanwhile taking any steps possible to treat the casualty.
■ To determine the length of time the casualty has been crushed, before starting treatment.

FOR A CASUALTY CRUSHED FOR LESS THAN 10 MINUTES

1 Release the casualty as quickly as possible.

2 Control any external bleeding and cover any wounds.

3 Secure and support any suspected fractures.

4 Examine and observe the casualty for signs of shock (*see page 78*), and treat accordingly.

☎ DIAL 999 OR 112 FOR AN AMBULANCE.

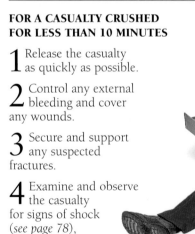

FOR A CASUALTY CRUSHED FOR MORE THAN 10 MINUTES

DO NOT release the casualty.

1 ☎ *DIAL 999 OR 112 FOR AN AMBULANCE.* Give clear details of the incident.

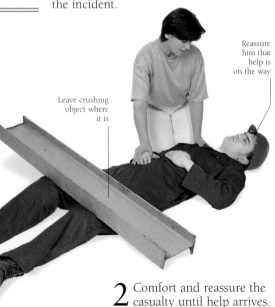

Reassure him that help is on the way

Leave crushing object where it is

2 Comfort and reassure the casualty until help arrives.

IMPALEMENT

If someone becomes impaled by, for example, falling on railings, you must never attempt to lift him or her off; you may worsen internal injuries. Give clear details to the emergency services; they will bring specialist cutting equipment.

TREATMENT

YOUR AIM IS:
- To prevent further injury.

1 ☎ *DIAL 999 OR 112 FOR AN AMBULANCE*. Explain the situation. Send someone to make the call, if possible.

2 Support the casualty's weight so that he or she is as comfortable as possible. Constantly reassure the casualty.

> **DO NOT** give the casualty anything to eat or drink.

AMPUTATION

The force and direction of an injury may be such that a limb, or part of a limb, is partially or completely severed. However, it is sometimes possible, using micro-surgical techniques, to "replant" an amputated part, so it is important to locate and preserve it. The sooner the casualty and the severed part reach hospital the better. Describe the accident clearly to the emergency services; they will alert the relevant specialist centre.

See also:
Shock, *page 78.*

TREATMENT

YOUR AIMS ARE:
- To minimise blood loss and shock.
- To preserve the amputated part.

CARE OF THE CASUALTY

1 Control blood loss by applying direct pressure, and raising the injured part, or apply indirect pressure (*see page 89*).

> **DO NOT** use a tourniquet.

2 Apply a sterile dressing or non-fluffy clean pad secured with a bandage.

3 Treat the casualty for shock (*see page 78*).

4 ☎ *DIAL 999 OR 112 FOR AN AMBULANCE*. Warn of amputation, and if the severed part has been recovered.

CARE OF THE AMPUTATED PART

1 Wrap the severed part in kitchen film or a plastic bag.

2 Wrap again in gauze or soft fabric, then place the package in another container (for example, another plastic bag) filled with crushed ice. Chilling will help to preserve the part.

3 Clearly mark the package with the time of injury and the casualty's name. Give it personally to medical personnel.

> **DO NOT** use cotton wool on surfaces of raw or open wounds.
>
> **DO NOT** wash the severed part.
>
> **DO NOT** allow the severed part to come into direct contact with ice.

EYE WOUNDS

The eye (*see page 178*) can be bruised or cut by direct blows or by sharp, chipped fragments of metal, grit, and glass. All eye injuries are potentially serious. Even superficial grazes to the surface (*cornea*) of the eye can lead to scarring or infection, with possible deterioration of vision.

A penetrating wound may rupture the eyeball and allow its clear fluid content to escape. Although this type of injury is very serious, it is now possible to repair eye wounds, and the sight in the eye may not be lost.

Recognition

◆ Intense pain in the affected eye, with spasm of the eyelids.

There may also be:

◆ A visible wound.
◆ A bloodshot appearance to the injured eye, even if there is no visible wound.
◆ Partial or total loss of vision.
◆ Leakage of blood or clear fluid from a wound, possibly with visible flattening of the eyeball.

TREATMENT

YOUR AIMS ARE:

■ To prevent further damage.
■ To arrange transport to hospital.

1 Lay the casualty on her back, holding her head to keep it as still as possible.

DO NOT touch or attempt to remove an embedded foreign body (*see page 105*).

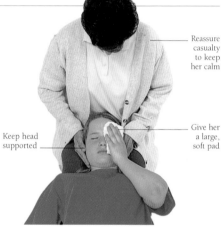

Reassure casualty to keep her calm

Keep head supported

Give her a large, soft pad

2 Tell the casualty to keep both eyes still; movement of the "good" eye will cause movement of the injured one, which may damage it further.

3 Ask the casualty to hold an eyepad, or sterile dressing, over the injured eye. This discourages the casualty from moving the eye and protects it from infection. If it will take some time to obtain medical help, bandage the pad in place for her.

4 Take or send the casualty to hospital in the treatment position.

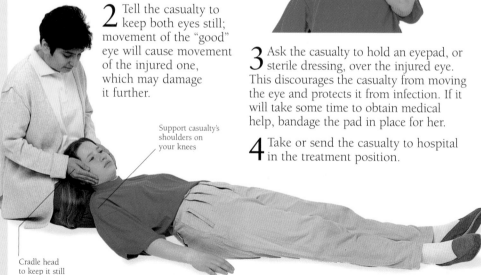

Support casualty's shoulders on your knees

Cradle head to keep it still

INTERNAL BLEEDING

Bleeding within the body cavities may follow injury, such as a fracture or penetrating wound, but can also occur spontaneously – for example, bleeding from a stomach ulcer.

Internal bleeding is serious; even if blood is not spilt from the body, it is still lost from the circulation, and shock can develop. Accumulated blood can also exert damaging pressure on organs such as the lungs or brain.

When to suspect internal bleeding

Suspect internal bleeding if, following injury, signs of shock develop without obvious blood loss. At the site of a violent injury, there may be "pattern bruising" – discolouration with the pattern of clothes or crushing objects. There may be blood at body orifices, either fresh or mixed with the contents of injured organs.

Recognition
There may be:
- Pallor.
- Cold, clammy skin.
- A rapid, weak pulse.
- Pain.
- Thirst.
- Confusion, restlessness, and irritability, possibly leading to collapse and unconsciousness.
- After violent injury, pattern bruising.
- Bleeding from orifices (*see overleaf*).
- Information from the casualty that indicates recent injury or illness, previous similar episodes, or if he or she takes drugs for a medical condition.

See also:
Cerebral Compression, *page 115.*
Crush Injuries, *page 96.*
Shock, *page 78.*
Unconsciousness, *page 110.*

TREATMENT

YOUR AIMS ARE:
- To arrange urgent removal to hospital.
- To minimise shock.

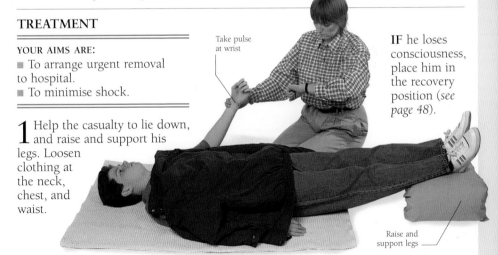

Take pulse at wrist

IF he loses consciousness, place him in the recovery position (*see page 48*).

Raise and support legs

1 Help the casualty to lie down, and raise and support his legs. Loosen clothing at the neck, chest, and waist.

2 ☎ *DIAL 999 OR 112 FOR AN AMBULANCE*. Insulate the casualty. Monitor and *record* breathing, pulse, and level of response every ten minutes.

3 Note the type, amount, and source of any blood loss from body orifices (*see overleaf*). If possible, send a sample with the casualty to hospital.

BLEEDING FROM ORIFICES

Site	Appearance	Cause
Mouth	Bright red, frothy, coughed-up blood (*haemoptysis*).	Bleeding in the lungs.
	Vomited blood (*haematemesis*), red or dark reddish-brown, resembling coffee grounds.	Bleeding within the digestive system.
Ear	Fresh, bright-red blood.	Injury to the inner or outer ear; perforated ear-drum.
	Thin, watery blood.	Leakage of cerebrospinal fluid following head injury.
Nose	Fresh, bright-red blood.	Ruptured blood vessel in the nostril.
	Thin, watery blood.	Leakage of cerebrospinal fluid following head injury.
Anus	Fresh, bright-red blood.	Injury to the anus or lower bowel.
	Black, tarry, offensive-smelling stool (*melaena*).	Injury causing bleeding from the upper bowel.
Urethra	Urine with a red or smoky appearance (*haematuria*) and occasionally clots.	Bleeding from the bladder or kidneys.
Vagina	Either fresh or dark blood.	Menstruation; miscarriage; disease of, or injury to, the vagina or womb.

BLEEDING FROM THE EAR

Bleeding that originates from inside the ear generally follows a rupture (*perforation*) of the ear-drum. Causes include a foreign body pushed into the ear, a blow to the side of the head, or an explosion. The casualty may experience a sharp pain as the ear-drum ruptures, followed by earache and deafness.

If bleeding follows a head injury, the blood may appear thin and watery. This is very serious, because it indicates that the skull is fractured and cerebrospinal fluid is leaking from around the brain.

See also:
Foreign Bodies in the Ear, *page 181.*
Head Injuries, *page 113.*

TREATMENT

YOUR AIMS ARE:
- To allow blood to drain away.
- To minimise the risk of infection.
- To arrange transport to hospital.

DO NOT plug the ear.

1 Help casualty to a half-sitting position, head inclined to the injured side.

2 Cover the ear with a sterile dressing. If a fractured skull is suspected treat as for head injuries.

3 Send or take the casualty to hospital in the treatment position.

BLEEDING FROM THE MOUTH

Cuts to the tongue, lips, or lining of the mouth range from trivial injuries to more serious wounds. The cause is usually the casualty's own teeth or dental extraction.

Bleeding from the mouth may be profuse and can be alarming. Profuse bleeding can be dangerous if inhaled; if the blood is swallowed, it can cause vomiting.

TREATMENT

YOUR AIMS ARE:
■ To control bleeding.
■ To safeguard the airway by preventing any inhalation of blood.

1 Sit the casualty down, with her head forward and inclined towards the injured side, to allow blood to drain.

Apply pressure on wound to control bleeding

2 Place a gauze dressing pad over the wound. Ask the casualty to squeeze the wound and the pad between finger and thumb, and press for ten minutes.

IF a tooth socket is bleeding, take a gauze pad that is thick enough to stop the casualty's teeth meeting, place it across the socket, and tell her to bite on it.

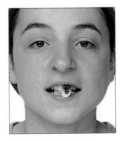

KNOCKED-OUT TOOTH

An adult tooth should be replanted in its socket as soon as possible after being knocked out. If it is lost, ask someone to look for it while you administer first aid. Do not replace a child's milk tooth.

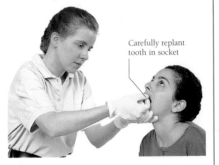

Carefully replant tooth in socket

Care of the tooth
Do not clean the tooth, as you may damage the tissues. Replace the tooth in its socket, keeping it in position by pressing a pad between the bottom and top teeth. If you cannot replant the tooth, keep it moist in water or milk, or in the casualty's cheek. Send the casualty to a dentist or hospital.

3 If bleeding persists, replace the pad with a fresh one. Tell the casualty to let any escaping blood dribble; if swallowed, it may induce vomiting.

DO NOT wash the mouth out, as this may disturb a clot.

4 Advise the casualty to avoid hot drinks for 12 hours.

IF the wound is large, or if bleeding persists beyond 30 minutes, or recurs, seek medical or dental advice.

NOSEBLEEDS

These most commonly occur when blood vessels inside the nostrils are ruptured, either by a blow to the nose, or as a result of sneezing, picking, or blowing the nose. Infection, such as a cold or 'flu, makes the blood vessels in the nose more fragile; nosebleeds may also occur as a result of high blood pressure. Nosebleeds are usually merely unpleasant, but they can be dangerous if the casualty loses a lot of blood. Where a nosebleed follows a head injury, the blood may appear thin and watery. This is very serious, as it is a sign that cerebrospinal fluid (*see page 108*) is leaking from around the brain.

See also:
Head Injuries, *page 113.*

TREATMENT

YOUR AIMS ARE:
- To control blood loss.
- To maintain an open airway.

1 Sit the casualty down with her head held well forward.

> **DO NOT** let her head tip back; blood may run down her throat and induce vomiting.

Pinch child's nose for her

Ask casualty to pinch fleshy part of nose

2 Ask the casualty to breathe through her mouth (this will also have a calming effect), and to pinch her nose just below the bridge. Help her if necessary.

3 Tell her to try not to speak, swallow, cough, spit, or sniff, as she may disturb blood clots. Give her a clean cloth or tissue to mop up dribble.

IF the casualty is a young child, let her dribble or spit into a bowl.

4 After ten minutes, tell the casualty to release the pressure. If her nose is still bleeding, reapply the pressure for further periods of ten minutes.

IF the nosebleed persists beyond 30 minutes, take or send the casualty to hospital in the treatment position.

5 Once the bleeding is under control, and with the casualty still leaning forward, gently clean around her nose and mouth with lukewarm water.

6 Advise the casualty to rest quietly for a few hours, and to avoid exertion and, in particular, not to blow her nose, as this will disturb any clot.

VAGINAL BLEEDING

Bleeding from the vagina is most likely to be menstrual bleeding, often with abdominal cramps, but it can also indicate miscarriage, recent abortion, internal disease or infection, or injury as a result of sexual assault. The history of the condition is vital to diagnosis, and has some bearing on the first aid given. If the bleeding is severe, shock may develop.

Always be sensitive to the woman's feelings. She may be embarrassed or may resent a male presence. Male First Aiders should, if possible, seek the help of a female chaperone.

See also:
Miscarriage, *page 202.*
Shock, *page 78.*

TREATMENT

YOUR AIMS ARE:
■ To make the woman comfortable and to reassure her.
■ To observe and treat for shock.
■ To arrange removal to hospital, if necessary.

1 Remove the woman, if possible, to a place with some privacy, or arrange for screening to be set up.

2 Find a sanitary pad or a clean towel and give it to her.

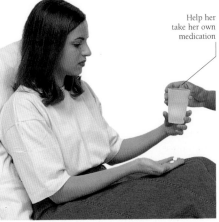

Help her take her own medication

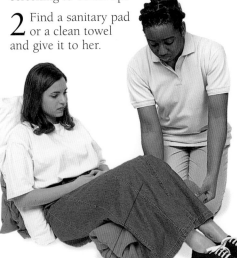

Bending knees eases strain on abdominal muscles

3 Make the casualty as comfortable as possible, in whichever position she prefers. If she chooses to sit up, prop her up with rolled-up clothing or cushions.

IF the casualty knows that her cramps are menstrual, she may take pain-killing tablets or drugs prescribed for relief.

IF bleeding continues and is severe, ☎ *DIAL 999 OR 112 FOR AN AMBULANCE.* Then treat for shock.

SEXUAL ASSAULT

If a woman has been assaulted, it is vital to preserve the evidence if possible. Gently encourage her to refrain from washing or using the toilet until a forensic examination has been performed by a trained police doctor, but do not insist. If she wishes to remove her clothing, keep it intact in a clean plastic bag if possible. A woman who has been recently assaulted may feel threatened by a male "rescuer".

MINOR WOUNDS

Prompt first aid can help nature heal small wounds and prevent infection. But you must seek medical advice:
• if there is a foreign body embedded in the wound (*see opposite*);
• if the wound is at special risk of infection (such as a dog bite, or a puncture by a dirty object);
• if an old wound shows signs of becoming infected (*see page 106*).

> ## GOOD WOUND CARE
> • First wash your hands thoroughly.
> • Cover your own sores or wounds with a waterproof dressing.
> • Avoid touching the wound with your fingers while treating it, and wear disposable gloves.
> • Don't talk, cough, or breathe over the wound or the dressing.
> For more details, see pages 14 and 215.

MINOR EXTERNAL BLEEDING

Minor bleeding is readily controlled by pressure and elevation. A small adhesive dressing is normally all that is necessary.

Medical aid need only be sought if the bleeding does not stop, or if the wound is at special risk of infection.

TREATMENT

YOUR AIM IS:
■ To minimise the risk of infection.

1 Before treating the wound, wash your hands well in soap and warm water. If possible, put on disposable gloves.

2 If the wound is dirty, clean it by rinsing lightly under running water, or use an antiseptic wipe. Pat dry with a gauze swab. Temporarily cover the wound with sterile gauze.

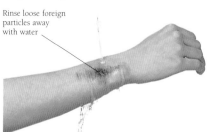

Rinse loose foreign particles away with water

3 Elevate the wounded part above the level of the heart, if possible. Avoid touching the wound directly. Support the affected limb with one hand.

Keep wounded part high

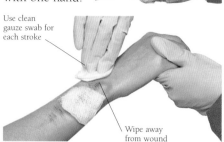

Use clean gauze swab for each stroke

Wipe away from wound

4 Clean the surrounding area with soap and water. Pat dry and remove the covering. Apply an adhesive dressing.

IF there is a special risk of infection, advise the casualty to see her doctor.

Foreign Bodies in Minor Wounds

Small pieces of glass or grit that are lying on a wound can be carefully picked off, or rinsed off with cold water before you give any treatment. Use tweezers if you have them. However, you must not attempt to remove objects that are embedded in the wound; you may cause further damage to the tissue around the injury and aggravate bleeding.

See also:
Fish Hooks, *page 177*.
Splinters, *page 176*.

TREATMENT

YOUR AIMS ARE:
- To control bleeding without pressing the object into the wound.
- To arrange transport to hospital.

1 Control any bleeding by applying firm pressure on either side of the object, and by raising the wounded part.

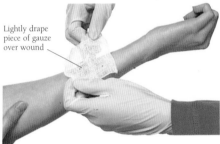

Lightly drape piece of gauze over wound

2 Cover the wound with gauze to minimise the risk of infection.

3 Pad around object so you can bandage it without pressing down, or use a ring pad. Hold padding in place while finishing the bandaging.

IF you cannot pad high enough, bandage *around* the object.

4 Arrange to take or send the casualty to hospital.

Bruises

These are caused by internal bleeding seeping through the tissues. Bruising can develop slowly, appearing days later. Bruising that develops rapidly and seems to be the main problem will benefit from first aid, although a bruise can indicate deeper injury. The elderly and those on anticoagulants can bruise easily.

See also:
Internal Bleeding, *page 99*.

TREATMENT

YOUR AIM IS:
- To reduce blood flow to the injury, and so minimise swelling, by means of cooling and compression.

Raise and support the injured part in a comfortable position. Apply a cold compress (*see page 221*) to the bruise.

IF you suspect more serious underlying injury, seek medical advice.

INFECTION IN WOUNDS

All open wounds are vulnerable to contamination by micro-organisms known as germs. These can come from the wounding source, from the air, from the breath or the fingers, or from particles of clothing embedded in a wound (such as with a gunshot wound). Bleeding flushes some of the dirt away and remaining germs may be destroyed by the white blood cells.

The dangers of infection

If dirt or dead tissue remain, there may be serious consequences. Germs can multiply and spread infection through the body (*septicaemia*), or tetanus infection (*see below*) can develop. A casualty with heavily contaminated or other susceptible wounds may need antibiotics or anti-tetanus injections. Wounds that do not begin to heal within 48 hours should be considered to be infected. In these cases, there may also be fever.

Recognition
As infection develops, there may be:

- Increasing pain and soreness.
- Swelling, redness, and a feeling of heat around the injury.
- Pus within, or oozing from, the wound.
- Swelling and tenderness of the glands in the neck, armpit, or groin.
- Faint red trails – leading to these glands – on the skin.
- In advanced infection, signs of fever: sweating, thirst, shivering, and lethargy.

TREATMENT

YOUR AIMS ARE:
- To prevent further infection.
- To obtain appropriate medical aid.

1 Wear disposable gloves. Cover the wound with a sterile dressing or a clean pad, and bandage it in place.

2 Raise and support the injured part to reduce swelling.

3 Tell the casualty to see her doctor. If severe, take or send her to hospital.

TETANUS

This is a dangerous infection that can develop if tetanus germs enter a wound. These germs are carried in the air and in soil as spores. When present in damaged and swollen tissues, they may release a poisonous substance (*toxin*) that spreads through the nervous system, causing muscle spasms and paralysis.

Preventing tetanus
Tetanus is very difficult to treat, but can be prevented by immunisation, which is part of a baby's vaccination programme. Children are given boosters on starting and leaving school. Adults should receive boosters every ten years. Always ask a wounded casualty when he or she last had a tetanus injection. Seek medical advice:
- if the casualty has never before been immunised;
- if the last injection was received more than ten years ago;
- if the casualty cannot remember when the last injection was given.

DISORDERS OF CONSCIOUSNESS

8

The nervous system is the most highly developed system in the body: it controls consciousness, contains centres for memory, speech, thought, and will, and correlates the activities of other body systems.

A fully conscious person is awake, alert, and aware of his or her surroundings. Sleep is a normal state of lowered consciousness, but *unconsciousness* is an abnormal state in which the body's control mechanisms are impaired or lost. When a person is asleep, vital functions such as breathing take place automatically. If a person is unconscious, muscle control is lost, so if the person is lying on his or her back, the tongue falls towards the back of the throat and may block the airway. An unconscious casualty will therefore require immediate first aid.

Unconsciousness and impaired consciousness

There are a number of disorders that cause varying levels of impaired or lost consciousness; after checking the airway, breathing, and pulse (*see page 52*), you must establish the *level of (un)consciousness*.

FIRST-AID PRIORITIES

◆ Open an unconscious casualty's airway. Every few minutes, check the airway, breathing, and circulation. Record the breathing and pulse rates.

◆ Protect the casualty from harm.

◆ Monitor and *record* the level of response.

◆ Look for, and treat, associated injuries.

◆ If unconsciousness lasts for more than three minutes or if you suspect a serious condition such as stroke or skull fracture, arrange urgent removal of the casualty to hospital.

CONTENTS

THE NERVOUS SYSTEM

This system consists of the brain and spinal cord (*central nervous system*), the motor and sensory nerves (*peripheral nervous system*), and the *autonomic nervous system*. The central nervous system analyses sensory information received via the nerves from all parts of the body and transmits appropriate responses back to the body through the nerves. The autonomic nervous system controls involuntary bodily functions.

CENTRAL NERVOUS SYSTEM

The brain and spinal cord consist of billions of interconnected nerve cells (*neurons*) and are enclosed by three protective membranes (*meninges*). Cerebrospinal fluid flows around the brain and spinal cord and between the meninges, acting as a shock absorber, providing oxygen and nutrients, and removing waste products.

The brain analyses and acts on most stimuli, but simple reflex actions (*see opposite*) are controlled solely by the spinal cord. Each side of the brain governs movement in the opposite side of the body, and specialised areas of the brain direct functions such as thinking or vision.

PERIPHERAL NERVOUS SYSTEM

This part of the nervous system consists of two parallel sets of nerves that connect the brain and spinal cord with the body. The cranial nerves emerge in 12 pairs directly from the base of the brain; 31 pairs of spinal nerves branch off at intervals from the spinal cord, passing into the body.

Nerves are rather like telephone cables, consisting of bundles of nerve fibres capable of relaying both incoming (*sensory*) and outgoing (*motor*) signals.

AUTONOMIC NERVOUS SYSTEM

Some cranial nerves and several small spinal nerves function as the *autonomic*, or *involuntary*, nervous system. This is concerned with vital bodily functions such as the heart rate, breathing, and body temperature. The system has two parts that counterbalance each other.

The sympathetic part prepares the body for action ("fight or flight") by releasing adrenaline (also called *epinephrine*) and related hormones that raise the heart and breathing rates, reduce blood flow to the skin and intestines, and increase sweating.

The parasympathetic part acts in opposition to the sympathetic by releasing other hormones; it also regulates many everyday functions, such as digestion.

WHAT CAN GO WRONG

Injury to the brain or spinal cord is very serious because damaged cells never recover. However, peripheral nerves can regenerate, especially if the severed nerve ends are rejoined surgically soon after an injury; muscle power and sensation may improve over several years.

◆ Injury to the brain or spinal cord from violent movement or impact, or pressure from tumours, blood clots, abscesses, or bleeding, may cause reduced sensation or paralysis.

◆ Impaired blood or oxygen supply, as occurs in stroke, leads to brain cell death within a few minutes.

◆ Infections, such as *meningitis* (*see page 204*), are rare but can be life-threatening.

◆ Degenerative diseases, such as *multiple sclerosis* or *Parkinson's disease*, attack the structure of the nerves, causing muscular degeneration.

Other common causes of unconsciousness are discussed in relevant sections of this chapter.

THE NERVOUS SYSTEM

This complex network of nerve cells and fibres carries electrical impulses at speeds of about 200 km (125 miles) per hour, conveying signals between the brain and the rest of the nervous system.

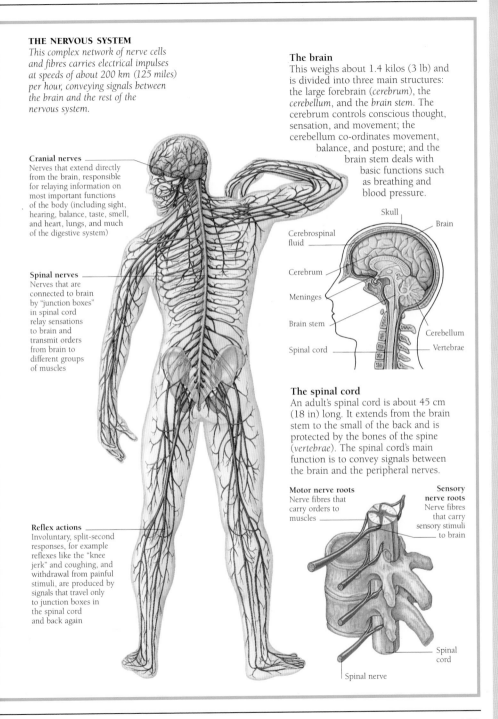

Cranial nerves
Nerves that extend directly from the brain, responsible for relaying information on most important functions of the body (including sight, hearing, balance, taste, smell, and heart, lungs, and much of the digestive system)

Spinal nerves
Nerves that are connected to brain by "junction boxes" in spinal cord relay sensations to brain and transmit orders from brain to different groups of muscles

Reflex actions
Involuntary, split-second responses, for example reflexes like the "knee jerk" and coughing, and withdrawal from painful stimuli, are produced by signals that travel only to junction boxes in the spinal cord and back again

The brain

This weighs about 1.4 kilos (3 lb) and is divided into three main structures: the large forebrain (*cerebrum*), the *cerebellum*, and the *brain stem*. The cerebrum controls conscious thought, sensation, and movement; the cerebellum co-ordinates movement, balance, and posture; and the brain stem deals with basic functions such as breathing and blood pressure.

Skull

Brain

Cerebrospinal fluid

Cerebrum

Meninges

Brain stem

Spinal cord

Cerebellum

Vertebrae

The spinal cord

An adult's spinal cord is about 45 cm (18 in) long. It extends from the brain stem to the small of the back and is protected by the bones of the spine (*vertebrae*). The spinal cord's main function is to convey signals between the brain and the peripheral nerves.

Motor nerve roots
Nerve fibres that carry orders to muscles

Sensory nerve roots
Nerve fibres that carry sensory stimuli to brain

Spinal cord

Spinal nerve

UNCONSCIOUSNESS

This results from an interruption of the brain's normal activity. Whatever the cause, follow these three rules:

1: Ensure that the airway is clear

An unconscious casualty's airway is in constant danger, particularly if he or she is lying face-up. The tongue may flop to the back of the throat and the muscles that normally keep the airway open, and the cough reflex that clears saliva from the throat, will not function. Stomach contents may also be regurgitated and inhaled.

2: Keep checking the response level

There are many degrees of impaired awareness and response short of full unconsciousness (*coma*). Make a rapid

assessment using the "AVPU" code (*below*). Make a detailed assessment using the simplified version of the Glasgow Coma Scale (*see bottom*). Repeat every ten minutes. This checklist is part of the chart on page 112.

THE "AVPU" CODE
A – **A**lert
V – responds to **V**oice
P – responds to **P**ain
U – **U**nresponsive time.

3: Examine the casualty thoroughly

Impaired consciousness can mask other injuries, so a full examination is vital. The casualty's condition and level of response may alter with time. To avoid aggravating any spinal injury, do not move him or her unnecessarily.

MAJOR CAUSES OF UNCONSCIOUSNESS

Cause	Effect
Head injury	Direct damage to the brain
Stroke • Fainting • Heart attack • Shock	Interference with blood supply to the brain
Head injury • Stroke • Some infections • Some tumours	Compression of the brain
Low blood oxygen (*hypoxia*) • Poisoning, including alcohol and drug intoxication • Low blood sugar (*hypoglycaemia*)	Disturbance of chemical content of blood supplied to the brain
Epilepsy • Abnormal body temperature	Fits

ASSESSING THE LEVEL OF RESPONSE (GLASGOW COMA SCALE)

Eyes – do they:	Movement – does the casualty:	Speech – does the casualty:
• Open spontaneously? • Open on command? • Open to a painful stimulus? • Remain closed?	• Obey commands? • Move in response to a painful stimulus? • Make no response?	• Respond sensibly to questions? • Appear confused? • Make incomprehensible sounds? • Make no response?

EXAMINING AND TREATING AN UNCONSCIOUS CASUALTY

YOUR AIMS ARE:
- To maintain an open airway.
- To assess and record the level of response.
- To treat any associated injuries.
- To arrange, if necessary, urgent removal to hospital.
- To gather and retain any circumstantial evidence of the cause of the condition.

DO NOT attempt to give an unconscious casualty anything by mouth.

DO NOT move the casualty unnecessarily, because of the possibility of spinal injury. *Never* attempt to make an unconscious person sit or stand upright.

DO NOT leave an unconscious casualty unattended at any time.

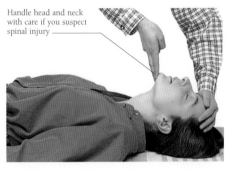

Handle head and neck with care if you suspect spinal injury

1 Open the airway by lifting the chin and tilting the head. Check breathing and pulse, and be prepared to resuscitate if necessary (*see pages 44–58*). Assess and *record* the level of response (*see overleaf*).

IF she starts to vomit, immediately place her in the recovery position (*see page 48*).

IF you suspect spinal injury, treat the casualty as described on pages 143–7.

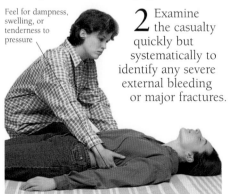

Feel for dampness, swelling, or tenderness to pressure

2 Examine the casualty quickly but systematically to identify any severe external bleeding or major fractures.

3 Control any bleeding (*see page 88*) and note and protect any suspected fractures (*see pages 123–54*).

4 As you work, look for less obvious injuries or conditions. Smell the casualty's breath and look for needle marks. Look for warning bracelets, lockets, or cards. Ask any bystanders for information.

Put in recovery position to maintain open airway

5 Place the casualty in the recovery position (*see page 48*).

IF the casualty does not regain full consciousness within three minutes, ☎ *DIAL 999 OR 112 FOR AN AMBULANCE.* Monitor and *record* breathing, pulse, and level of response every ten minutes, using the observation chart (*see overleaf*). Send the chart with the casualty to hospital.

IF the casualty regains full consciousness within three minutes, and remains well after a further ten minutes, advise her to see her doctor as soon as possible.

OBSERVATION CHART

The information from this chart will be very valuable when decisions are taken about further treatment:
* use a photocopy of it to record your observations while waiting for help;
* tick the appropriate boxes;
* update them at ten-minute intervals;
* send the completed chart, and any notes, with the casualty when he or she leaves your care.

DATE . . . .   CASUALTY'S NAME . . . .

Time of observation (10-minute intervals)		10	20	30	40	50	60
Eyes Observe for reaction while testing other responses.	Open spontaneously						
	Open to speech						
	Open to painful stimulus						
	No response						
Movement Apply painful stimulus: pinch ear lobe or skin on back of hand.	Obeys commands						
	Responds to painful stimulus						
	No response						
Speech When testing responses, speak clearly and directly, close to casualty's ear.	Responds sensibly to questions						
	Seems confused						
	Uses inappropriate words						
	Incomprehensible sounds						
	No response						
Pulse (beats per minute) Take pulse at wrist (*see page 77*) or at neck on adult (*page 52*); at inner arm on baby (*page 57*). Note rate, and whether beats are weak (**w**) or strong (**s**), regular (**reg**), or irregular (**irreg**).	Over 110						
	101-110						
	91-100						
	81-90						
	71-80						
	61-70						
	Below 61						
Breathing (breaths per minute) Note rate, and whether breathing is quiet (**q**) or noisy (**n**), easy (**e**) or difficult (**diff**).	Over 40						
	31-40						
	21-30						
	11-20						
	Below 11						

HEAD INJURIES

All injuries to the head are potentially dangerous, and require proper assessment, particularly if the casualty's consciousness is impaired; this may indicate damage to the brain, damage to blood vessels inside the skull, or skull fracture. A scalp wound (see page 90) may raise your suspicions, but often deeper, underlying damage will leave little visible evidence. Conversely, impaired consciousness may mask the presence of other injuries: examine the casualty fully. Remember that while unconsciousness can result from a head injury, the casualty may have lost consciousness for another reason and have sustained the head injury in a fall.

CONCUSSION

The brain is free to move a little within the skull, and can thus be "shaken" by a violent blow. This may cause concussion, a condition of widespread but temporary disturbance of the brain. There will be a period of unconsciousness, but it is always brief and is followed by complete recovery – by definition, concussion can only be safely diagnosed once the casualty has completely recovered.

Recognition

♦ Brief or partial loss of consciousness following a blow to the head.

There may also be:

♦ Dizziness or nausea on recovery.
♦ Loss of memory of events at the time of, or immediately preceding, the injury.
♦ A mild, generalised headache.

See also:
Unconsciousness, page 110.

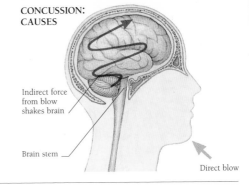

CONCUSSION: CAUSES

Indirect force from blow shakes brain

Brain stem

Direct blow

TREATMENT

YOUR AIMS ARE:
■ To ensure that the casualty recovers fully and safely.
■ If necessary, to seek medical aid.

1 Place an unconscious casualty in the recovery position (see page 48). Monitor and *record* breathing, pulse, and level of response every ten minutes.

IF the casualty is unconscious after three minutes, suspect a more serious injury.
☎ *DIAL 999 OR 112 FOR AN AMBULANCE.*

IF the casualty regains consciousness within three minutes, watch closely for any deterioration in the level of response, even after an apparent full recovery.

2 Place the casualty in the care of a responsible person. Do not allow a casualty who has been injured on the sports field to "play on" without the approval of a doctor.

3 Advise the casualty to see his or her own doctor if headache, sickness, or tiredness occur after injury.

SKULL FRACTURE

A head wound may alert you to possible skull fracture; the casualty may or may not be unconscious. A skull fracture is dangerous as there may be brain damage; also germs that cause infection can enter the brain. Clear fluid (*cerebrospinal fluid, see page 108*) or watery blood leaking from the ear or nose are signs of serious injury and an entry point for germs.

Suspect a fractured skull in any casualty who has received a head injury resulting in unconsciousness. Bear in mind, however, that if violent head movements (especially "fore-and-aft") have caused unconsciousness, there may also be an associated neck injury.

Recognition

- A wound or bruise on the head.
- A soft area or depression of the scalp.
- Impairment of consciousness.
- A progressive deterioration in the level of response.
- Clear fluid or watery blood coming from the nose or ear.
- Blood in the white of the eye.
- Distortion or lack of symmetry of the head or face.

See also:
Back Injuries, *page 142.*
Bleeding From the Scalp, *page 90.*
Unconsciousness, *page 110.*

TREATMENT

YOUR AIMS ARE:
- To resuscitate if necessary.
- To maintain an open airway.
- To arrange urgent removal to hospital.

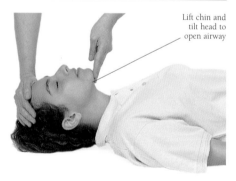

Lift chin and tilt head to open airway

1 If the casualty is unconscious, open the airway, check breathing and pulse, and be prepared to resuscitate if necessary (*see pages 44–58*). Place her in the recovery position (*see page 48*).

IF you suspect spinal injury, treat the casualty as described on pages 143–7.

2 Help a conscious casualty to lie down, with the head and shoulders raised.

IF there is discharge from an ear, position the casualty so that the affected ear is lower. Cover the ear with a sterile dressing or clean pad, lightly secured with a bandage. Do not plug the ear.

3 Control any bleeding from the scalp. Look for, and treat, other injuries.
☎ *DIAL 999 OR 112 FOR AN AMBULANCE.*

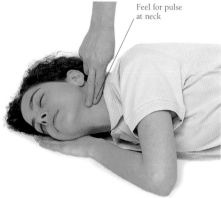

Feel for pulse at neck

4 Monitor and *record* breathing, pulse, and level of response every ten minutes until help arrives. Make sure your notes accompany the casualty to hospital.

DIAGNOSIS OF A FRACTURE

Many types of skull fracture, particularly linear fractures (*cracks*) in the domed vault and fractures to the base of the skull, can only be diagnosed by X-ray or other imaging methods in hospital. Severe injuries may cause multiple cracking ("eggshell" fracture), which may extend to the base of the skull. A depressed fracture may cause bone fragments to be driven in, to injure, and exert damaging pressure on the brain.

Causes of a fracture
A depressed fracture is caused by a direct blow; a fracture of the base of the skull may be caused by landing heavily on the feet or the base of the spine.

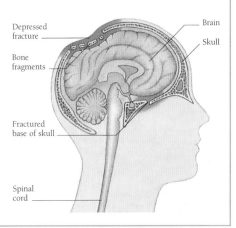

Depressed fracture

Bone fragments

Fractured base of skull

Spinal cord

Brain

Skull

CEREBRAL COMPRESSION

This is a very serious condition that almost invariably requires surgery. It occurs when pressure is exerted on the brain within the skull, for example, by an accumulation of blood or by swelling of an injured brain. It is often associated with head injury and skull fracture, but can be due to other causes, for example, stroke, infection, or tumour.

Cerebral compression may develop immediately after a head injury, or may be delayed for some hours, or even days, so you should always try to find out if there is any recent history of head injury.

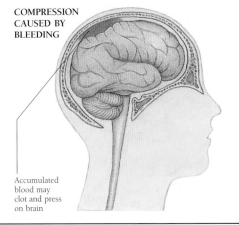

COMPRESSION CAUSED BY BLEEDING

Accumulated blood may clot and press on brain

Recognition

◆ As the condition develops, the casualty's level of consciousness will deteriorate.

There may also be:

◆ A recent head injury, followed by an apparently full recovery. Later on, the casualty may deteriorate and become disorientated.
◆ An intense headache.
◆ Noisy breathing, becoming slow.
◆ A slow, yet full and strong pulse.
◆ Unequal or dilated pupils.
◆ Weakness or paralysis down one side of the face or body.
◆ Drowsiness.
◆ A noticeable change in personality or behaviour, such as irritability.

TREATMENT

☎ *DIAL 999 OR 112 FOR AN AMBULANCE.*

IF the casualty is unconscious, follow the treatment on page 111.

IF the casualty is conscious, support him or her in a comfortable position. Monitor and *record* breathing, pulse, and level of response every ten minutes.

CONVULSIONS

A convulsion, or fit, consists of involuntary contractions of many of the muscles in the body, caused by a disturbance in the function of the brain. Convulsions usually result in loss of, or impaired, consciousness.

There are a number of possible causes, including head injury, some brain-damaging diseases, shortage of oxygen to the brain, and the intake of certain poisons. In babies and young children, fits may be triggered by a high temperature. Fits are also a feature of *epilepsy*.

No matter what the cause of the fit, you must observe the three rules of treatment for the unconscious casualty (*see page 110*), protect the casualty from further harm during a fit, and arrange appropriate aftercare.

MINOR EPILEPSY

Short of major epilepsy, there are many forms of epilepsy, including *absence seizures* which cause only a brief blurring of consciousness, like daydreaming. On recovery, the casualty may simply have lost the thread of what he or she was doing. The level of consciousness varies in all forms of minor epilepsy, but a major fit sometimes follows a minor one.

Recognition
There may be:

◆ Sudden "switching off"; the casualty may be staring blankly ahead.
◆ Slight or localised twitching or jerking of the lips, eyelids, head, or limbs.
◆ Odd "automatic" movements, such as lip-smacking, chewing, or making noises.

TREATMENT

YOUR AIM IS:
■ To protect the casualty until she is fully recovered.

1 Help the casualty to sit down in a quiet place. Remove any possible sources of harm, for example hot drinks or sharp objects, from the immediate vicinity.

2 Talk to her calmly and reassuringly. Do not pester her with questions. Stay with her until you are sure she is herself again.

IF the casualty does not recognise and know about her condition, advise her to consult her own doctor as soon as possible.

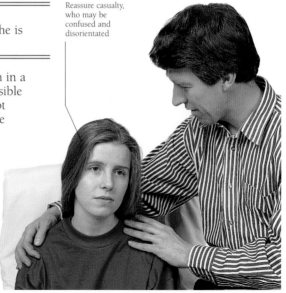
Reassure casualty, who may be confused and disorientated

MAJOR EPILEPSY

This condition is characterised by recurrent, major disturbances of brain activity, resulting in violent seizures (*tonic-clonic*) and severe impairment of consciousness. Epileptic fits can be sudden and dramatic, but the casualty may have a brief warning period (*aura*) with, for example, a strange feeling or a special smell or taste.

Recognition

An epileptic fit usually follows a pattern:

◆ The casualty suddenly falls unconscious, often letting out a cry.
◆ He becomes rigid, arching his back (this is known as the *tonic* phase).
◆ Breathing may cease. The lips may show a grey-blue tinge (*cyanosis*) and the face and neck may become congested.
◆ Convulsive movements begin (the *clonic* phase). The jaw may be clenched and breathing may be noisy. Saliva may appear at the mouth, blood-stained if lips or tongue have been bitten. There may be loss of bladder or bowel control.
◆ The muscles relax and breathing becomes normal; the casualty recovers consciousness, usually within a few minutes. He may feel dazed, or behave strangely in a state of "automatism", being unaware of his actions. A fit may also be followed by a deep sleep.
◆ There may be evidence of injury, such as burns or scars, from previous fits.

TREATMENT

YOUR AIMS ARE:

■ To protect the casualty from injury while the fit lasts.
■ To provide care when consciousness has been regained.

DO NOT lift or move the casualty unless he is in immediate danger.

DO NOT use force to restrain him, or put anything in his mouth.

1 If you see the casualty falling, try to support him or ease his fall. Make space around him and ask bystanders to move away.

2 Loosen clothing around his neck and, if possible, protect his head.

3 When the convulsions cease, place him in the recovery position (*see page 48*). Check breathing and pulse, and be prepared to resuscitate if necessary (*see pages 44–58*). Stay with him until he is fully recovered.

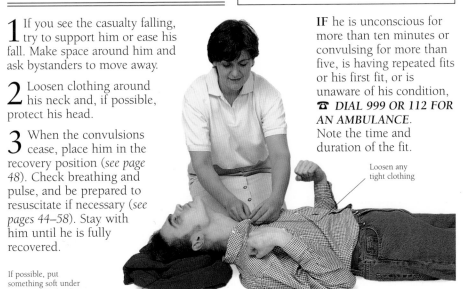

If possible, put something soft under or around his head

IF he is unconscious for more than ten minutes or convulsing for more than five, is having repeated fits or his first fit, or is unaware of his condition, ☎ *DIAL 999 OR 112 FOR AN AMBULANCE*. Note the time and duration of the fit.

Loosen any tight clothing

CONVULSIONS IN YOUNG CHILDREN

Although young children can have epileptic fits just like adults (*see page 116*) they may, more commonly, develop fits at the onset of an infectious disease, or a throat or ear infection associated with a greatly raised body temperature or fever (*febrile convulsion*).

These convulsions can be alarming, but they are rarely dangerous if properly managed. For safety's sake, the child should be seen at a hospital to eliminate any serious condition. This may be upsetting if you are the child's parent, but be reassured that, in nearly all cases, no problems occur once the fit passes.

Recognition

♦ Clear signs of fever: hot, flushed skin, and perhaps sweating.
♦ Violent muscle twitching, with clenched fists and an arched back.

There may also be:

♦ Twitching of the face with squinting, fixed, or upturned eyes.
♦ Breath-holding, with congested face and neck or drooling at the mouth.
♦ Loss of, or altered, consciousness.

See also:

Unconsciousness, *page 110*.

TREATMENT

YOUR AIMS ARE:

■ To protect the child from injury.
■ To cool the child.
■ To reassure the parents.
■ To arrange removal to hospital.

Use pillows or rolled blankets for padding

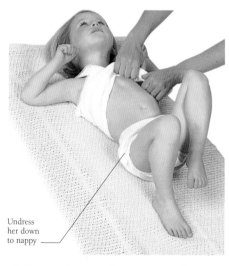

Undress her down to nappy

1 Remove any clothes or covering bedclothes. Ensure a good supply of cool, fresh air (although you should be careful not to overcool the child).

2 Position pillows or soft padding around the child so that even violent movement will not result in injury.

3 Sponge the child with tepid water to help cooling; start at her head and work down.

4 Keep the airway open, by using the recovery position (*page 48*) if possible.

☎ *DIAL 999 OR 112 FOR AN AMBULANCE.*

5 Reassure the child and parents or carer until the ambulance arrives.

STROKE

This term is used to describe a condition in which the blood supply to part of the brain is suddenly and seriously impaired by a blood clot or a ruptured artery.

Strokes are more common in later life, and in those who suffer from high blood pressure or some other circulatory disorder. The effect of a stroke depends on how much, and which part, of the brain is affected. Major strokes can be fatal, but many people make complete recoveries from minor strokes.

Recognition
There may be:

◆ A sudden, severe headache.
◆ A confused, emotional mental state that could be mistaken for drunkenness.
◆ Sudden or gradual loss of consciousness.
◆ Signs of weakness or paralysis, possibly on one side of the body, such as a drooping, dribbling mouth; slurred speech; loss of power or movement in the limbs; pupils of unequal size; loss of bladder or bowel control.

See also:
Unconsciousness, *page 110.*

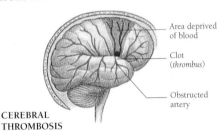

Area deprived of blood

Clot (*thrombus*)

Obstructed artery

CEREBRAL THROMBOSIS

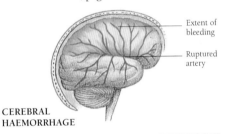

Extent of bleeding

Ruptured artery

CEREBRAL HAEMORRHAGE

TREATMENT

YOUR AIMS ARE:

■ To maintain an open airway.
■ To minimise brain damage.
■ To arrange urgent removal of the casualty to hospital.

FOR AN UNCONSCIOUS CASUALTY

1 Open the airway, check breathing and pulse, and be prepared to resuscitate if necessary (*see pages 44–58*). Place her in the recovery position (*see page 48*).

2 Monitor and *record* breathing, pulse, and the level of response every ten minutes.

3 Loosen any clothing that might impede the casualty's breathing. ☎ *DIAL 999 OR 112 FOR AN AMBULANCE.*

FOR A CONSCIOUS CASUALTY

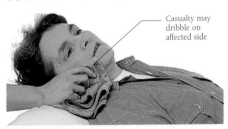

Casualty may dribble on affected side

Lay her down with her head and shoulders slightly raised and supported. Incline her head to one side, and place a towel or cloth on her shoulder to absorb dribbling. ☎ *DIAL 999 OR 112 FOR AN AMBULANCE.*

DO NOT give the casualty anything to eat or drink.

OTHER DISORDERS

The nervous system is vulnerable to disorder and damage not only by physical injury and disruptive conditions such as epilepsy, but also by changes in the composition of the blood supplied to the brain.

Chemical changes to which the brain is particularly sensitive include an insufficiency of oxygen in the blood (*see page 62*), altered blood sugar levels, or the presence of toxins such as poisons, alcohol, or drugs.

The problems of substance abuse

The abuse of alcohol, drugs, and other substances is an emotive subject, but you must never let your feelings on this subject impair your judgement and management of the unconscious casualty. He or she may be doubly at risk – from the dangers of unconsciousness as well as from the effects of the intoxicating substance.

The importance of examination

Remember that the symptoms and signs of conditions such as stroke and diabetic emergency can closely resemble, and easily be mistaken for, intoxication. You should, having ensured an open airway and breathing, examine every such casualty thoroughly to check for other possible causes.

DIABETES MELLITUS

This is a condition in which the body fails to regulate the concentration of sugar (*glucose*) in the blood. Blood-sugar levels are normally controlled by a hormone (*insulin*) produced by the pancreas.

Without insulin, sugar accumulates in the blood, and can cause *hyperglycaemia* (*see below*). Diabetics must carefully balance the amount of sugar in their diet and regulate their blood sugar with insulin injections or tablets; too much insulin or too little sugar can cause *hypoglycaemia* (*see opposite*).

Most diabetics are aware of the risk of hypoglycaemia if, for example, they miss a meal or over-exert themselves, and may carry sugar lumps or glucose tablets to raise their blood-sugar level quickly.

HYPERGLYCAEMIA

Prolonged high blood sugar can result in unconsciousness and then diabetic coma, although a diabetic often drifts into this state over a few days. This condition requires urgent medical treatment with insulin and intravenous infusion of fluids.

Recognition

- ◆ Dry skin and a rapid pulse.
- ◆ Deep, laboured breathing.
- ◆ A faint smell of acetone (as in nail-varnish remover) on the casualty's breath.

TREATMENT

YOUR AIM IS:

■ To arrange urgent removal of the casualty to hospital.

☎ *DIAL 999 OR 112 FOR AN AMBULANCE.* Treat unconscious casualty as detailed on page 111. Check casualty's condition every ten minutes.

HYPOGLYCAEMIA

When the blood-sugar level falls below normal (*hypoglycaemia*), brain function is affected rapidly. This can occur in sufferers of *diabetes mellitus* and, more occasionally, accompany an epileptic fit or follow an episode of binge drinking. Hypoglycaemia can also complicate heat exhaustion or hypothermia.

Diabetics may carry their own blood-testing kits with which to check their blood-sugar levels, and are usually well prepared for emergencies. If the "hypo" attack is advanced, however, consciousness may be impaired or lost.

Recognition
There may be:

◆ A history of diabetes; the casualty will sometimes, but not always, recognise the onset of a "hypo" attack.

◆ Weakness, faintness, or hunger.
◆ Palpitations and muscle tremors.
◆ Strange actions or behaviour; the casualty may seem confused, belligerent, or may even be violent.
◆ Sweating.
◆ Pallor.
◆ Cold, clammy skin.
◆ A strong, bounding pulse.
◆ A deteriorating level of response.
◆ Shallow breathing.
◆ A diabetic's warning card (medic-alert) or bracelet, sugar lumps, tablets, or an insulin syringe (which may look like a pen) among the casualty's possessions.

See also:
Convulsions, *page 116.*
Heat Exhaustion, *page 173.*
Hypothermia, *page 170.*
Unconsciousness, *page 110.*

TREATMENT

YOUR AIMS ARE:
■ To raise the sugar content of the blood as quickly as possible.
■ To obtain appropriate medical aid.

FOR AN UNCONSCIOUS CASUALTY

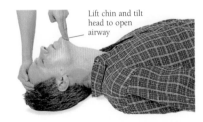

Lift chin and tilt head to open airway

1 Open the airway, check breathing and pulse, and be prepared to resuscitate if necessary (*see pages 44–58*). Place the casualty in recovery position (*see page 48*).

2 Monitor and *record* breathing, pulse, and response every ten minutes. ☎ *DIAL 999 OR 112 FOR AN AMBULANCE.*

FOR A CONSCIOUS CASUALTY

Give a sugary drink, which allows rapid absorption of sugar into blood

1 Help the casualty to sit or lie down, and give her a sugary drink, sugar lumps, chocolate, or other sweet food.

2 If the casualty responds quickly, give more food or drink, and let her rest until she feels better. Tell her to see her doctor even if she feels fully recovered.

IF her condition does not improve, examine her for other causes of tremor and confusion, and treat as necessary.

DRUNKENNESS

The unconscious casualty who has drunk excessive alcohol risks a blocked airway, especially if he is lying face-up or has vomited. There may be head or neck injuries resulting from an assault or fall, or a stroke may have occurred. Fits (*see page 116*) are common in binge drinking, and there is also a risk of hypothermia.

See also:
Alcohol Poisoning, *page 188.*
Hypothermia, *page 170.*
Stroke, *page 119.*
Unconsciousness, *page 110.*

TREATMENT

YOUR AIMS ARE:
- To maintain an open airway.
- To obtain medical aid if necessary.

1 Open the casualty's airway by lifting the chin and tilting the head (*see page 47*). Make sure that there is no vomit causing an obstruction in the airway.

IF the casualty starts to vomit, place him in the recovery position (*see page 48*) immediately to drain his mouth, and check that his airway is still clear.

2 Check the casualty's breathing, pulse, and level of response (*see page 46*), and be prepared to resuscitate if necessary (*see pages 44–58*).

3 Place or keep the casualty in the recovery position (*see page 48*). Keep a close watch on his condition; monitor and *record* breathing, pulse, and level of response every ten minutes. If in doubt, take or send the casualty to hospital.

4 Keep the casualty warm, especially in cold, wet conditions.

IF the casualty is totally unresponsive (for example, to a firm pinch on the hand) or is having fits, ☎ *DIAL 999 OR 112 FOR AN AMBULANCE.*

SUBSTANCE MISUSE

A variety of illicit or prescribed drugs and substances may be taken by accident, for "kicks" or in a suicide attempt, by mouth, by injection or by inhalation ("snorting"). Some drugs can cause unconsciousness and severely impair breathing. If you are in doubt about the cause of unconsciousness, particularly if treating a casualty in unusual circumstances, suspect drug abuse or overdose. Beware of uncapped needles.

See also:
Drug Poisoning, *page 186.*
Unconsciousness, *page 110.*

TREATMENT

YOUR AIMS ARE:
- To maintain an open airway.
- To arrange removal to hospital.

1 Open the airway, and check breathing, pulse, and level of response. Be prepared to resuscitate if necessary (*see pages 44–58*).

Always wear gloves

Put in recovery position to help breathing

2 Place the casualty in the recovery position (*see page 48*). ☎ *DIAL 999 OR 112 FOR AN AMBULANCE.*

3 Monitor and *record* breathing, pulse, and level of response every ten minutes.

BONE, JOINT, AND MUSCLE INJURIES 9

The skeleton is the hard framework around which the body is constructed, and on which all the body's tissues depend for support. The skeleton is jointed in many places, and muscles attached to the bones enable them to move. Most of these movements are controlled at will, and co-ordinated by impulses that travel from the brain via nerves to every muscle and joint in the body.

Diagnosing types of injury

It can be difficult to distinguish between bone, joint, and muscle injuries, so it helps to understand how the bones and muscles attached to them function, and how and why injury can happen. This information is given here, together with the general principles of treatment for different types of injury. You will also find specific first-aid treatments for injuries to bones, joints, and muscles in every part of the body.

The only type of fracture not covered in these pages is skull fracture, which, because of the potential effect on the brain, is discussed in the chapter *Disorders of Consciousness* (*pages 107–22*).

FIRST-AID PRIORITIES

◆ Maintain an open airway.

◆ Steady and support the injured part, if possible.

◆ Provide more permanent support, with padding and firm bandaging or splinting. An uninjured part of the body is the best form of "splint".

◆ If a broken bone lies within a large bulk of tissue (for example, the thigh), treat the casualty for shock.

◆ Obtain appropriate medical treatment.

CONTENTS

BONES, JOINTS, AND MUSCLES

The body is built on a framework of bones – the skeleton – that supports the muscles, blood vessels, and nerves of the body, and protects organs such as the heart. Movement is made possible by muscles attached to the bones, and by movable joints where the bones meet.

THE SKELETON
The bones of the skeleton are composed of calcium and phosphorus, which makes them hard and rigid, providing a protective framework for the body.

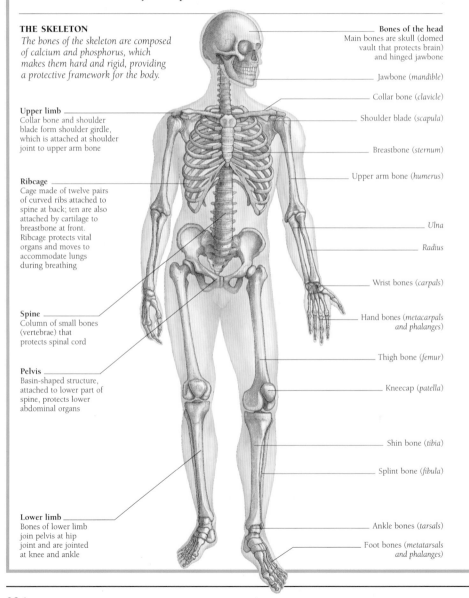

Upper limb
Collar bone and shoulder blade form shoulder girdle, which is attached at shoulder joint to upper arm bone

Ribcage
Cage made of twelve pairs of curved ribs attached to spine at back; ten are also attached by cartilage to breastbone at front. Ribcage protects vital organs and moves to accommodate lungs during breathing

Spine
Column of small bones (vertebrae) that protects spinal cord

Pelvis
Basin-shaped structure, attached to lower part of spine, protects lower abdominal organs

Lower limb
Bones of lower limb join pelvis at hip joint and are jointed at knee and ankle

Bones of the head
Main bones are skull (domed vault that protects brain) and hinged jawbone

Jawbone (*mandible*)

Collar bone (*clavicle*)

Shoulder blade (*scapula*)

Breastbone (*sternum*)

Upper arm bone (*humerus*)

Ulna

Radius

Wrist bones (*carpals*)

Hand bones (*metacarpals and phalanges*)

Thigh bone (*femur*)

Kneecap (*patella*)

Shin bone (*tibia*)

Splint bone (*fibula*)

Ankle bones (*tarsals*)

Foot bones (*metatarsals and phalanges*)

THE JOINTS

Wherever one bone meets another, there is a movable or immovable joint. Immovable joints are those where the bone edges fit firmly into each other, or are fused together, like the pelvic bones.

Movable joints allow movement between adjacent bones and are of three types: slightly movable, ball-and-socket, and hinge joints (*see below*). The degree of movement depends on the shape of the bone ends, the arrangement of muscles controlling the limb, and the strength of the surrounding ligaments.

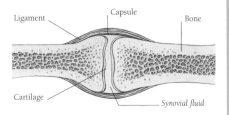

Cross-section of a movable joint
Smooth cartilage covering the bone ends minimises friction. Elastic bands of tissue (ligaments) hold the ends together. The joint is enclosed in a capsule filled with a lubricant (synovial fluid).

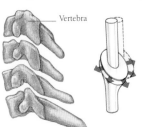

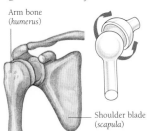

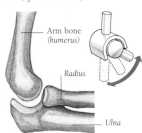

Slightly movable joints
These allow only slight gliding or rocking movements. Examples are joints between the spinal vertebrae, and in the feet.

Ball-and-socket joints
The round head of one bone fits into the cup-shaped end of another, allowing a swivelling action in all directions, as, for example, in the shoulder.

Hinge joints
The bone ends are contoured to allow bending (flexion) and straightening (extension) in only one plane, as in the elbow.

THE MUSCLES

Muscles cause the various parts of the body to move. Skeletal (voluntary) muscles are controlled by the will. They are attached to the bones by bands of strong, fibrous tissue (tendons), and operate in groups; as one group of muscles contracts, its paired group relaxes. Muscles also work constantly to maintain the position or stability of the body.

Smooth (involuntary) muscles operate the internal organs, such as the heart, and work constantly, even when we are asleep. They are controlled by the autonomic nervous system (*see page 108*).

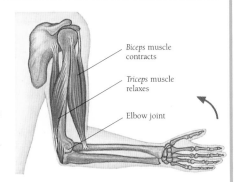

How voluntary muscles of the arm work
The biceps contracts, drawing the lower arm towards it. At the same time, its opposite muscle, the triceps, relaxes to allow the arm to bend.

TYPES OF INJURY

Bones may be broken (fractured), displaced at a joint (dislocated), or both. Muscles, and the tendons that attach them to bones, may be strained or torn, and the ligaments holding the joints together can tear. If you have any doubt about which type of injury you are dealing with, it is best to opt for the most serious, which is generally a fracture.

FRACTURES

A fracture is a break or crack in a bone. Bones are not brittle structures like blackboard chalk, but are tough and resilient. When struck or twisted, bones bend like the branches of a healthy tree. Generally, considerable force is required to break a bone, unless it is diseased or old (*see opposite*). Conversely, young bones that are still growing are supple and may split, bend, or crack just like a young sapling – hence the name "greenstick fracture" for this type of injury.

Any type of fracture may be accompanied by an open wound, and complicated by injury to adjoining nerves, muscles, blood vessels, and organs.

Simple fracture
This is a clean break or a crack in the bone.

Comminuted fracture
This type of fracture produces multiple bone fragments.

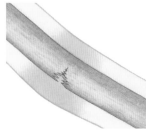

Greenstick fracture
A split in a young, immature bone is common in children.

OPEN AND CLOSED FRACTURES

In an *open* or compound fracture, part of the bone breaks through the skin, causing bleeding. The exposed bone is vulnerable to contamination from bacteria on the skin surface and in the air.

When the skin around a broken bone is intact, the injury is known as a *closed* fracture. There will often be bruising and swelling around the fracture site.

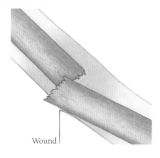

Wound

Open fracture
The wound may be caused by the injuring force, or by internal bone fragments perforating the skin.

Swelling

Unbroken skin

Closed fracture
The surrounding skin is unbroken; but internal injury to surrounding tissues may cause local swelling.

HOW FRACTURES ARE CAUSED

Both direct and indirect force can cause bones to fracture. A bone may break at the point where a heavy blow is received. For example, the direct impact of a moving vehicle's bumper can break the shin bone.

Indirect force may be produced by a twist or a wrench: a trip or stumble can break a leg bone, for example. Force may travel from the point of impact through the body to break bones elsewhere. Rarely, violent muscle contraction can fracture a bone to which the muscle is attached.

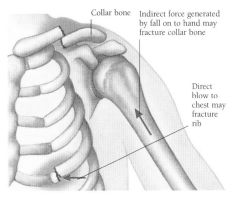

Collar bone

Indirect force generated by fall on to hand may fracture collar bone

Direct blow to chest may fracture rib

OLD OR DISEASED BONES

Age and disease can weaken bones, making them brittle and susceptible to breaking or crumbling when stressed. Such conditions include:
♦ osteoporosis, a condition where the bone loses density, usually in old age;
♦ congenital abnormalities; where bones are naturally brittle;
♦ benign or cancerous tumours or cysts. With any of these conditions, a simple movement may result in a spontaneous fracture, often causing severe pain.

People who are known to have a susceptibility to breaks or fractures should always be handled with care. Remember to move old people carefully, even if there is no history of violent injury or movement to the bones.

BONE STRUCTURE

Bones can be long, short, or flat. They have blood vessels which supply the inner cells and are dense and heavy because they are mainly composed of calcium. Bones grow from birth to early adulthood by continually laying down calcium on the outside. They are also able to generate new tissue after an injury.

Bones are vulnerable during the growing process, and any damage during adolescence can lead to a shortened bone or impaired movement.

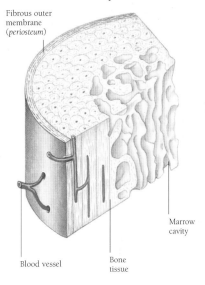

Fibrous outer membrane (*periosteum*)

Marrow cavity

Blood vessel

Bone tissue

BONES OF THE SKULL

By adulthood, the bones of the skull fuse together to form a protective casing for the brain and the top of the spinal cord.

Within the bone are air spaces (*sinuses*) that lighten the skull. Sinuses are weak points in the skull and, if fractured, can allow the cerebrospinal fluid that cushions the brain (*see page 108*) to leak out. This is a serious injury because the brain may become infected.

It is not uncommon for broken bones around the eye socket to be mistaken for a simple black eye, because bruising can disguise this type of fracture.

DISLOCATIONS

This is partial or full displacement of bones at a joint. There may be an associated fracture, tearing of the ligaments (*see below*), or damage to the membrane that encases the joint (*joint capsule*). Dislocation can be caused by a strong force wrenching the bone into an abnormal position, or by violent muscle contraction. This very painful injury most often occurs to the shoulder, thumb, finger, and jaw.

If the spine is dislocated, the spinal cord can be injured, and shoulder or hip dislocation may damage major nerves to the limbs and result in paralysis. A severe dislocation of any joint may also fracture the bones involved. It can often be difficult to distinguish a dislocation from a fracture. Never try to manipulate a dislocated joint back into place, as this may cause further injury.

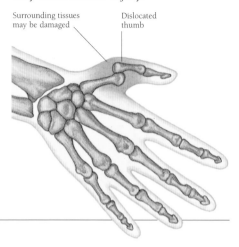

Surrounding tissues may be damaged

Dislocated thumb

SOFT TISSUE INJURIES

These are injuries that affect the tendons, ligaments and muscles. A sprain is an injury to a ligament at, or near, a joint. It is often the result of a sudden or unexpected wrenching movement at the joint, that pulls the bones within the joint too far apart and tears the tissues surrounding the joint.

Muscles and their tendons may be overstretched and torn by violent or sudden movement. Damage to muscle tissue can occur in one of three ways.

◆ *Strain*: overstretching of the muscle, which may result in a partial tearing or pull. This often occurs at the junction of the muscle and the tendon that joins it to a bone.

◆ *Rupture*: complete tearing of the muscle, which may occur in the fleshy part or in the tendon.

◆ *Deep bruising*: this may be extensive in parts of the body where there is a large bulk of muscle. These injuries are usually accompanied by bleeding into the damaged area, which can lead to pain, swelling, and bruising.

Strains and ruptures are frequently suffered by athletes; ligament strains and muscle tears are also common causes of non-specific back pain.

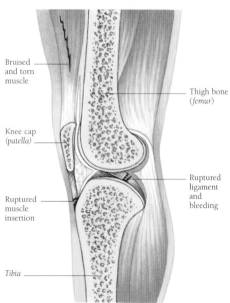

Bruised and torn muscle

Thigh bone (*femur*)

Knee cap (*patella*)

Ruptured ligament and bleeding

Ruptured muscle insertion

Tibia

ASSESSMENT OF BONE, JOINT, AND MUSCLE INJURIES

Some injuries, such as an open fracture or a dislocated thumb, are obvious. Others may only be revealed by X-ray examination. When you are assessing an injury, note as many features as possible, without moving the injured part unnecessarily. Try to visualise how the injury was caused, and how much force might have been involved.

Compare the shape, position, and appearance of the injured part with the uninjured side. If in doubt about the severity of an injury, treat it as a fracture.

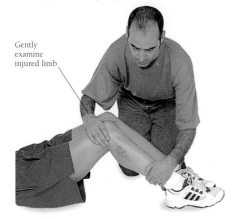

Gently examine injured limb

Recognition

There may have been:

◆ A recent violent blow or a fall.
◆ The snapping sound of a broken bone or torn ligament.
◆ The sharp pain of a muscle tear.

There may also be:

◆ Difficulty in moving a limb normally, or at all (for example, inability to walk).
◆ Pain at or near the site of injury, made worse by movement. "Sickening" and severe pain often indicates dislocation; tenderness over a bone if gently touched is a sign of fracture.
◆ Distortion, swelling, and bruising at the site of the fracture.
◆ Coarse grating of the bone ends (*crepitus*) may be heard or felt – do not try to produce this deliberately.
◆ Signs of shock, if the fracture is to the thigh bone, ribcage, or pelvis.
◆ A shortening, bending, or twisting of the affected limb.

See also:
Shock, *page 78.*

STABLE AND UNSTABLE INJURIES

Stable injuries

The force causing what is known as a "stable injury" may either fail to break the bone completely, or may act in such a way that the broken ends are jammed together or impacted. Such injuries are fairly common at the wrist, shoulder, ankle, and hip. Because there is little movement at the site, stable injuries can usually be gently handled without causing more damage.

Unstable injuries

With this injury, the bone is completely broken, or the ligaments are ruptured, in such a way that a broken bone or bone end may become displaced. Handle such injuries carefully to avoid causing further damage.

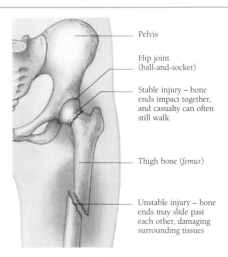

Pelvis

Hip joint (ball-and-socket)

Stable injury – bone ends impact together, and casualty can often still walk

Thigh bone (*femur*)

Unstable injury – bone ends may slide past each other, damaging surrounding tissues

TREATMENT FOR OPEN FRACTURES

YOUR AIMS ARE:
■ To prevent blood loss, movement, and infection at the site of injury.
■ To arrange removal to hospital, with comfortable support during transport.

DO NOT move the casualty until the injured part is secured and supported, unless she is in danger.

DO NOT let the casualty have anything to eat or drink.

IF you can, get a helper to support the limb while you work on the wound.

1 Cover the wound with a clean pad or sterile dressing, and apply pressure to control the bleeding (*see page 88*).

Always work from uninjured side

Pad larger than wound

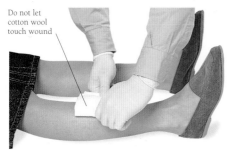

DO NOT press down directly on a protruding bone end.

Do not let cotton wool touch wound

2 Without touching an open wound with your fingers, carefully place a ring pad, cotton wool, or some other clean padding over and around the dressing.

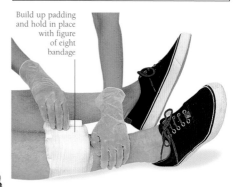

Build up padding and hold in place with figure of eight bandage

IF bone is protruding, use a ring pad, or pad soft, non-fluffy material around the bone until you can bandage over the pads.

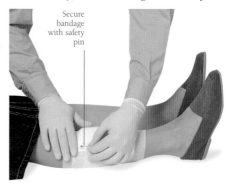

Secure bandage with safety pin

3 Secure the dressing and padding; bandage firmly, but not so tightly that the circulation is impeded.

4 Immobilise the injured part as for a closed fracture (*see opposite*).

☎ *DIAL 999 OR 112 FOR AN AMBULANCE.*

5 Treat the casualty for shock (*see page 78*). Check the circulation beyond the bandage (*see page 223*) every ten minutes.

TREATMENT FOR CLOSED FRACTURES AND DISLOCATIONS

YOUR AIMS ARE:
- To prevent movement at the injury site.
- To arrange removal to hospital, with comfortable support during transport.

1 Tell the casualty to keep still, and steady and support the injured part with your hands until it is immobilised.

Support above and below injury

2 Secure the injured part to a sound part of the body. If this causes pain, simply support it in a comfortable position.
- *For upper limb fractures*, always support the arm against the trunk with a sling and, if needed, bandaging (*see page 137*).
- *For lower limb fractures*, if removal to hospital will be delayed, bandage the sound leg to the injured one (*see page 150*).

DO NOT move the casualty until the injured part is secured and supported, unless she is in danger.

DO NOT let the casualty eat or drink.

DO NOT try to replace a dislocated bone into its socket.

3 ☎ *DIAL 999 OR 112 FOR AN AMBULANCE.* Treat the casualty for shock (*see page 78*).

4 Check the circulation beyond any bandages (*see page 223*) every ten minutes, and loosen if necessary.

TRACTION

If a fractured leg is bent or angled so it cannot be immobilised, apply gentle traction to pull it straight. This overcomes the pull of the muscles, and reduces pain and bleeding at the fracture site.

To apply traction, pull steadily in the line of the bone until the leg is securely immobilised. You can do no harm if you pull only in a straight line, but do not persist if traction causes intolerable pain.

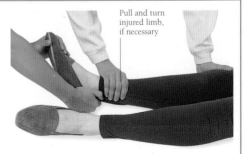

Pull and turn injured limb, if necessary

TREATMENT FOR SOFT TISSUE INJURIES

Follow the "RICE" procedure (*see right*) to treat sprains, strains, and deep bruising initially. This treatment may be sufficient, but if you are in doubt as to the severity of the injury, treat it as a fracture (*see page 130*).

(*see page 130*)

> **THE RICE PROCEDURE**
> **R**   **R**est the injured part.
> **I**   Apply **I**ce or a cold compress.
> **C**   **C**ompress the injury.
> **E**   **E**levate the injured part.

YOUR AIMS ARE:
- To reduce swelling and pain.
- To obtain medical aid if necessary.

1 Rest, steady, and support the injured part in the most comfortable position for the casualty.

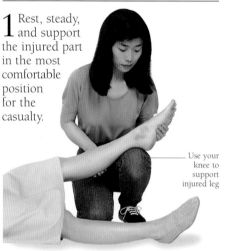

Use your knee to support injured leg

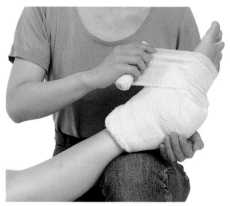

3 Apply gentle, even pressure, or compression, to the injured part by surrounding the area with a thick layer of soft padding, such as cotton wool or foam, secured with a bandage. Check the pulse below the bandage.

Elevate limb

2 If the injury has just happened, cool the area by applying an ice pack or cold compress (*see page 221*). This will reduce swelling, bruising, and pain.

(*see page 221*)

4 Raise and support the injured limb, to reduce blood flow to the injury and to minimise swelling.

5 Take or send the casualty to hospital or, if the injury seems very minor, advise the casualty to rest the injured part and to see her doctor if necessary.

INJURIES TO THE FACE AND JAW

Common injuries to the face include a broken nose, cheekbone, or jaw. The jaw can also be dislocated. The main danger is obstruction of the airway, either by swollen, displaced, or lacerated tissue, by loose teeth, or by blood and saliva (because the casualty cannot swallow adequately). There may also be damage to the brain, skull, or neck.

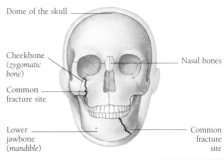

Dome of the skull

Cheekbone (*zygomatic bone*)

Nasal bones

Common fracture site

Lower jawbone (*mandible*)

Common fracture site

MAJOR FACIAL FRACTURES

Serious or combined facial fractures may appear horrifying, with distortion of the eye sockets, nose, upper teeth, and palate. Swelling and bruising may rapidly develop, and bleeding may occur from the nose or mouth, or displaced tissue. The danger is that these may cause breathing difficulties. Check also for signs of head and neck injury. Take care not to dismiss a facial fracture as a black eye (*see page 127*).

See also:
Head Injuries, *page 113*.
Spinal Injury, *page 143*.

TREATMENT

YOUR AIMS ARE:
■ To keep the airway open.
■ To arrange urgent removal to hospital.

IF you have to carry the casualty on a stretcher, you should ensure that he remains in the recovery position in order to protect his airway.

Keep lower leg straight and bend upper leg to prevent casualty from rolling forward

Tilt head very gently if you suspect neck injury

1 Open and, if necessary, clear the airway (*see page 47*).

2 Place the casualty in the recovery position (*see page 48*). ☎ *DIAL 999 OR 112 FOR AN AMBULANCE.*

IF the jawbone is injured, place soft padding under the head to keep weight off the jaw.

DO NOT apply a jaw bandage.

CHEEKBONE AND NOSE FRACTURES

Fractures of the cheekbone and nose are common, and are usually the result of fighting. The associated swelling is uncomfortable, and may block the air passages in the nose. These injuries should always be checked at hospital.

TREATMENT

YOUR AIMS ARE:

- To minimise pain and swelling.
- To arrange removal to hospital.

1 Quickly apply a cold compress (*see page 221*) to the injured area in order to reduce swelling.

2 Treat an associated nosebleed if necessary (*see page 102*).

3 Arrange to take or send the casualty to hospital.

IF straw-coloured (*cerebrospinal*) fluid leaks from the nose, treat as for skull fracture (*see page 114*).

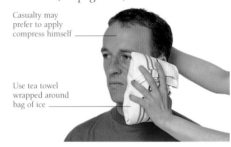

Casualty may prefer to apply compress himself

Use tea towel wrapped around bag of ice

INJURIES TO THE LOWER JAW

Jaw fractures are usually the result of direct force, such as a heavy blow to the jaw. Because of its shape, a blow to one side of the jaw may cause a fracture on the other side. A fall on to the point of the chin can fracture both sides. A blow, or even yawning, may dislocate the jaw.

Recognition

There may be:

- Pain and sickness when moving the jaw.
- Distortion of the teeth and dribbling.
- Swelling, tenderness, and bruising.
- A wound or bruising inside the mouth.

TREATMENT

YOUR AIMS ARE:

- To protect the airway.
- To arrange removal to hospital.

IF the casualty is seriously injured, treat as a major facial fracture (*see page 133*).

1 Help a casualty who is not seriously injured to sit up with her head well forward, to allow any blood, mucus, or saliva to drain away. Encourage her to spit out any loose teeth (*see page 101*).

IF she vomits, support her jaw and head, then gently clean out her mouth.

2 Give the casualty a soft pad to hold against her jaw and ask her to hold it firmly in place to support the jaw.

DO NOT bandage the pad in place.

3 Take or send the casualty to hospital, keeping her jaw supported.

INJURIES TO THE UPPER LIMB

The term "upper limb" is used to describe the shoulder girdle (the collar bone and shoulder) and the arm. Casualties with injuries to the upper limb can often walk or be transported to hospital seated.

FRACTURED COLLAR BONE

The collar bones (*clavicles*) form struts between the shoulder blades and the breastbone, to support the arms. It is rare for collar bones to be broken by a direct blow. They are usually broken by indirect force, transmitted from impact at the shoulder or a fall on to an outstretched hand.

Recognition

There may be:

◆ Pain and tenderness at the site of the injury, increased by movement.
◆ Attempts to relax muscles and relieve pain; the casualty may support the arm at the elbow, and incline the head to the injured side.

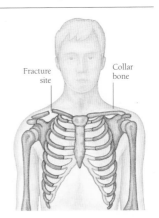

Fracture site

Collar bone

TREATMENT

YOUR AIMS ARE:

■ To immobilise the injured upper limb.
■ To arrange removal to hospital.

1 Sit the casualty down. Place the arm on her injured side across her chest, and ask her to support it at the elbow.

Rest fingertips against opposite shoulder

Head inclined to injured side

Remove bra strap if it is uncomfortable

Support elbow

2 Support the arm in an elevation sling (*see page 233*).

3 Gently place some soft padding, such as a small towel or folded clothing, between the injured arm and the body to make the casualty more comfortable.

4 Secure the arm to the chest with a broad-fold bandage (*see page 229*) tied around the chest and over the sling.

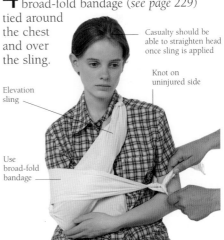

Casualty should be able to straighten head once sling is applied

Knot on uninjured side

Elevation sling

Use broad-fold bandage

5 Take or send the casualty to hospital, keeping her seated.

DISLOCATED SHOULDER

A fall directly on to the shoulder or on to the outstretched arm, or a wrenching force, may cause the head of the arm bone (*humerus*) to come out of the shoulder joint socket. This is a painful injury, and some people suffer repeated dislocations until a strengthening operation is carried out.

Recognition

♦ Pain, increased by movement.
♦ Reluctance to move because of the pain.
♦ The casualty often supports the arm, and inclines the head to the injured side.
♦ A flat, angular look to the shoulder.

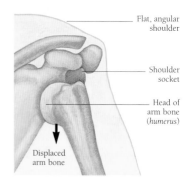

Flat, angular shoulder

Shoulder socket

Head of arm bone (*humerus*)

Displaced arm bone

TREATMENT

YOUR AIMS ARE:
■ To support the injured limb.
■ To arrange removal to hospital.

1 Sit the casualty down. Gently place the affected arm across her chest at an angle that causes the least pain.

2 Place a triangular bandage between the affected limb and the chest, as for an arm sling (*see page 232*).

3 Insert soft padding between the arm and the chest on the affected side.

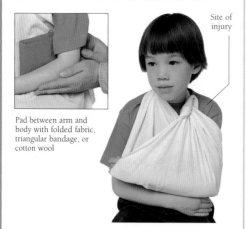

Site of injury

Pad between arm and body with folded fabric, triangular bandage, or cotton wool

4 Finish tying the arm sling so that the arm and its padding are supported.

DO NOT attempt to replace the bone into its socket.

DO NOT allow the casualty to eat or drink, as an anaesthetic may be necessary.

5 Take or send the casualty to hospital, keeping her seated.

SHOULDER SPRAIN

A fall on to the point of the shoulder may sprain the ligaments that brace the collar bone at the shoulder. Other sprains affect the capsule and tendons around the shoulder joint; these sprains are common in older people. To treat, follow the RICE procedure (*see page 132*).

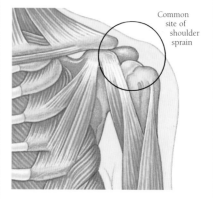

Common site of shoulder sprain

FRACTURED UPPER ARM

The long bone of the upper arm may be fractured across its shaft by a direct blow, but it is much more common, especially in the elderly, for the neck of the arm bone (*humerus*) at the shoulder to break, usually in a fall.

Because this type of fracture is a stable injury (*see page 129*), a casualty may put up with the pain and walk around with an untreated fracture for some time without seeking medical advice.

Recognition

◆ Pain, increased by movement.

There may also be:

◆ Tenderness over the fracture site.
◆ Rapid swelling.
◆ Bruising, which may develop more slowly.

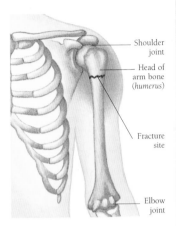

Shoulder joint

Head of arm bone (*humerus*)

Fracture site

Elbow joint

TREATMENT

YOUR AIMS ARE:

■ To immobilise the arm.
■ To arrange removal to hospital.

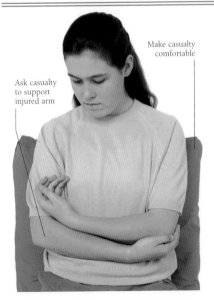

Ask casualty to support injured arm

Make casualty comfortable

1 Sit the casualty down. Gently place the injured arm across her chest in the position that is most comfortable. Ask her to support the arm, if possible.

2 Place the affected arm in an arm sling (*see page 232*), and place soft padding between the arm and the chest.

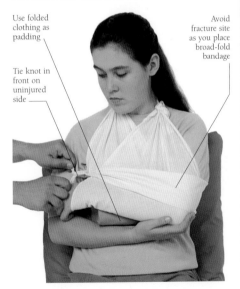

Use folded clothing as padding

Tie knot in front on uninjured side

Avoid fracture site as you place broad-fold bandage

3 Secure the limb to the chest by tying a broad-fold bandage (*see page 229*) around the chest and over the sling.

4 Take or send the casualty to hospital, keeping her seated.

INJURIES AROUND THE ELBOW

Fractures at the elbow are fairly common, often resulting from a fall on to the hand. A fracture or dislocation of the forearm bones is characterised by a stiff elbow that cannot be fully straightened.

Children often fracture the upper arm bone (*humerus*) just above the elbow. This is an unstable injury: the broken bone ends may move and damage nearby blood vessels and nerves, so it is vital to check frequently the pulse at the affected wrist and the circulation.

Recognition

- Pain, increased by movement.
- Tenderness over the fracture site.
- Possible swelling and bruising.
- Fixed elbow if the head of the radius is fractured.

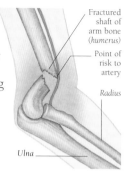

Fractured shaft of arm bone (*humerus*)

Point of risk to artery

Radius

Ulna

TREATMENT

YOUR AIMS ARE:
- To immobilise the arm without further injury to the joint.
- To arrange removal to hospital.

FOR AN ELBOW THAT CAN BEND

Treat as for a fracture of the upper arm (*see page 137*). Check the affected wrist pulse (*see page 77*) every ten minutes.

IF the pulse is not present, gently straighten the elbow until the pulse returns and support it in that position.

FOR AN ELBOW THAT CANNOT BEND

DO NOT try to move the injured limb.

1 Lay the casualty down. Place padding, such as cushions or towels, around the elbow for comfort and support.

2 ☎ *DIAL 999 OR 112 FOR AN AMBULANCE.* Check the injured wrist pulse every ten minutes until help arrives.

DO NOT attempt to bandage the casualty if medical help is on its way.

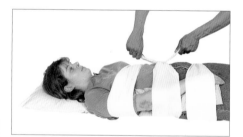

IF it is necessary to transport the casualty, put soft padding between the injured limb and body. Bandage the injured limb to the trunk, first at the wrist and hips, then above and below the elbow.

Casualty may be more comfortable lying down

Use towels and pillows as padding

INJURIES TO THE FOREARM AND WRIST

The bones of the forearm (the *radius* and *ulna*) may be fractured across their shafts by a heavy blow. As the bones have little fleshy covering, these fractures are often open, that is, associated with a wound.

The most common wrist fracture is a Colles' fracture (*see right*), usually suffered by older women who fall on to an outstretched hand. In a young adult, such a fall may break one of the small wrist bones. The complex wrist joint is rarely dislocated, but often sprained. It can be quite difficult to distinguish between a sprained and fractured wrist, especially if the *scaphoid* bone (*see right*) is injured.

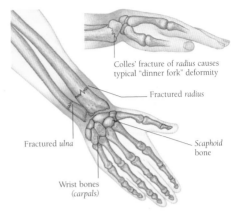

Colles' fracture of *radius* causes typical "dinner fork" deformity

Fractured *radius*

Fractured *ulna*

Scaphoid bone

Wrist bones (*carpals*)

TREATMENT

YOUR AIMS ARE:

■ To immobilise the arm.
■ To arrange removal to hospital.

1 Sit the casualty down. Gently steady and support the injured forearm across his chest. If necessary, carefully expose and treat any wound (*see page 130*).

Ask casualty to support injured arm

Cradle arm in folds of soft padding

2 Place a triangular bandage between the chest and the injured arm, as for an arm sling (*see page 232*). Gently surround the forearm in soft padding.

3 Tie the arm and its padding in an arm sling to support it (*see page 232*).

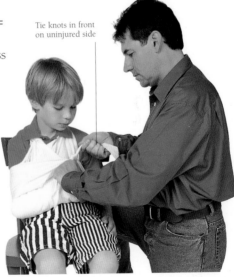

Tie knots in front on uninjured side

4 You may, if necessary, secure the limb to the chest, using a broad-fold bandage (*see page 229*). Tie it over the sling, positioning it close to the elbow.

5 Take or send the casualty to hospital, keeping him seated.

INJURIES TO THE HAND AND FINGERS

Any one of the many small bones and movable joints in the hand may be injured by direct or indirect force.

Minor fractures are usually caused by direct force. The most common injury often results from a misdirected punch and consists of a fracture of the knuckle between the little finger and the hand. Multiple fractures, affecting all of the bones in the hand, are usually caused by crushing injuries, and may produce severe bleeding and swelling.

Dislocations and sprains may affect any of the fingers. Falls on to the hand (for example, while skiing) are a common cause of dislocations of the thumb.

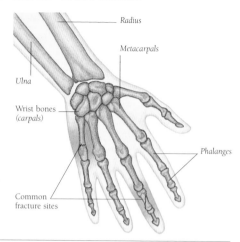

Radius

Metacarpals

Ulna

Wrist bones (carpals)

Phalanges

Common fracture sites

TREATMENT

YOUR AIMS ARE:

- To immobilise and elevate the hand.
- To arrange removal to hospital.

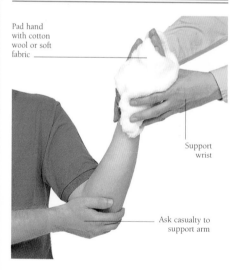

Pad hand with cotton wool or soft fabric

Support wrist

Ask casualty to support arm

1 Remove any rings before the hand begins to swell and keep the hand raised to reduce swelling. Protect the injured hand by wrapping it in folds of soft padding.

2 Gently support the affected arm in an elevation sling (*see page 233*).

3 You may, if necessary, secure the arm to the chest by tying a broad-fold bandage (*see page 229*) around the chest and over the sling.

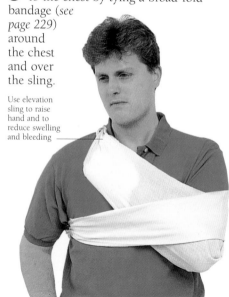

Use elevation sling to raise hand and to reduce swelling and bleeding

4 Take or send the casualty to hospital, keeping him seated.

FRACTURES OF THE RIBCAGE

Ribs may be fractured by direct force to the chest, from a blow or a fall, or by indirect force produced in a crush injury. If the rib fracture is complicated by a penetrating wound, breathing may be seriously impaired.

Flail chest injuries

Multiple rib fractures can result in part of the chest wall moving contrary to normal chest movement: moving in when the casualty breathes in, and out when he or she breathes out. This "paradoxical breathing" will cause severe respiratory difficulties.

Recognition

Depending on severity, there may be:

- Sharp pain at the site of the fracture.
- Pain on taking a deep breath.
- Distressed, paradoxical breathing.
- An open wound over the fracture, through which you might hear air being "sucked" into the chest cavity.
- Features of internal bleeding (*see page 99*) and shock (*see page 78*).
- Grey-blue skin (*cyanosis*)

See also:
Penetrating Chest Wounds, *page 94.*
Process of Breathing, *page 61.*

TREATMENT

YOUR AIMS ARE:

- To support the chest wall.
- To arrange removal to hospital.

FOR A FRACTURED RIB

Support the limb on the injured side in an arm sling (*see page 232*). Take or send the casualty to hospital.

FOR OPEN OR MULTIPLE FRACTURES

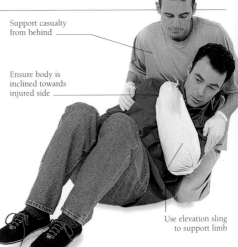

Support casualty from behind

Ensure body is inclined towards injured side

Use elevation sling to support limb

1 Immediately cover and seal any wounds to the chest wall (*see page 95*).

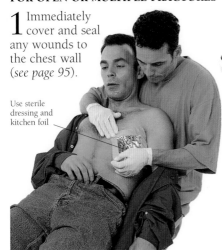

Use sterile dressing and kitchen foil

2 Place casualty in the most comfortable position, which may be half-sitting; head, shoulders, and body turned towards injured side. Support limb on the injured side in an elevation sling (*see page 233*).

☎ *DIAL 999 OR 112 FOR AN AMBULANCE.*

IF the casualty becomes unconscious, or breathing becomes difficult or noisy, place him in the recovery position (*see page 48*), uninjured side uppermost.

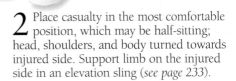

BACK INJURIES

Injuries to the back include fractures, fracture-dislocations of the bones of the spine, a displaced intervertebral disc ("slipped disc"), and muscle and ligament strains. The main danger, particularly with fracture-dislocations and disc injuries, is damage to the spinal cord or the nerves.

THE SPINE

The spine, or backbone, is actually made up of a column of small bones, each of which is called a *vertebra*. The spine supports the trunk and head, and surrounds and protects the spinal cord (*see page 108*). The spinal column is supported by many strong ligaments and the muscles of the trunk.

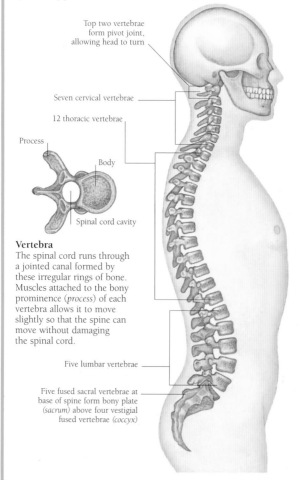

Top two vertebrae form pivot joint, allowing head to turn

Seven cervical vertebrae

12 thoracic vertebrae

Process

Body

Spinal cord cavity

Vertebra
The spinal cord runs through a jointed canal formed by these irregular rings of bone. Muscles attached to the bony prominence (*process*) of each vertebra allows it to move slightly so that the spine can move without damaging the spinal cord.

Five lumbar vertebrae

Five fused sacral vertebrae at base of spine form bony plate (*sacrum*) above four vestigial fused vertebrae (*coccyx*)

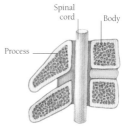

Spinal cord

Body

Process

Spinal cord
Part of the nervous system (*see page 108*), this is composed of nerve fibres that pass messages from the brain to the organs and other parts of the body. At each junction between the first cervical and the fifth sacral vertebra, nerves issue from the spinal cord and supply different areas of the body.

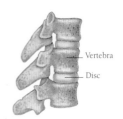

Vertebra

Disc

Intervertebral discs
These thick pads of gristle separate almost all the vertebrae. They act as shock absorbers, cushioning the impact on the spine when, for example, landing on the feet.

SPINAL INJURY

The danger of any spinal injury is that the spinal cord may be affected. The spinal cord is delicate and, if damaged, loss of power or sensation can occur in parts of the body below the injured area. Temporary damage can be caused if the cord or nerve roots are pinched by displaced or dislocated discs or bone fragments; permanent damage results if the cord is partly or completely severed.

Dangers of spinal fracture

Although the spinal cord may be injured without any damage to the bones, spinal fracture vastly increases the risk. Such fractures can be caused by both direct and indirect force. The most vulnerable parts of the spine are the bones in the neck and in the lower back.

What causes spinal injury?

Always suspect spinal injury when unusual or abnormal forces have been exerted on the back or neck, and particularly if the casualty complains of any disturbance of feeling or movement.

The history of the injury is the most important indicator. If the accident involved a violent forward bending, a backward bending, or a twisting of the spine, you must treat as for a fractured spine (*see overleaf*).

Recognition

When only the bones of the spinal column are damaged, there may be:

◆ Pain in the neck or the back at the level of the injury; this may be masked by other, more painful injuries.
◆ A step, irregularity, or twist in the normal curve of the spine.
◆ Tenderness on gently feeling the spine.

When the spinal cord is also damaged, there may be:

◆ Loss of control over limbs; movement may be weak or absent.
◆ Loss of sensation.
◆ Abnormal sensations, for example burning or tingling. The casualty may say that limbs feel "stiff", "heavy", or "clumsy".
◆ Breathing difficulties.

SOME CAUSES OF SPINAL INJURY

◆ Falling from a height.
◆ Falling awkwardly while doing gymnastics or trampolining.
◆ Diving into a shallow pool and hitting the bottom.
◆ Being thrown from a horse or from a motorbike.
◆ Being in a collapsed rugby scrum.
◆ Sudden deceleration in a motor vehicle (for example, in a head-on crash).
◆ A heavy object falling across the back.
◆ Injury to the head or the face.

Checking for spinal cord injury
Examine the casualty carefully in the position found.

Ask helper to maintain support at head

Touch casualty without him knowing to test for loss of sensation

Ask him to move his limbs to test for loss of power

TREATMENT FOR A CONSCIOUS CASUALTY

YOUR AIMS ARE:
- To prevent further injury.
- To arrange urgent removal to hospital.

> **DO NOT** move the casualty from the position found, unless she is in danger or becomes unconscious (*see opposite*). If she must be moved, use a scoop stretcher (*see page 244*) or a log-roll (*see opposite*).

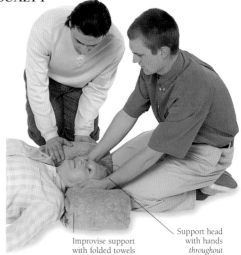

Improvise support
with folded towels

Support head
with hands
throughout

1 Reassure the casualty, and tell her not to move.

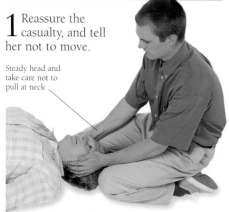

Steady head and
take care not to
pull at neck

2 Steady and support her head in the neutral position (*see page 147*) by placing your hands at either side of her head. Maintain this support throughout.

IF you suspect neck injury, get a helper to place rolled-up blankets or sandbags either side of the casualty's neck and shoulders.

☎ *DIAL 999 OR 112 FOR AN AMBULANCE.*

IF arrival of the ambulance is imminent, maintain support of the head and the neck with your hands until it arrives.

IF removal to hospital is delayed and the neck is injured, you may apply a rigid collar if trained to do so. You must continue to hold the head and neck while, and after, the collar is fitted.

RIGID NECK COLLARS

Rigid neck collars provide support to a casualty with a suspected neck injury. They should only be used by First Aiders who have been fully trained and are competent in their use. Use the correct size of collar for the casualty. Do not use a soft or improvised collar.

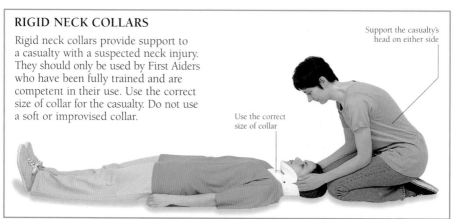

Support the casualty's
head on either side

Use the correct
size of collar

TREATMENT FOR AN UNCONSCIOUS CASUALTY

YOUR AIMS ARE:

- To resuscitate the casualty if necessary.
- To maintain an open airway.
- To prevent further damage to the spine or spinal cord.
- To arrange urgent removal to hospital.

Check the casualty's breathing and pulse. If necessary, move the casualty: resuscitating or protecting the casualty's airway must always take precedence over any risk of exacerbating spinal injury.

IF BREATHING AND PULSE ARE PRESENT

Place the casualty in a modified recovery position (*see overleaf*). ☎ *DIAL 999 OR 112 FOR AN AMBULANCE.*

IF BREATHING AND PULSE ARE ABSENT

1 ☎ *DIAL 999 OR 112 FOR AN AMBULANCE.* Open and, if necessary, clear the airway. Tilt the head more gently than usual so that the head and neck stay in the neutral position (*see overleaf*).

2 Recheck breathing and pulse. If they have not returned, position the casualty using the log-roll technique (*see below*) so that you can resuscitate him.

3 Combine artificial ventilation (*see pages 50–51*) with chest compressions (*see page 53*) until help arrives.

IF pulse and breathing return, place the casualty in a modified recovery position (*see overleaf*).

LOG-ROLL TECHNIQUE

If you have to turn the casualty on to his back to resuscitate, you should keep his head, trunk, and toes in a straight line at all times during the manoeuvre. While you maintain support at the neck, ask helpers to gently straighten the casualty's limbs, and "log-roll" him over on to his back.

Ideally, you need five helpers to carry out this manoeuvre. This technique can also be used to roll the casualty on to a stretcher.

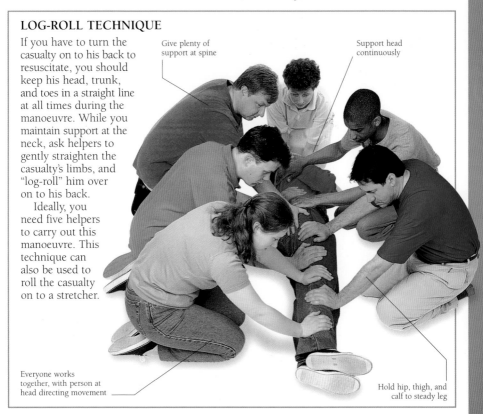

Give plenty of support at spine

Support head continuously

Everyone works together, with person at head directing movement

Hold hip, thigh, and calf to steady leg

THE RECOVERY POSITION IN SPINAL INJURY

If the casualty is unconscious with breathing and pulse present, you must place him in the recovery position (*see page 48*) in order to protect the airway. With spinal injuries, you should, ideally, modify the recovery position to keep the casualty's head and trunk aligned at all times so that the spine is protected.

You will need at least one helper to do this successfully (*see below*); use more helpers if they are available. Even if you are alone with the casualty, the ABC of resuscitation (*see page 44*) must always be followed, and the casualty must be turned to protect the airway, even if there is some risk of damaging the spine.

THE NEUTRAL HEAD POSITION

The least harmful position for a casualty with a suspected spinal injury is the neutral position, when the head, neck, and spine are aligned. When moving the head, grip it firmly over the ears and move it *slowly* into position. To ensure that the casualty is in the correct position, check that the nose is in line with the navel.

METHOD

1 Steady and support the casualty's head in the neutral position by placing your hands over his ears. Maintain this support until help arrives.

Support head and neck with your hands *at all times*

Leave limbs in position found until help arrives

Another person can help align the rest of the casualty's body

DO NOT pull on the neck.

2 Ask your helper to straighten the casualty's legs carefully. He should support the legs, while moving them.

Straighten legs carefully

Keep head and trunk aligned

3 While you continue to support the head, tell your helper to kneel beside the casualty and carefully place the nearest arm under the nearest thigh, palm upwards.

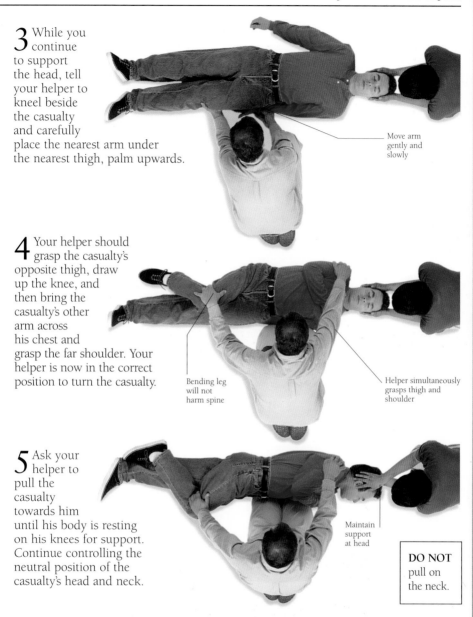

Move arm gently and slowly

4 Your helper should grasp the casualty's opposite thigh, draw up the knee, and then bring the casualty's other arm across his chest and grasp the far shoulder. Your helper is now in the correct position to turn the casualty.

Bending leg will not harm spine

Helper simultaneously grasps thigh and shoulder

5 Ask your helper to pull the casualty towards him until his body is resting on his knees for support. Continue controlling the neutral position of the casualty's head and neck.

Maintain support at head

DO NOT pull on the neck.

IF you have to send your helper to summon aid, place rolled blankets, coats, or similar articles on either side of the casualty to keep him in the neutral position. This will keep him steady until help arrives.

IF the neck is injured, a cervical collar may be applied for further support but only use this if you have had specific training in the use of a collar (*see page 144*). This is *not* a substitute for supporting the neck with the hands.

BACK PAIN

The lower back and neck are the most common sites of muscle or ligament sprain. Damage to the discs between the vertebrae may irritate or pinch the spinal cord or adjoining nerve roots.

How back pain is caused

Prolonged bending, lifting heavy weights, strenuous exercise, or an awkward fall can all lead to back and neck strain. Other causes of backache include kidney disease, pregnancy, and menstruation. A common cause of neck sprain is the "whiplash" effect produced in a car accident.

Dangerous complications

Hospital treatment is needed if back pain is accompanied by muscle spasms, fever, headaches, vomiting, nausea, impaired consciousness, incontinence, or loss of sensation or movement.

Recognition

There may be:

◆ Dull or severe pain in the back or neck, which is usually increased by movement.
◆ Pain travelling down any of the limbs, possibly together with tingling and numbness.
◆ Spasm of the muscles, causing the neck or back to be held rigid or bent.
◆ Tenderness in the muscles.

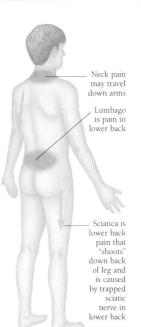

Neck pain may travel down arms

Lumbago is pain in lower back

Sciatica is lower back pain that "shoots" down back of leg and is caused by trapped sciatic nerve in lower back

---

TREATMENT

YOUR AIMS ARE:
■ To relieve pain.
■ To seek medical aid if necessary.

FOR MINOR BACK PAIN

He may be more comfortable without pillow

Ask casualty to lie as still as possible to ease pain

1 Help the casualty to lie down in the most comfortable position, either on the ground or on a firm mattress.

FOR SEVERE BACK PAIN

Help the casualty to lie down and make him as comfortable as possible (*see below*). Call a doctor. If the pain is in the neck, a collar (*see page 144*) should provide some relief.
☎ *DIAL 999 OR 112 FOR AN AMBULANCE,* if there are complications (*see above*), or if you are at all worried about the casualty's condition.

2 Advise the casualty to rest until the pain eases, and to see his doctor if symptoms persist.

FRACTURED PELVIS

Injuries to the pelvis are usually caused by indirect force, such as in a car crash or by crushing. The impact of a car dashboard on a knee can force the head of the thigh bone through the hip socket.

Pelvic injuries may be complicated by injury to internal tissues and organs, such as the bladder and urinary passages, which the pelvis protects. Because of the bulk of body tissue around the pelvis, internal bleeding associated with the fracture may be severe, and shock often develops.

Recognition

There may be:

◆ Inability to walk or even stand, although the legs appear uninjured.
◆ Pain and tenderness in the region of the hip, groin, or back, increased when the casualty moves.
◆ Blood at the urinary orifice, especially in a male casualty. The casualty may not be able to pass urine or may find this painful.
◆ Signs of shock and internal bleeding.

See also:
Internal Bleeding, *page 99.*
Shock, *page 78.*

Common fracture site   Ilium

Pubis   Ischium

The pelvic girdle
This consists of two hip bones formed by the fusions of three paired bones, the *ischium*, the *ilium*, and the *pubis*.

TREATMENT

YOUR AIM IS:

■ To arrange urgent removal to hospital.

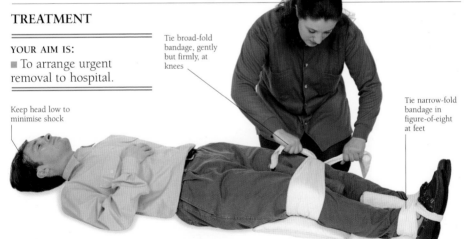

Tie broad-fold bandage, gently but firmly, at knees

Keep head low to minimise shock

Tie narrow-fold bandage in figure-of-eight at feet

1 Help the casualty to lie on his back either with his legs straight or, if it is more comfortable, help him to bend his knees slightly and support them.

2 Immobilise his legs by bandaging them together, placing padding between the bony points.

3 ☎ *DIAL 999 OR 112 FOR AN AMBULANCE.* Treat him for shock.

DO NOT bandage the legs together if this causes intolerable pain.

INJURIES TO THE LOWER LIMB

Injuries that may affect the lower limb, from the hip joint to the toes, include fractures, dislocations, sprains, and strains. It is important that casualties with lower limb injuries do not put weight on the injured leg.

INJURIES TO THE HIP AND THIGH

It takes considerable force (such as in road accidents or falls from heights) to fracture the shaft of the thigh bone. This is a serious injury because, in most cases, a large volume of blood is lost into the tissues, which may cause shock to develop.

Fractures of the neck of the thigh bone (*femur*) at the hip joint are common in the elderly, particularly in elderly women, whose bones become more porous and brittle as they age. This can be a stable injury (*see page 129*); the casualty may be able to walk around for some time before the fracture is discovered. The hip may also, more rarely, be dislocated.

Recognition
There may be:

◆ Pain at the site of the injury.
◆ Inability to walk.
◆ Signs of shock.
◆ Shortening of the thigh, as powerful muscles pull broken bone ends together.
◆ A turning outwards of the knee and foot.

See also:
Shock, *page 78.*

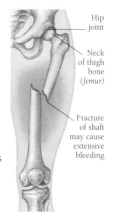

Hip joint

Neck of thigh bone (*femur*)

Fracture of shaft may cause extensive bleeding

TREATMENT

YOUR AIMS ARE:
■ To immobilise the lower limb.
■ To arrange urgent removal to hospital.

3 ☎ *DIAL 999 OR 112 FOR AN AMBULANCE.* Support the leg until the ambulance arrives.

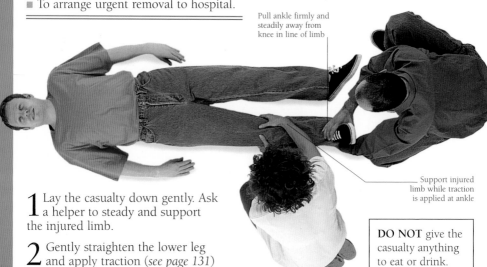

Pull ankle firmly and steadily away from knee in line of limb

Support injured limb while traction is applied at ankle

1 Lay the casualty down gently. Ask a helper to steady and support the injured limb.

2 Gently straighten the lower leg and apply traction (*see page 131*) at the ankle, if appropriate.

DO NOT give the casualty anything to eat or drink.

150

4 Take any steps possible to treat the casualty for shock; insulate him from the cold, but do not raise his legs.

IF the ambulance is delayed, immobilise the limb by securing or splinting it to the uninjured limb.
◆ Gently bring the casualty's sound limb alongside the injured one.
◆ Maintaining traction throughout at the ankle, gently slide two bandages under the knees. Ease them into place above and below the fracture by sliding them backwards or forwards. Position more bandages under the knees and ankles.
◆ Insert padding between the thighs, knees, and ankles, to stop the bandages displacing the broken bone once tied.

◆ Tie the bandages around his ankles and knees. Then tie the bandages above and below the fracture site.
◆ Release traction only when all bandaging knots are tied.

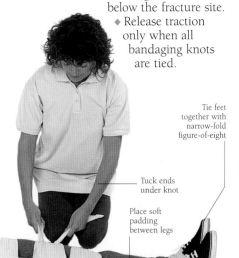

Tie feet together with narrow-fold figure-of-eight

Tuck ends under knot

Place soft padding between legs

Fracture site

Use broad-fold bandages around legs

TRANSPORTING A CASUALTY OVER DISTANCE

Log-roll casualty on to carrying canvas or blanket after bandaging

Splint from armpit to foot

Fracture site

If you have to transport a casualty on a stretcher to reach help (for example, across a moor), sturdier support for the leg will be needed. If you have been trained to do it, use a purpose-made malleable splint.

Alternatively, place a leg splint, such as a fence post, reaching from the armpit to the foot, against the injured side. Pad between the legs and between the splint and body.

Secure the splint to the pelvis with broad-fold bandages at the chest (1), pelvis (2), ankles (3), knees (4), above and below the fracture site (5 and 6) and at one extra point for support (7). *Do not* bandage over the fracture. Move the casualty on to the stretcher using the log-roll technique (*see page 145*). While carrying the stretcher, raise the feet to reduce swelling and shock.

INJURIES TO THE KNEE JOINT

The knee is the strong hinge joint between the thigh bone (*femur*) and shin bone (*tibia*). It is capable of bending, straightening, and, in the bent position, slight rotation. The knee joint is supported by strong muscles and ligaments, and protected in front by a disc of bone, the kneecap (*patella*). Any of these structures may be damaged by direct blows, violent twists, or strains.

Recognition

There may be:

◆ A recent twist or blow to the knee.
◆ Pain, spreading from the injury to become deep-seated in the joint.
◆ If the bent knee has "locked", acute pain on attempting to straighten the leg.
◆ Rapid swelling at the knee joint.

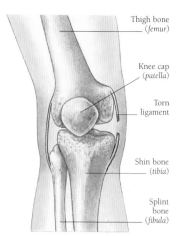

Thigh bone (*femur*)

Knee cap (*patella*)

Torn ligament

Shin bone (*tibia*)

Splint bone (*fibula*)

TREATMENT

YOUR AIMS ARE:

■ To protect the knee in the most comfortable position.
■ To arrange transport to hospital.

1 Help the casualty to lie down. Place soft padding, such as a blanket, under her injured knee to support it in the most comfortable position.

DO NOT attempt to straighten the knee forcibly. Displaced cartilage or internal bleeding may make the joint impossible to straighten safely.

DO NOT give the casualty anything to eat or drink; she may need an anaesthetic.

DO NOT allow the casualty to walk.

2 Wrap soft padding around the joint, and bandage it carefully in place.

3 Take or send the casualty to hospital, transporting her on a stretcher (*see pages 241–8*).

Keep your body clear of injury as you work

Use roller bandage to hold padding in place

Support casualty's knee with pillow, folded blanket, or coat

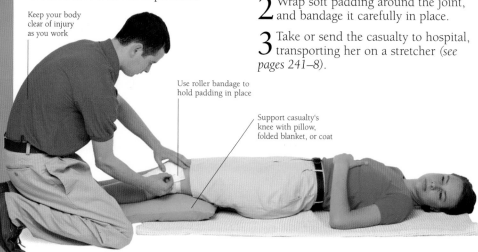

INJURIES TO THE LOWER LEG

The sturdy shin bone (*tibia*) of the lower leg will usually be broken only by a heavy blow (for example, from the bumper of a moving vehicle).

The thinner splint bone (*fibula*) can be broken by the type of twisting injury that sprains the ankle. If the load-bearing shin bone remains intact, the casualty may be able to walk, and may be unaware that a fracture has occurred.

Recognition

♦ Localised pain.

There may also be:

♦ A recent blow or wrench of the foot.
♦ An open wound.
♦ Inability to walk.

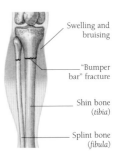

Swelling and bruising

"Bumper bar" fracture

Shin bone (*tibia*)

Splint bone (*fibula*)

TREATMENT

YOUR AIMS ARE:

■ To immobilise the leg.
■ To arrange urgent removal to hospital.

1 Help the casualty to lie down, and carefully steady and support the injured leg. If necessary, gently expose and treat any wound (*see page 130*).

Support leg at knee and ankle

2 Straighten the leg using traction (*see page 131*); pull in the line of the shin.

3 ☎ DIAL 999 OR 112 FOR AN AMBULANCE. Support the leg with your hands until the ambulance arrives.

IF the ambulance is delayed, splint the injured limb to the sound one.
♦ Bring the sound limb to the injured one.

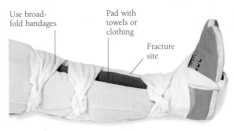

Use broad-fold bandages

Pad with towels or clothing

Fracture site

♦ Gently slide bandages under the knees and ankles. Slide them to the knees and ankles, and above and below the fracture; avoid the fracture if it is close to a joint.
♦ Insert padding between the knees and ankles and between the calves.
♦ Tie the bandages firmly around ankles and knees, then above and below the fracture. Knot on the uninjured side.

TRANSPORTING THE CASUALTY

If you are transporting the casualty on a stretcher, place extra padding (such as blankets) on either side of the legs, from the upper thigh to the foot. Secure with broad-fold bandages at the thigh and knee, and above and below the fracture.

IF the ankle is broken, bandage above the ankle and around the toes, rather than in a figure-of-eight.

Sprained Ankle

If the ankle is broken, treat it as a fracture of the lower leg (*see page 153*); a sprain (usually caused by a wrench) can be treated by the RICE procedure (*see page 132*).

Recognition

◆ Pain, increased either by movement or by putting weight on the foot.
◆ Swelling.

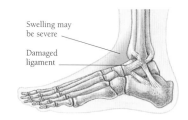

Swelling may be severe

Damaged ligament

TREATMENT

YOUR AIMS ARE:
■ To relieve pain and swelling.
■ To seek medical aid if necessary.

IF you suspect a broken bone, secure and support it (*see page 131*), and take or send the casualty to hospital.

1 Rest, steady, and support the ankle in the most comfortable position.

2 Apply an ice pack or a cold compress (*see page 221*) to a recent injury to reduce swelling.

3 Wrap the ankle in a thick layer of padding and bandage firmly.

4 Raise and support the injured limb to reduce swelling.

5 Advise the casualty to rest the ankle, and to see a doctor if pain persists.

Fractures of the Foot

Fractures affecting the many small bones of the foot are usually caused by crushing injuries. These types of fractures are best treated at hospital.

Recognition

There may be:

◆ Difficulty in walking.
◆ Stiffness of movement.
◆ Bruising and swelling.

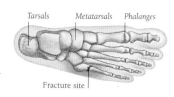

Tarsals   Metatarsals   Phalanges

Fracture site

TREATMENT

YOUR AIMS ARE:
■ To minimise swelling.
■ To arrange removal to hospital.

1 Quickly raise and support the foot to reduce blood flow to the foot and so minimise swelling.

2 Apply an ice pack or cold compress (*see page 221*).

3 Arrange to take or send the casualty to hospital. Try to ensure that the foot remains elevated while the casualty is being transported.

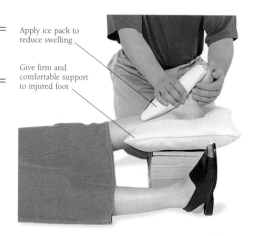

Apply ice pack to reduce swelling

Give firm and comfortable support to injured foot

BURNS AND SCALDS

10

Burns result from dry heat, extreme cold, corrosive substances, friction, or radiation, including the sun's rays; scalds are caused by wet heat from hot liquids and vapours.

Burns and scalds may be associated with conditions that pose a greater threat to life or there may be other serious injuries caused, for example, by an explosion or a jump from a burning building. Once the burns are treated, the casualty should be thoroughly examined.

Dealing with a burns incident

The approach to an accident resulting in burns is frequently complicated by the presence of fire, an explosion, electricity, smoke, toxic fumes, or other hazards (*see* Action at an Emergency, *pages 15–28*). Burns can be very distressing, and both you and the casualty may be upset by the smell of singed hair and burned flesh.

CONTENTS

FIRST-AID PRIORITIES

◆ Establish your own safety before attempting to treat the casualty.

◆ Deal with any airway problems.

◆ Stop the burning, by rapid cooling, to prevent further tissue damage, reduce swelling, minimise shock, and alleviate pain.

◆ Cover the injury to protect it from infection.

◆ Check for other injuries.

◆ Except in the case of very minor burns, assess the burns and obtain appropriate medical aid.

THE SKIN

One of the largest organs of the body, the skin is made up of two layers of tissue, the outer *epidermis* and the inner *dermis*, and lies on a layer of *subcutaneous* fat.

The epidermis contains a fatty substance that makes the skin waterproof. The dermis contains blood vessels, nerves, muscles, oil (*sebaceous*) glands, sweat glands, and hair roots (*follicles*). The sensory nerves within the dermis ensure that the body's surface area is sensitive to heat, cold, pain, and the slightest touch. As well as protecting the body from injury, bacterial and

viral infections, and minor burns, the skin's key function is to maintain a constant body temperature. It does this by varying the blood flow into capillary vessels beneath the skin surface and by producing *perspiration,* which evaporates cooling the body.

The blood capillaries dilate and perspiration increases when the body is too warm. If the body needs to conserve heat, the blood vessels constrict and small muscles attached to the hair follicles contract, pulling the skin into "goose-pimples". The body also creates heat by shivering.

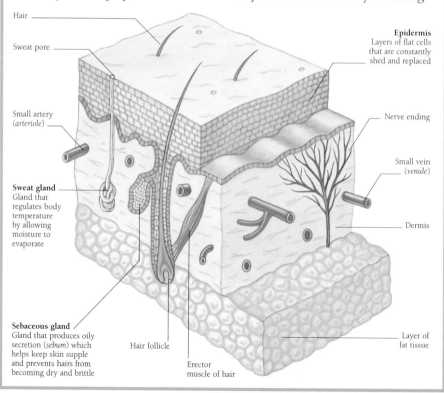

Hair

Sweat pore

Small artery
(*arteriole*)

Sweat gland
Gland that regulates body temperature by allowing moisture to evaporate

Sebaceous gland
Gland that produces oily secretion (*sebum*) which helps keep skin supple and prevents hairs from becoming dry and brittle

Hair follicle

Erector
muscle of hair

Epidermis
Layers of flat cells that are constantly shed and replaced

Nerve ending

Small vein
(*venule*)

Dermis

Layer of
fat tissue

ASSESSING A BURN

Before treating a burn, it is important to consider the extent and the depth of the burn, its cause, and whether the airway is affected.

The extent of the burn will tell you whether shock is likely to develop because of excessive loss of tissue fluid (*serum*). Burns destroy the skin, the body's natural barrier against airborne bacteria, and therefore carry a serious risk of infection: the deeper the burn, the higher the risk (*see overleaf*).

Once you are able to establish the cause of the burn, you can decide on the treatment. If the airway has been injured, the casualty may experience breathing difficulties, which will require urgent attention (*see page 162*).

How the skin reacts to a burn

When the skin is burned, the small blood vessels within the skin leak fluid. This fluid either gathers in tissue spaces to form blisters or it leaks through the skin surface. In a burn over a large surface area, this loss of fluid can lead to a marked drop in the blood volume and loss of blood proteins, a condition which may result in shock.

If the burn is on a limb, the fluid may accumulate in the tissues, causing swelling and pain. This is particularly dangerous if the limb is being constricted, for example by clothing or footwear.

See also:
Burns to the Airway, *page 162.*
Shock, *page 78.*

HOW BURNS ARE CAUSED	
Type of burn	**Causes**
Dry burn	• Flames • Contact with hot objects, for example domestic appliances or cigarettes • Friction, for example rope burns
Scald	• Steam • Hot liquids, such as tea and coffee, or hot fat
Electrical burn	• Low-voltage current, as used by domestic appliances • High-voltage currents, as carried in mains overhead cables • Lightning strikes
Cold injury	• Frostbite • Contact with freezing metals • Contact with freezing vapours, such as liquid oxygen or liquid nitrogen
Chemical burn	• Industrial chemicals, including inhaled fumes and corrosive gases • Domestic chemicals and agents, such as paint stripper, caustic soda, weedkillers, bleach, oven cleaner, or any other strong acid or alkali
Radiation burn	• Sunburn • Over-exposure to ultra-violet lamp ("sunlamp") • Exposure to radioactive source, such as an X-ray

EXTENT OF BURNS

It is vital to assess the extent of the area affected by a burn, as the greater the surface area, the greater the fluid loss and risk of shock. By using a simple formula, the "rule of nines", that divides the body into areas of about nine per cent, you can calculate the extent and decide what medical aid is needed. If in doubt, call a doctor. For an adult:

♦ any partial-thickness burn of one per cent or more must be seen by a doctor;
♦ a partial-thickness burn of over nine per cent will cause shock to develop and the casualty will need hospital treatment;
♦ any full-thickness burn requires hospital treatment. A child with any partial- or full-thickness burns needs medical attention.

If 60% of the skin surface (40% in the very young or old) is burned, kidney failure is likely to occur up to six weeks after the burn is sustained.

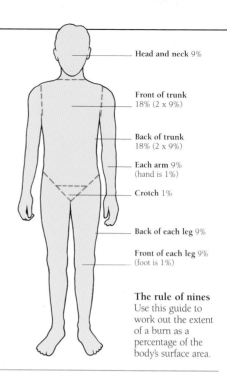

Head and neck 9%

Front of trunk 18% (2 x 9%)

Back of trunk 18% (2 x 9%)

Each arm 9% (hand is 1%)

Crotch 1%

Back of each leg 9%

Front of each leg 9% (foot is 1%)

The rule of nines
Use this guide to work out the extent of a burn as a percentage of the body's surface area.

DEPTH OF BURNS

There are three types of burn injury: superficial, partial-thickness, and full thickness. A casualty may suffer one or more depths of burn in an incident.

In very deep burns, pain sensation is usually lost, which may mislead both you and the casualty about the true severity of the injury.

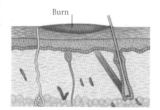

Burn

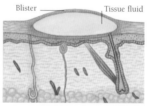

Blister — Tissue fluid

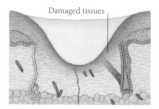

Damaged tissues

Superficial burn

This involves only the outermost layer of skin and is characterised by redness, swelling, and tenderness. It usually heals well if first aid is given promptly, and should not require medical attention unless it is extensive.

Partial-thickness burn

Any one per cent burn affecting layers of the epidermis, giving rise to rawness and blisters, needs medical treatment. Such burns can heal well, but if they affect very large areas (i.e. over 60%) of the body, they can be fatal.

Full-thickness burn

With this type of burn, all the layers of the skin are burned and there may be some damage to nerves, fat tissue, and muscles. The skin may look waxy, pale, or charred. Urgent medical attention is always essential for these burns.

MINOR BURNS AND SCALDS

Small, superficial burns are often caused by domestic accidents. Most can be treated by a First Aider and will heal naturally. If you are in any doubt as to the severity of the injury, seek medical advice.

TREATMENT

YOUR AIMS ARE:
- To stop the burning.
- To relieve pain and swelling.
- To minimise the risk of infection.

Cool with plenty of water

1 Flood the injured part with cold water for at least ten minutes to stop the burning and relieve the pain. If water is not available, any cold, harmless liquid, such as milk or canned drinks, will do.

2 Gently remove any jewellery, watches, belts, or constricting clothing from the injured area before it begins to swell.

> **DO NOT** break blisters or otherwise interfere with the injured area.
>
> **DO NOT** apply adhesive dressings or adhesive tape to the skin; the burn may be more extensive than it first appears.
>
> **DO NOT** apply lotions, ointments, or fats to the injury; they can further damage the tissues and increase the risk of infection.

3 Cover the area with a sterile dressing, or any clean, non-fluffy material, and bandage loosely in place. A plastic bag (*see page 161*) or some kitchen film makes a good temporary covering.

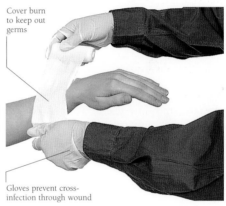

Cover burn to keep out germs

Gloves prevent cross-infection through wound

BLISTERS

Thin "bubbles", known as blisters, form on skin that has been damaged by heat or friction. They are caused by tissue fluid (*serum*) leaking into the burned area below the skin's surface. During healing, new skin forms at the base of the blister; the serum is re-absorbed and the outer layer of dead skin will eventually peel off.

What you should do

Never break a blister as you may introduce infection into the wound. A blister usually needs no treatment. However, if it breaks, or is likely to be damaged, cover the injured area with a dry, non-adhesive dressing that extends well beyond the edges of the blister. Leave in place until the blister subsides.

SEVERE BURNS AND SCALDS

Great care must be taken when treating burns that are deep or extend over a large area. The longer the burning continues, the more severe the injury will be. If the casualty has been burned in a fire, it should be assumed that smoke or hot air has also affected the respiratory system.

The two essential priorities for you, therefore, are to initiate rapid cooling of the burn, and to check the casualty's breathing. Follow the ABC of resuscitation if necessary (*see pages 44–58*). A casualty with a severe burn or scald injury will almost certainly be affected by shock and may require first aid.

See also:
Burns to the Airway, *page 162.*
Fires, *page 22.*
Resuscitation, *pages 44–58.*
Shock, *page 78.*

TREATMENT

YOUR AIMS ARE:
■ To stop the burning and relieve pain.
■ To maintain an open airway.
■ To treat associated injuries.
■ To minimise the risk of infection.
■ To arrange removal to hospital.
■ To gather relevant information for the emergency services.

1 Lay the casualty down. Protect the burned area from contact with the ground, if possible.

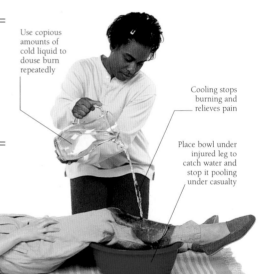

Use copious amounts of cold liquid to douse burn repeatedly

Cooling stops burning and relieves pain

Place bowl under injured leg to catch water and stop it pooling under casualty

2 Douse the burn with plenty of cold liquid. Thorough cooling may take at least ten minutes, but must not delay the casualty's removal to hospital.

3 While cooling the burn, watch for signs of difficulty in breathing, and be ready to resuscitate if necessary (*see pages 44–58*).
☎ *DIAL 999 OR 112 FOR AN AMBULANCE.*

DO NOT overcool the casualty; this treatment carries with it the risk of lowering the body temperature to a dangerous level (*hypothermia*) if the burns cover a large part of the body.

DO NOT remove anything sticking to the burn; you may cause further damage and introduce infection into the wound.

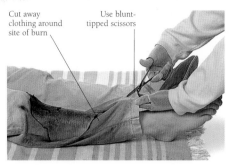

Cut away clothing around site of burn

Use blunt-tipped scissors

DO NOT interfere with the injured area. Wear gloves and a mask if possible.

DO NOT burst any blisters.

DO NOT apply lotions, ointment, fat, or adhesive tape to the injury.

4 Gently remove any rings, watches, belts, shoes, or smouldering clothing from the injured area, before it begins to swell. Carefully remove burned clothing, unless it is sticking to the burn.

Hold clean pad by edges to avoid infection

Wear plastic gloves to reduce risk of infection

5 Cover the injury with a sterile dressing or some other suitable material (*see box, below*) to protect it from germs and infection.

IF the casualty has a burn to the face, it does not need to be covered. Keep cooling a facial injury with water to relieve the pain until help arrives.

6 Gather and *record* details of the casualty's injuries, circumstances, and potential hazards such as gas.

7 While waiting for help, reassure the casualty and treat for shock. Monitor and *record* her breathing and pulse rates (*see page 40*), and be prepared to resuscitate if necessary (*see pages 44–58*).

DRESSING A BURN

Burns and scalds must be covered to protect them from infection by airborne bacteria, although the dressing does not need to be secured unless it is on an awkward part of the body. Use a sterile dressing if possible, or improvise a dressing with clean, non-fluffy material, such as:

◆ a portion of a clean sheet or pillowcase;
◆ plastic kitchen film – discard the first two turns from the roll;
◆ a folded triangular bandage;

◆ a clean plastic bag for a burned hand or foot. Secure it with a bandage or adhesive tape over the plastic, not the skin.

Clean plastic bag protects burn on hand

SPECIAL TYPES OF BURN

Many burns are caused not by direct contact with a naked flame, but by scorching air or heat produced within the body tissues by, for example, electricity. The damage caused is the same as that in thermal burns, and first aid follows the same principles. With accidents involving high-voltage electricity or harmful chemicals, remember that your own safety comes first. Do not endanger yourself or others by treating a casualty in hazardous circumstances, however urgent the casualty's needs appear.

See also:
Action at an Emergency, *pages 15–28.*

BURNS TO THE AIRWAY

Burns to the face and within the mouth or throat are very dangerous, as the air passages rapidly become inflamed and swollen. Usually, signs of burning will be evident, but you should always suspect burns to the airway if the injury has been sustained in a confined space, as the casualty may have inhaled hot air or gases.

There is no specific first-aid treatment for an extreme case; the swelling will rapidly block the airway, and there is a serious risk of suffocation. Immediate and specialised medical aid is required.

Recognition
There may be:

- ◆ Soot around the nose or mouth.
- ◆ Singeing of the nasal hairs.
- ◆ Redness, swelling, or actual burning of the tongue.
- ◆ Damaged skin around the mouth.
- ◆ Hoarseness of the voice.
- ◆ Breathing difficulties.

See also:
Shock, *page 78.*

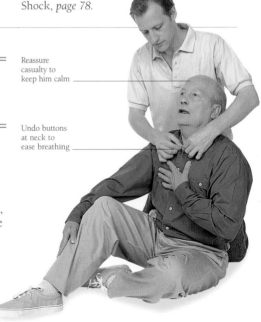

Reassure casualty to keep him calm

Undo buttons at neck to ease breathing

TREATMENT

YOUR AIMS ARE:
- ■ To obtain specialist medical aid as quickly as possible.
- ■ To maintain an open airway.

1 ☎ *DIAL 999 OR 112 FOR AN AMBULANCE.* Tell the control officer that you suspect burns to the airway.

2 Take any steps possible to improve the casualty's air supply; for example, loosening clothing around his neck. Give oxygen, if you are trained to do so.

IF the casualty becomes unconscious, open the airway, check breathing and pulse, and be prepared to resuscitate if necessary (*see pages 44–58*). Place him in the recovery position (*see page 48*).

Electrical Burns

Burns may occur when electricity passes through the body. Much of the visible damage occurs at the points of entry and exit of the current. However, there may also be a track of internal damage. The position and direction of entry and exit wounds will alert you to the likely extent of hidden injury, and to the degree of shock that may ensue.

Dangers of electrical burns

Burns may be caused by a lightning strike or by low or high-voltage current. An electric shock can cause cardiac arrest. If the casualty is unconscious, your immediate priority, once you are sure it is safe, is the ABC of resuscitation (*see pages 44–58*).

Recognition

There may be:

◆ Unconsciousness.
◆ Full-thickness burns, with swelling, scorching, and charring, at both the point of entry and exit.
◆ Signs of shock.
◆ A brown, coppery residue on the skin, if the casualty has been a victim of "arcing" high-voltage electricity. (Do not mistake this for injury.)

See also:
Cardiac Arrest, *page 84.*
Electrical Injuries, *page 24.*
Severe Burns and Scalds, *page 160.*
Shock, *page 78.*
Unconsciousness, *page 110.*

TREATMENT

YOUR AIMS ARE:

■ To treat the burns and shock.
■ To arrange removal of the casualty to hospital.

1 Make sure that contact with the electrical source is broken (*see page 25*).

IF the casualty is unconscious, open the airway, check breathing and pulse, and be prepared to resuscitate if necessary (*see pages 44–58*).

2 Flood the sites of injury with plenty of cold water to cool the burns (*see page 160*), and cut away any burned clothing if necessary.

3 Place a sterile dressing, a clean, folded triangular bandage, or some other clean, non-fluffy material over the burns to protect them against any airborne infection.

☎ *DIAL 999 OR 112 FOR AN AMBULANCE.*

4 Reassure the casualty and treat for shock (*see page 78*).

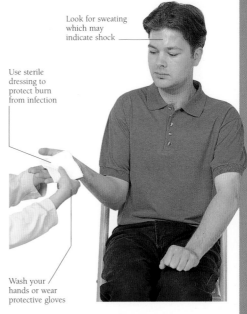

Look for sweating which may indicate shock

Use sterile dressing to protect burn from infection

Wash your hands or wear protective gloves

DO NOT approach a victim of high-voltage electricity until you are officially informed that the current has been switched off and isolated.

CHEMICAL BURNS

Certain chemicals may irritate, harm, or be absorbed through the skin, causing widespread and sometimes fatal damage. Unlike thermal burns, the signs develop slowly, but the first aid is the same.

Most strong corrosives are found in industry, although chemical burns do occur in the home, especially from dishwasher products (the most frequent cause of alkali burns in children), oven cleaners, and paint stripper.

Chemical burns are always serious and may require urgent hospital treatment. If possible, note the name or brand name of the substance. Ensure your own safety: some chemicals give off deadly fumes.

Recognition
There may be:

◆ Evidence of chemicals in the vicinity.
◆ Intense, stinging pain.
◆ Later, discolouration, blistering, peeling, and swelling of the affected area.

See also:
Assess the Situation, *page 16.*
Hazardous Substances, *page 20*
Industrial Poisons, *page 187.*
Inhalation of Fumes, *page 70.*

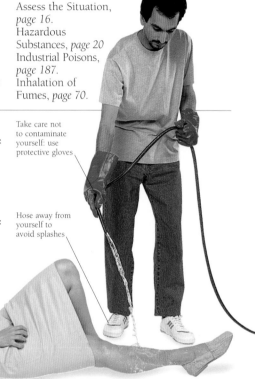

Take care not to contaminate yourself: use protective gloves

Hose away from yourself to avoid splashes

TREATMENT

YOUR AIMS ARE:

■ To disperse the harmful chemical.
■ To arrange transport to hospital.
■ To make the area safe and inform the relevant authority.

1 First make sure that the area is safe. Ventilate the area and, if possible, seal the chemical container. Remove the casualty from the area if necessary.

Ask casualty if she can identify chemical

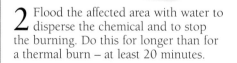

2 Flood the affected area with water to disperse the chemical and to stop the burning. Do this for longer than for a thermal burn – at least 20 minutes.

> **NEVER** attempt to neutralise acid or alkali burns unless trained to do so.
>
> **DO NOT** delay starting treatment by searching for an antidote.

3 Gently remove any contaminated clothing while flooding the injury.

4 Take or send the casualty to hospital; watch her airway and breathing closely. Note and pass on any details about the chemical to medical personnel.

IF in the workplace, notify the local Safety Officer or emergency services.

CHEMICAL BURNS TO THE EYE

Splashes of chemicals in the eye can cause serious injury if not treated quickly. Chemicals can damage the surface of the eye, resulting in scarring and even blindness. When irrigating the eye, be especially careful that the contaminated rinsing water does not splash you or the casualty. Wear protective gloves if they are available.

Recognition

There may be:

- ◆ Intense pain in the eye.
- ◆ Inability to open the injured eye.
- ◆ Redness and swelling around the eye.
- ◆ Copious watering of the eye.
- ◆ Evidence of chemical substances or containers in the immediate area.

TREATMENT

YOUR AIMS ARE:

- ■ To disperse the harmful chemical.
- ■ To arrange removal to hospital.

> **DO NOT** allow the casualty to touch the injured eye or forcibly remove contact lens.

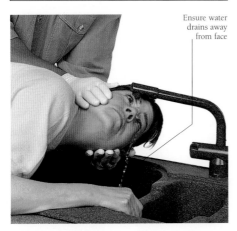

Ensure water drains away from face

1 Hold the affected eye under gently running cold water for at least ten minutes. Make sure that you irrigate both sides of the eyelid thoroughly. You may find it easier to pour the water from an eye irrigator or a glass.

IF the eye is shut in a spasm of pain, gently but firmly pull the eyelids open. Be careful that contaminated water does not splash the uninjured eye.

2 Ask the casualty to hold a sterile eye pad or a pad of clean, non-fluffy material over the injured eye.

Put bandage over eye pad

IF some time elapses before the casualty receives medical attention, bandage the pad loosely in position.

3 Take or send the casualty to hospital. Identify the chemical, if possible.

> **USING CHEMICAL ANTIDOTES**
>
> **DO NOT** use chemical antidote on a chemical burn to the eye, as the heat generated by the reaction may increase the degree of injury and cause more lasting damage. Alkalis may continue to cause damage for several hours after exposure to the chemical.
>
> *What you should do*
>
> Further treatment to relieve the pain and to limit corneal damage is usually required, and the patient should be referred to an ophthalmologist as soon as possible.

FLASH BURNS TO THE EYE

In this painful condition, which usually affects both eyes, the surface (*cornea*) of the eyes may be damaged by exposure to ultra-violet light, or to prolonged glare from the reflection of the sun's rays off a bright surface. It can take up to a week to recover. When the burn is caused by a welding torch, the condition is known as "welder's flash" or "arc eye".

Recognition

The symptoms and signs do not usually appear for some time after exposure.

◆ Intense pain in the affected eye(s).

There may also be:

◆ A "gritty" feeling in the eye(s).
◆ Sensitivity to light.
◆ Redness and watering of the eye(s).

TREATMENT

YOUR AIMS ARE:

■ To prevent further damage.
■ To obtain medical attention.

DO NOT remove contact lenses, if any.

1 Reassure the casualty. Ask him or her to hold eye pad(s) to the injured eye(s). If it will take some time to obtain medical help, bandage the pad(s) in place.

2 Arrange to take or send the casualty to hospital.

SUNBURN

This can be caused by over-exposure to the sun or a sunlamp or, rarely, by exposure to radioactivity. Most sunburn is superficial; in severe cases, the skin is lobster-red and blistered and the casualty may suffer heatstroke. Some medicines trigger severe reactions to sunlight. At high altitudes, sunburn can occur even on an overcast summer's day from "skyshine" or reflection from winter snow. If a mole changes after exposure to sun, tell the casualty, without causing alarm, to seek early medical advice.

See also:
Heatstroke, *page 174.*

TREATMENT

YOUR AIMS ARE:

■ To move the casualty out of the sun.
■ To relieve discomfort and pain.

1 Cover the casualty's skin with light clothing or a towel. Help her into the shade or, preferably, indoors.

2 Cool her skin by sponging with cold water, or by soaking the affected area in a cold bath for ten minutes.

IF there is extensive blistering or other skin damage, seek medical advice.

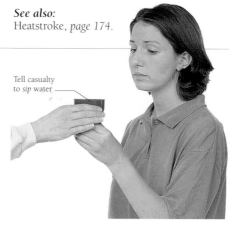

Tell casualty to *sip* water

3 Give her frequent sips of cold water. If the burns are mild, calamine or an after-sun preparation may soothe them.

EFFECTS OF HEAT AND COLD 11

The human body is designed to work best at, or close to, a temperature of 37°C (98.6°F). To maintain this temperature, the body possesses mechanisms that generate and conserve heat when the environment is cold and, conversely, that lose heat when it is hot. These mechanisms are controlled by a special centre in the brain. In addition, humans control their environment to some degree through clothing, heating, and air-conditioning, which make it easier for the body to perform well in a wide range of temperatures. In spite of all this, excessive heat or cold can still cause serious or even fatal injury.

The dangers of extreme temperatures

The harmful effects of extreme heat or cold can be localised, as is the case with frostbite and sunburn, or generalised, as with hypothermia, heat exhaustion, and heatstroke. The generalised effects of extremes of temperature occur more often in the very young and the very old, whose temperature-regulation systems may, respectively, be under-developed or impaired.

CONTENTS

THE FIRST AIDER SHOULD

◆ Remove, or protect, the casualty from excessively hot or cold surroundings.

◆ Restore normal body temperature: if the condition has been rapid in onset (for example, heat exhaustion), reverse it rapidly; if it has developed slowly (for example, hypothermia of slow onset affecting an elderly person), the casualty's body temperature must be gradually restored to normal.

◆ Obtain appropriate medical attention.

THE BODY TEMPERATURE

To keep the body temperature within its optimum range of 36–38°C (97.8–100.4°F), the body must maintain a constant balance between heat gain and heat loss. A "thermostat" deep within the brain regulates the balance.

The body's steady heat gain, produced by the conversion of food to energy (metabolism) and by muscular activity, is normally offset by continuous heat loss. Some methods of heat loss are passive, for example, the natural tendency of body heat to be lost to cool air; some are active, notably, changes within the circulatory system and at the skin.

In hot conditions, blood vessels dilate so that more blood heat may be lost by radiation from the skin. For heat to be conserved, this process is reversed. A rise in temperature beyond the normal range (fever, *see page 204*) most commonly occurs with infections.

HOW THE BODY KEEPS WARM

Heat is generated in the tissues by:
• Conversion of food to energy in the body's cells • Muscle activity, either voluntary (exercise) or, in cold conditions, involuntary (shivering)

Heat is absorbed:
• From outside sources – sun, fire, hot air, hot food or drink, or any hot object in contact with the skin

In cold conditions, the body saves heat by:
• Constricting blood vessels at the body surface to keep warm blood in the main part of the body (core) • Reducing sweating • Erecting body hairs to "trap" warm air at the skin • Burning the body's fat

HOW THE BODY LOSES HEAT

Heat may be lost to:
• Cool surrounding air – by radiation and by evaporation from the skin, and in the breath • Cool objects in contact with the skin, which provide a "pathway" for heat to escape

In hot conditions, the body reacts and loses heat by:
• Blood vessels that lie in or near the skin dilating to lose blood heat • Sweat glands becoming active and secreting sweat; heat is then lost as the sweat evaporates from the skin into the cooler air
• Increased rate and depth of breathing: warm air is expelled, and cool air is drawn in to replace it, cooling the blood as it passes through the lungs

KEEPING WARM IN THE COLD

Muscles contract to erect hairs   Vessels constrict to preserve blood heat

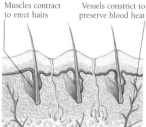

STAYING COOL IN THE HEAT

Vessels dilate to allow blood heat to escape   Hairs lie flat

Sweat

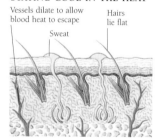

EFFECTS OF EXTREME COLD

The body reacts to cold by shutting down blood vessels in the skin to stop "core heat" escaping. When deprived of warm blood, extremities such as fingers or toes may freeze in severe conditions, causing frostbite. If the body's core temperature becomes dangerously low, bodily functions slow down (*hypothermia*) and may cease altogether.

FROSTBITE

This condition usually occurs in freezing and often dry and windy conditions. Those who cannot move are particularly vulnerable. The tissues of the extremities freeze – in severe cases this can lead to permanent loss of sensation and, eventually, gangrene.

Frostbite is often accompanied by hypothermia, which should be treated accordingly (*see pages 170–72*).

Recognition
There may be:

♦ At first, "pins-and-needles".
♦ Paleness, followed by numbness.
♦ A hardening and stiffening of the skin.
♦ A colour change to the skin of the affected area: first red and swollen, then white and mottled, and eventually black when gangrene occurs.

TREATMENT

YOUR AIMS ARE:
■ To warm the affected area slowly, to prevent further tissue damage.
■ To obtain medical aid if necessary.

1 Very gently remove gloves, rings, and any other constrictions, such as boots. Warm the affected part with your hands, in your lap, or in the casualty's armpit. Avoid rubbing because it can damage skin and tissues.

Allow casualty to warm affected part

DO NOT put affected part by direct heat, or thaw it if there is danger of it refreezing.

2 Move the casualty into warmth before you thaw the affected part; carry her if possible when the feet are affected.

3 Place the affected part in warm water. Dry carefully, and apply a light dressing of fluffed-up, dry gauze bandage.

4 Raise and support the limb to reduce swelling. An adult casualty may take two paracetamol tablets for intense pain. Take or send her to hospital, if necessary.

IMMERSION (TRENCH) FOOT

This is caused by prolonged exposure to near-freezing temperatures in damp, slushy conditions, and can be aggravated by lack of mobility, tight shoes, and wet socks. The feet will be white, cold, and numb, then red, hot, and painful on rewarming. Treat as for frostbite.

HYPOTHERMIA

This condition develops when the body temperature falls below 35°C (95°F). The effects vary with the speed of onset, and the level to which the temperature falls. Moderate hypothermia can usually be completely reversed. However, deep hypothermia (core temperature below 26°C / 79°F) is often, though not always, fatal: it is always worth persisting with resuscitation (*see pages 44–58*) until a doctor arrives to assess the condition.

How hypothermia can be caused

Hypothermia may develop over several days in poorly heated houses. Infants, homeless people, elderly people, and the thin and frail are particularly vulnerable. Lack of agility, chronic illness, and fatigue all increase the risk; alcohol and drugs can exacerbate the condition.

Hypothermia can also be caused by prolonged exposure to cold out of doors (*see page 172*), especially in wet and windy conditions. Moving air has a much greater cooling effect than still air: a high "wind-chill factor" can, therefore, substantially increase the risk of a person developing hypothermia.

Death from immersion in cold water may be caused by hypothermia, not drowning. When surrounded by cold water, the body cools 30 times faster than in dry air, leading to a dangerously rapid lowering of body temperature.

Recognition

As hypothermia develops, there may be:

◆ Shivering, and cold, pale, dry skin.
◆ Apathy, disorientation, or irrational behaviour; occasionally belligerence.
◆ Lethargy or failing consciousness.
◆ Slow and shallow breathing.
◆ A slow and weakening pulse.
◆ In extreme cases, cardiac arrest.

See also:
Cardiac Arrest, *page 84*.
Drowning, *pages 26 and 68*.

HYPOTHERMIA IN THE ELDERLY

Frail, infirm, and elderly people are at risk from hypothermia if the weather is very cold. They often have inadequate food or heating, and are more likely to suffer from conditions such as arthritis, making them relatively immobile and at greater risk.

As the body ages, it loses its sensitivity to cold, so the elderly may not feel a drop in body temperature. In addition, an elderly person's body is less able to compensate for an extreme temperature change.

What to do

Hypothermia in the home may often develop slowly, and warming should also be gradual (*see right*). Rapid warming, for example in a hot bath, should be avoided as this may send cold blood from the body surfaces to the heart and brain too suddenly. Always call a doctor, because this type of hypothermia may disguise the symptoms of, or accompany, a stroke or a heart attack.

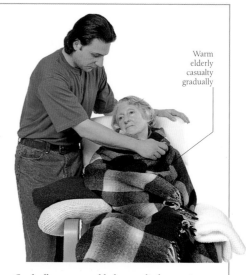

Warm elderly casualty gradually

Gradually warm an elderly casualty by covering her with layers of blankets in a room temperature of approximately 25°C (77°F).

TREATMENT

YOUR AIMS ARE:
■ To prevent the casualty losing more body heat.
■ To rewarm the casualty.
■ To obtain medical aid.

FOR A CASUALTY INDOORS

1 For a casualty brought in from outside, quickly replace any wet clothing with warm, dry garments.

2 The casualty can be rewarmed by bathing if she is young, fit, and able to climb into the bath unaided. The water should be warm (40°C / 104°F).

> **DO NOT** allow an elderly casualty to have a bath (*see opposite*).

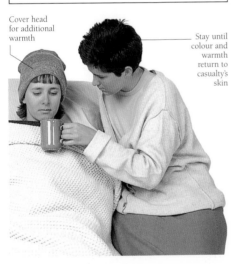

Cover head for additional warmth

Stay until colour and warmth return to casualty's skin

3 Put the casualty in a bed and ensure that she is well covered. Give her warm drinks, soup, or high-energy foods such as chocolate.

> **DO NOT** place heat sources, such as hot-water bottles or fires, next to the casualty.

> **DO NOT** give the casualty any alcohol.

4 It is important that you call a doctor if you have any doubts about the casualty's condition, or if the casualty is elderly (*see opposite*) or an infant.

IF the casualty becomes unconscious, open the airway, check breathing and pulse, and be prepared to resuscitate if necessary (*see pages 44–58*). ☎ *DIAL 999 OR 112 FOR AN AMBULANCE.*
As the casualty warms up, continue resuscitation, if needed, until help arrives.

HYPOTHERMIA IN INFANTS

Warm baby gradually and keep head covered

A baby's mechanisms for regulating temperature are under-developed, so an infant may develop hypothermia in a cold room. The baby's skin may look healthy, but feel cold, and she may be limp, unusually quiet, and refuse to feed.

Rewarm a hypothermic baby gradually. Wrap her in blankets and warm the room. A doctor *must* examine the child.

171

Hypothermia (continued)

YOUR AIMS ARE:
- To prevent the casualty from losing more body heat.
- To rewarm the casualty.
- To obtain medical aid.

FOR A CASUALTY OUTDOORS

Make sure casualty has enough clothing, but do not give him yours

1 Insulate the casualty with extra clothing or blankets, and cover his head.

2 Take or carry the casualty to a sheltered place as quickly as possible.

3 Protect the casualty from the ground and the elements. Put him in a dry sleeping bag, cover him with blankets or newspapers, or enclose him in a plastic or foil survival bag.

PREVENTING HYPOTHERMIA OUTDOORS

Plan outdoor expeditions carefully, and make sure participants are properly supervised. Anyone with even minor illness should not participate; take anyone who is unwell or is injured during the expedition to a safe place without delay.

Be equipped for an emergency

Always take a spare sweater, dry socks, dry and well-aired sleeping bags, and a survival bag. Take extra high-energy food and drink, but not alcohol; it dilates the blood vessels and accelerates heat loss.

Dress to beat the cold

Layers of clothing are more effective than one warm garment. The outer layer should be wind- and water-proof, and capable of being loosened at the neck and wrists. Coats and boots become heavy when wet; if you fall into cold water, lie as still as possible and remove them, as the weight may drag you down.

Shelter and warm him with your body

Lay casualty on thick layer of dry insulating material, such as pine branches, heather, or bracken

Protect him from wind and rain with survival bag

4 Send for help; in an ideal situation, two people should go. However, it is important that you do not leave the casualty alone; someone must remain with him at all times.

5 Give a conscious casualty warm drinks, if available.

6 When help arrives, evacuate the casualty to hospital by stretcher.

IF the casualty becomes unconscious, open the airway, check breathing and pulse, and resuscitate if necessary (*see pages 44–58*). If necessary, continue resuscitation until medical help arrives.

EFFECTS OF EXTREME HEAT

When the atmospheric temperature is the same as your body temperature, the body cannot lose heat by radiation or by evaporation. If there is also a humid atmosphere, sweat will not evaporate from the body. In these circumstances, particularly during strenuous exercise when the body generates more heat, heat exhaustion or heatstroke can occur.

> **RECREATIONAL DRUG USE**
> A dangerous and common cause of raised body temperature is that resulting from certain drugs, such as Ecstasy, taken for pleasure. The casualty sweats profusely due to prolonged overactivity and becomes dehydrated, leading to heat exhaustion. This, coupled with the drug's effect on the brain, can lead to heatstroke.

HEAT EXHAUSTION

This condition usually develops gradually and is caused by loss of salt and water from the body through excessive sweating. It usually happens to people who are unaccustomed to a hot, humid environment. Those who are unwell, especially with illnesses that cause vomiting and diarrhoea (*see page 210*), are also vulnerable.

Recognition

As the condition develops, there may be:

◆ Headache, dizziness, and confusion.
◆ Loss of appetite, and nausea.
◆ Sweating, with pale, clammy skin.
◆ Cramps in the arms, legs, or the abdominal wall.
◆ Rapid, weakening pulse and breathing.

TREATMENT

YOUR AIMS ARE:
■ To cool down the casualty.
■ To replace lost fluid and salt.

1 Help the casualty to a cool place. Lay him down and raise his legs.

2 Give him plenty of water; follow, if possible, with weak salt solution (one teaspoon of salt per litre of water).

3 Even if the casualty recovers quickly, ensure he sees a doctor.

IF the casualty's responses deteriorate, place him in the recovery position (*see page 48*).
☎ *DIAL 999 OR 112 FOR AN AMBULANCE.*
Monitor and *record* breathing, pulse, and response every ten minutes, and be ready to resuscitate if needed (*see pages 44–58*).

Support casualty's head as he drinks water

Raise feet to improve blood flow to brain

Place cushion under his feet for comfort

Heatstroke

A failure of the "thermostat" in the brain causes this condition. The body becomes dangerously overheated due to a high fever or prolonged exposure to heat. In some cases, it follows heat exhaustion when sweating ceases, and the body cannot be cooled by evaporation. Heatstroke can occur suddenly, causing unconsciousness within minutes. This may be signalled by the casualty feeling uneasy and ill.

Recognition
There may be:

- Headache, dizziness, and discomfort.
- Restlessness and confusion.
- Hot, flushed, and dry skin.
- A rapid deterioration in the level of response (*see page 110*).
- A full, bounding pulse.
- Body temperature above 40°C (104°F).

TREATMENT

YOUR AIMS ARE:
- To lower the casualty's body temperature as quickly as possible.
- To arrange removal of the casualty to hospital.

1 Quickly move the casualty to a cool place. Remove as much of his outer clothing as possible.
☎ *DIAL 999 OR 112 FOR AN AMBULANCE.*

TAKING A TEMPERATURE

- Hold the thermometer at the opposite end from the silver mercury bulb.
- Shake the thermometer, ensuring that the mercury drops well below the normal mark, 37°C (98.6°F).
- Place the thermometer under the tongue (or armpit for a child), and leave for three minutes. Read the temperature at the point at which the mercury has stopped.

IF the casualty's responses deteriorate, or he becomes unconscious, open the airway, check breathing and pulse, and be prepared to resuscitate if necessary (*see pages 44–58*). Place him in the recovery position (*see page 48*).

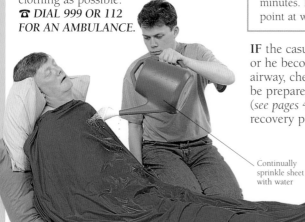

Continually sprinkle sheet with water

Wrap casualty in wet sheet

2 Wrap the casualty in a cold, wet sheet and keep it wet until his temperature falls to 38°C / 100.4°F (under the tongue) or 37.5°C / 99.5°F (under the armpit).

IF no sheet is available, constantly fan the casualty or sponge with cold water.

3 When the casualty's temperature has fallen to a safe level, replace the wet sheet with a dry one. Monitor the casualty carefully until help arrives.

IF the casualty's temperature rises again, repeat the cooling process (*see step 2*).

FOREIGN BODIES

12

Any object, large or small, that finds its way into the body either through a wound in the skin or via one of the body's orifices, such as the ear, nose, eye, vagina, or rectum, is called a "foreign body". Foreign bodies – commonly, specks of dirt or grit – can also rest on, or enter, the eye. These types of injury are often seen by a First Aider. While they are not usually serious, they can be distressing and painful for the casualty. Calm, reassuring, and prompt treatment is essential.

Understanding treatment procedures

This chapter explains how to treat foreign bodies in the skin, eye, nose, and ear. The structure of the eyes, nose, and ears are illustrated and explained to help you understand the treatment required, and to recognise any potential problems. Advice is also given on what to do when an object has been swallowed or inhaled.

Casualties with foreign bodies in the ano-genital orifices should be referred to a doctor or nurse. For advice on treating foreign bodies embedded in an open wound, see page 105.

FIRST-AID PRIORITIES

◆ Decide if it is safe to remove the foreign body. Do not remove large or deeply embedded objects. If it cannot be removed, obtain medical help.

◆ If the foreign body is small, loose, or superficial, and can easily be removed, reassure the casualty and ask him or her to keep still.

◆ Once the object has been removed, take any necessary further action. If you suspect infection or internal injury, seek a doctor's advice.

175

FOREIGN BODIES IN THE SKIN

Small foreign bodies such as wood splinters or shards of glass usually cause minor puncture wounds with little or no bleeding. If a portion of the object protrudes from the skin, you may attempt to draw it out. If a foreign body is deeply embedded in a wound, do not remove it; you may cause further injury by doing so.

Foreign bodies in wounds are often contaminated with bacteria and dirt. Always ensure the wound is clean, and the casualty's immunisation for tetanus is up to date (*see page 106*).

See also:
Foreign Bodies in Minor Wounds, *page 105*.
Infection in Wounds, *page 106*.
Severe External Bleeding, *page 88*.

SPLINTERS

Small splinters of wood, metal, or glass in the skin, particularly of the hands, feet, and knees, are common injuries. The splinter can usually be successfully drawn out using tweezers. If the splinter is deeply embedded, lies over a joint, or is difficult to remove, leave it in place and tell the casualty to consult a doctor.

TREATMENT

YOUR AIMS ARE:
■ To remove the splinter.
■ To minimise the risk of infection.

DO NOT probe the wound with a sharp object, such as a needle, in an attempt to lever out the splinter.

1 Gently clean the area around the splinter with soap and warm water. Sterilise a pair of tweezers by passing them through a flame and allow to cool.

IF the splinter does not come out easily, or breaks, treat it as an embedded foreign body (*see page 105*), and seek medical advice.

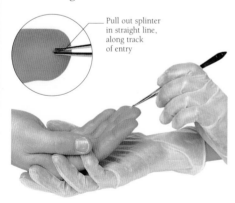

Pull out splinter in straight line, along track of entry

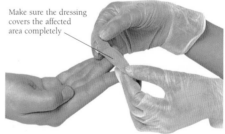

Make sure the dressing covers the affected area completely

3 Clean the area and apply an adhesive dressing (plaster) that is larger than the affected area, to prevent infection.

2 Grasp the splinter with the tweezers as close to the skin as possible, and draw it out at the angle it went in.

4 Check that the casualty's tetanus immunisation is up to date (*see page 106*). If it is not, or if in doubt, advise the casualty to see a doctor.

FISH HOOKS

Embedded fish hooks are difficult to draw out because of their barbs; you should only attempt to remove one if medical aid is not available. If you do remove it, advise the casualty to see a doctor if tetanus immunity is in doubt (*see page 106*).

TREATMENT

YOUR AIMS ARE:
■ To seek medical aid. If unavailable, to remove the fish hook without causing the casualty any further injury and pain.

WHEN MEDICAL AID IS EXPECTED

1 Cut the fishing line as close as possible to the hook.

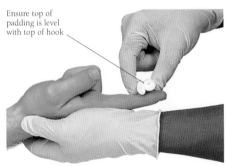

Ensure top of padding is level with top of hook

2 Build up pads of gauze around the hook until you can bandage over it without pushing it in further.

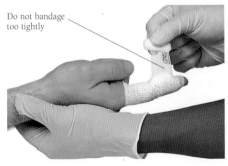

Do not bandage too tightly

3 Bandage over the padding and the fish hook; take care not to press down on the hook. Ensure that the casualty receives medical care as soon as possible.

WHEN MEDICAL AID IS NOT READILY AVAILABLE

If the barb is visible

> **DO NOT** pull out a hook unless the barb is cut off.

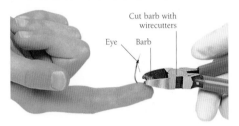

Cut barb with wirecutters

Eye   Barb

1 Cut the barb away, and then carefully withdraw the hook by its eye.

2 Clean the wound, then pad around it with gauze and bandage it. Ensure that tetanus immunity is up to date.

If the barb is not visible

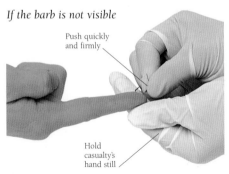

Push quickly and firmly

Hold casualty's hand still

1 If possible, push the hook forwards through the wound, until the barb emerges from the skin.

2 Cut the barb away, then withdraw the fish hook, and dress the wound as described above.

THE EYES, NOSE, AND EARS

These vital parts of the body relay sensory information to the brain for interpretation. Each has a complex, delicate structure and is susceptible to damage by foreign bodies. A basic knowledge of their anatomy will help you understand the treatment for injuries to these organs.

THE EYES

The eyes allow us to see. Each one is about 2.5 cm (1 in) across, but only a small part is visible, as each eye sits in a protective bony socket in the skull.

Each eye has a coloured part (*iris*) with a small opening (*pupil*) that lets in light. A lens in the centre focuses light on to a "screen" (*retina*) at the back of the eye to form an image. Nerve cells in the retina translate images into electrical impulses that travel via the optic nerve to the brain to be analysed. The front of the eye has a protective layer (*cornea*) and an outer membrane (*conjunctiva*) that is constantly bathed in fluid to keep the surface clean.

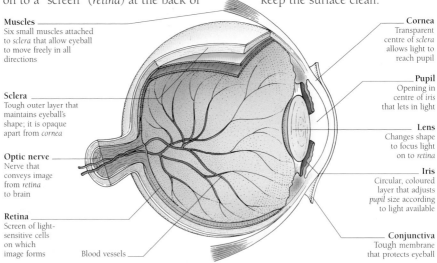

Muscles
Six small muscles attached to *sclera* that allow eyeball to move freely in all directions

Sclera
Tough outer layer that maintains eyeball's shape; it is opaque apart from *cornea*

Optic nerve
Nerve that conveys image from *retina* to brain

Retina
Screen of light-sensitive cells on which image forms

Blood vessels

Cornea
Transparent centre of *sclera* allows light to reach pupil

Pupil
Opening in centre of *iris* that lets in light

Lens
Changes shape to focus light on to *retina*

Iris
Circular, coloured layer that adjusts *pupil* size according to light available

Conjunctiva
Tough membrane that protects eyeball

WHAT CAN GO WRONG

◆ Increasing pressure inside the eyeball may damage the optic nerve, and cause a gradual loss of vision. This progressive condition is called *glaucoma*.
◆ A cataract is caused by the lens of the eye becoming opaque and reducing the amount of light reaching the retina.

◆ Inflammation of the conjunctiva and cornea (*conjunctivitis*) is a common and painful eye condition, characterised by redness, irritation, and rapid blinking.
◆ Damage to the cornea through injury or infection may lead to build-up of scar tissue and a permanent defect in vision.

THE NOSE

This delicate organ forms an entrance to the respiratory tract (*see page 60*). It allows air to enter the respiratory system, and also interprets smell and enhances taste.

The nasal cavities are lined with blood vessels and mucous membranes that warm and moisten the air to prevent damage to the lungs' membranes. The mucus also traps debris, which is moved by minute hairs (*cilia*) down the throat to be coughed up or swallowed. Special cells (*olfactory epithelia*) in the nasal cavities detect and transmit smells to the brain via *olfactory nerve fibres*.

> ## WHAT CAN GO WRONG
> ◆ Inflamed nasal membranes, sneezing, and congestion are caused by hay fever, a reaction to allergens such as pollen, dust mites, or fungal spores, and by viral infections such as the common cold.
> ◆ Fractures of the nasal bones are often sustained while playing sport.
> ◆ Nosebleeds (*see page 102*) are due to infection, raised blood pressure, or damage to the blood vessels lining the nasal cavity.

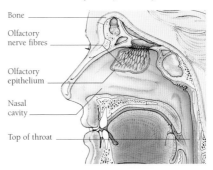

Bone
Olfactory nerve fibres
Olfactory epithelium
Nasal cavity
Top of throat

THE EARS

The ears control hearing and balance. Each ear has three parts. The outer ear consists of the visible part (*auricle*), the ear canal, and ear-drum. The auricle funnels sound waves into and through the ear canal to vibrate the ear-drum. Fine hairs in the canal filter out dust, and glands secrete wax to trap other small foreign particles.

The middle ear is an air-filled cavity with three small bones that transmit sound waves from the ear-drum to the inner ear. The middle ear is linked to the back of the nose by the Eustachian tube which equalises air pressure.

The inner ear has two small organs: the *cochlea* and *vestibular apparatus*. The cochlea converts sound vibrations from the ear-drum into impulses, and sends them to the brain via the auditory nerve. The vestibular apparatus monitors balance and position.

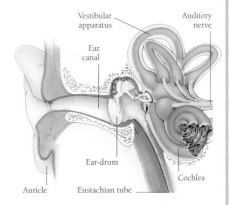

Vestibular apparatus
Auditory nerve
Ear canal
Ear-drum
Cochlea
Auricle
Eustachian tube

> ## WHAT CAN GO WRONG
> Earache can indicate infection of the outer ear (often after swimming). Infection usually reaches the middle ear via the Eustachian tube. The fluid from infections can become sticky ("glue ear"), often a cause of temporary deafness in children.

FOREIGN BODIES IN THE EYE

A speck of dust, loose eyelash, or even a contact lens can literally float on the white of the eye, and is usually easily removed. However, anything that sticks to the eye, penetrates the eyeball, or rests on the coloured part of the eye (the pupil and iris, *see page 178*) should not be touched.

Recognition
There may be:

- Blurred vision.
- Pain or discomfort.
- Redness and watering of the eye.
- Eyelids screwed up in spasm.

See also:
Eye Wounds, *page 98*.

TREATMENT

YOUR AIM IS:
- To prevent injury to the eye.

1 Advise the casualty not to rub her eye. Sit her down facing the light.

> **DO NOT** touch anything that is sticking to, or embedded in, the eyeball, or over the coloured part of the eye.

2 Gently separate the eyelids with your finger and thumb. Examine every part of her eye.

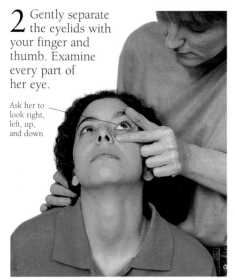

Ask her to look right, left, up, and down

Pour water on inner corner of eye

Let water drain on to towel

3 If you can see a foreign body on the white of the eye, wash it out with a glass or an eyebath, and clean water.

4 If this is unsuccessful, providing the foreign body is not stuck in place, lift it off with a moist swab, or the damp corner of a tissue or clean handkerchief.

Ask casualty to pull down upper lid

Lower lashes may brush particle clear

IF the foreign body is sticking to or embedded in the eye, cover the affected eye with an eye pad and a bandage, then take or send the casualty to hospital.

IF the object is under the upper eyelid, ask her to grasp her lashes and pull the lid over the lower lid. Blinking under water may also make the object float clear.

FOREIGN BODIES IN THE NOSE

Young children may push small objects up their noses. These can cause blockage and infection and, if they are sharp, may also damage the tissues of the nostrils. You must not try to extricate these items; you may cause injury or push the object in further.

Recognition
There may be:

◆ Difficulty in breathing, or noisy breathing through the nose.
◆ Swelling of the nose.
◆ Smelly or blood-stained discharge; this may indicate an object that has been lodged for some time.

TREATMENT

YOUR AIM IS:
■ To obtain medical attention.

DO NOT attempt to remove the foreign body with your fingers or any instrument, even if you can see it.

1 Keep the casualty quiet and calm. Tell him or her to breathe through the mouth at a normal rate.

2 Arrange to take or send the casualty to hospital.

FOREIGN BODIES IN THE EAR

If an object becomes lodged in the ear, it can cause temporary deafness by blocking the ear canal, or may damage the ear-drum. Young children often push objects into their ears; people leave cotton wool in the ear after cleaning it. Insects can fly or crawl into the ear; their buzzing or movement may cause alarm.

TREATMENT

YOUR AIMS ARE:
■ To prevent injury to the ear.
■ To obtain medical attention for a lodged foreign body.
■ To remove a trapped insect.

FOR A LODGED FOREIGN BODY

DO NOT attempt to remove the object. You may cause serious injury and push the foreign body in even further.

Arrange to take or send the casualty to hospital as soon as possible. Reassure the casualty during the journey, or until medical help arrives.

FOR AN INSECT IN THE EAR

1 Reassure the casualty, and sit her down.

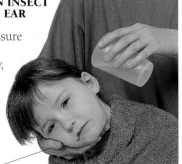

Support head with affected ear uppermost

2 Gently flood the ear with tepid water so that the insect floats out.

3 If this is unsuccessful, take or send the casualty to hospital.

SWALLOWED FOREIGN BODIES

Small objects such as coins, safety pins, or buttons can easily be swallowed by young children. If the object is sharp, it may damage the digestive tract. Small, smooth objects are unlikely to cause this type of injury, but they are still dangerous as they can lead to choking.

See also:
Choking Baby and Child, *page 66.*

TREATMENT

YOUR AIM IS:
■ To obtain medical attention.

FOR SHARP OR LARGE OBJECTS

☎ *DIAL 999 OR 112 FOR AN AMBULANCE.* Reassure the casualty while waiting for medical help to arrive.

DO NOT give the casualty anything to eat or drink – an anaesthetic may be administered at hospital.

FOR SMALL, SMOOTH OBJECTS

Reassure the casualty, and take or send him or her to hospital or to a doctor.

INHALED FOREIGN BODIES

Small, smooth objects can slip past the protective mechanisms within the throat and enter the air passages. Dry peanuts, which can swell up when in contact with body fluids, pose a particular danger in young children as they can be inhaled into the lungs, causing serious damage. Some people are allergic to nuts, which may cause anaphylactic shock (*see page 81*).

Recognition
There may be:
◆ Some sign or noise of choking, which quickly passes.
◆ A persistent dry cough.
◆ Difficulty in breathing.

See also:
Choking,
pages 64–7.

TREATMENT

YOUR AIM IS:
■ To obtain urgent medical attention.

1 Treat the casualty for choking, if necessary (*see pages 64–7*).

☎ *DIAL 999 OR 112 FOR AN AMBULANCE.*

2 Reassure the casualty while waiting for the ambulance. Try to discover from him or any bystanders what kind of foreign body has been inhaled, and inform the medical services.

Choking casualty
If back slaps and chest thrusts fail, apply abdominal thrusts.

Hold casualty around central upper abdomen and give up to five quick, upward thrusts

POISONING

13

Poisoning is often accidental, but can also be deliberate (for example, in cases of attempted suicide). It can occur as a result of accidents, or be caused by eating contaminated food or poisonous plants. Drugs and alcohol can also poison the body.

Recognising and treating poisoning

The effects of poisoning vary depending on the type and amount of poison absorbed, and it is advisable to seek medical attention. Although poisoning can be fatal, most cases are treatable. In all cases, it will help the doctor if you can identify the poison involved. If a conscious casualty or an onlooker cannot identify it, look for clues, such as tablets, a suspect container, or alcohol on the breath. If you suspect the poisoning is caused by a drug overdose, take care – an addict may be carrying syringe needles which may be dirty.

This chapter deals with acute poisoning – most often encountered by a First Aider in an emergency. Acute poisoning comes on suddenly, as opposed to chronic poisoning, for example by lead, which affects the body over a longer period of time.

FIRST-AID PRIORITIES

◆ Open an unconscious casualty's airway, and monitor airway, breathing, and circulation.

◆ Prevent further injury from:
SWALLOWED POISONS: do not attempt to induce vomiting, as this may harm the casualty further.
INHALED POISONS: remove the casualty from danger and into fresh air. Do not endanger yourself.
ABSORBED POISONS: flush away any residual chemical on the skin.

◆ Obtain appropriate medical assistance.

WHAT IS A POISON?

A poison is a substance which, if taken into the body in sufficient quantity, may cause temporary or permanent damage. Poisons may be swallowed, inhaled, absorbed through the skin, splashed into the eye, or injected. Natural poisons (*toxins*) are those which originate from bacteria or certain plants, and animals such as snakes.

Once in the body, poisons may work their way into the bloodstream and be swiftly carried to all the tissues of the body. Signs and symptoms vary depending on the poison and its method of entry, and can be delayed in onset.

Vomiting is common in many cases, and carries with it the additional danger of the casualty inhaling his or her own vomit, and choking.

THE EXCRETORY SYSTEM

The body "processes" food to extract its nutrients and eliminate waste that has many mildly poisonous elements. From the stomach, food passes into the small intestine, where nutrients are absorbed into the blood.

Blood is filtered through the liver, which inactivates many poisons. The kidneys also filter the blood and excrete impurities in urine. The food residue passes to the large intestine, and waste is expelled at the anus.

HOW POISONS ENTER THE BODY

Poisons may enter an eye, possibly causing chemical burns

Poisonous gases, solvents, vapours, or fumes may be inhaled

Injected poisons and drugs enter bloodstream rapidly; dangerous drugs, particularly narcotics, are injected by abusers; poisonous snakes, fish, or insects may inject venom into skin

Liver

Swallowed poisons may enter circulatory system through walls of digestive tract

Strong chemicals, such as corrosives and pesticides, or plant toxins may be absorbed through skin, and cause burns

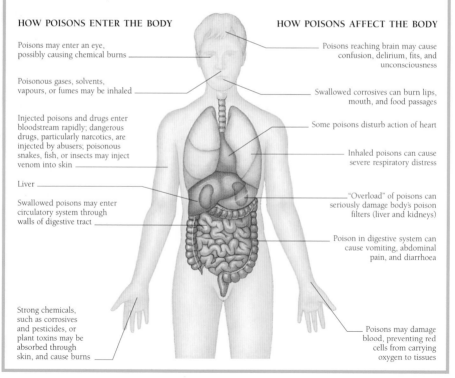

HOW POISONS AFFECT THE BODY

Poisons reaching brain may cause confusion, delirium, fits, and unconsciousness

Swallowed corrosives can burn lips, mouth, and food passages

Some poisons disturb action of heart

Inhaled poisons can cause severe respiratory distress

"Overload" of poisons can seriously damage body's poison filters (liver and kidneys)

Poison in digestive system can cause vomiting, abdominal pain, and diarrhoea

Poisons may damage blood, preventing red cells from carrying oxygen to tissues

HOUSEHOLD POISONS

Almost every home has poisonous substances, such as bleach, detergent, or weedkiller. These can spill, resulting in chemical burns, or be swallowed, causing poisoning. In Ireland in 1993, 170 people died from poisoning, including small children. Prevention of accidental poisoning is essential.

See also:
Chemical Burns, *page 164.*
Drug Poisoning, *page 186.*
Inhalation of Fumes, *page 70.*
Unconsciousness, *page 110.*

HOW TO PREVENT POISONING

◆ Keep toxic chemicals out of children's reach and sight (*not* under the sink).
◆ Keep medicines in a locked cupboard.
◆ Leave poisonous household substances in their original containers. Never store them in old soft-drinks bottles; children are commonly misled by such containers and try to drink the contents.
◆ Buy medicines and household substances in child-resistant containers.
◆ Dispose appropriately of unwanted medicines, as detailed in the instructions.

TREATMENT

YOUR AIMS ARE:
▧ To maintain the airway, breathing, and circulation.
▧ To remove any contaminated clothing.
▧ To identify the poison.
▧ To obtain medical aid.

To use a face shield, place the oval tube between the casualty's teeth. Seal your lips around the top of the tube to begin mouth-to-mouth respiration.

FOR SWALLOWED POISONS

1 Check and, if necessary, clear the casualty's airway (*see page 47*). Use protective gloves if possible.

Pinch shield over nose

Blow until chest rises

IF the casualty becomes unconscious, check breathing and pulse, and be prepared to resuscitate if necessary (*see pages 44–58*). Place him in the recovery position (*see page 48*).

IF you need to give mouth-to-mouth ventilation and there are chemicals on the casualty's mouth, use a plastic face shield, if possible, to protect yourself.

NEVER attempt to induce vomiting.

2 ☎ *DIAL 999 OR 112 FOR AN AMBULANCE.* Give information about the swallowed poison, if possible.

IF a conscious casualty's lips are burned by corrosive substances, give him frequent sips of cold water.

DRUG POISONING

This condition can result from an accidental or deliberate overdose of prescribed or over-the-counter drugs, or from drug abuse. The signs and symptoms of drug poisoning vary depending on the type of drug taken and the method of entry into the body (*see chart below*).

See also:
Unconsciousness, *page 110*.

TREATMENT

YOUR AIMS ARE:
■ To maintain the airway, breathing, and circulation.
■ To arrange removal to hospital.

1 Check and, if necessary, clear the casualty's airway (*see page 47*).

IF the casualty is unconscious, check breathing and pulse, and be prepared to resuscitate the casualty if necessary (*see pages 44–58*).

2 Place the casualty in the recovery position (*see page 48*).

> **DO NOT** induce vomiting. It is often ineffective, and it may cause the casualty further harm.

3 ☎ *DIAL 999 OR 112 FOR AN AMBULANCE*. Keep samples of vomited material. Look for clues to the identity of the drug, such as containers. Send these with the casualty to hospital.

DRUG	EFFECTS
Painkillers: Aspirin	• Upper abdominal pain, nausea, and vomiting (possibly blood-stained) • Ringing in the ears • "Sighing" when breathing • Confusion and delirium
Painkillers: Paracetamol	• Little effect at first • Later, features of liver damage: upper abdominal pain and tenderness, nausea, and vomiting
Nervous system depressants and tranquillisers Barbiturates and benzodiazepines (such as valium)	• Lethargy and sleepiness, leading to unconsciousness • Shallow breathing • A weak, irregular, or abnormally slow or fast pulse
Stimulants and hallucinogens Amphetamines (such as Ecstasy) and LSD (commonly swallowed); cocaine (commonly inhaled or "snorted")	• Excitable, hyperactive behaviour, wildness, and frenzy • Sweating • Tremor of the hands • Hallucinations: the casualty may be "hearing" voices or "seeing" things • Seizures • Respiratory or cardiac arrest
Narcotics (commonly injected) Morphine, heroin	• Constricted pupils • Sluggishness and confusion, possibly leading to unconsciousness • Slow, shallow breathing; cardiac arrest may occur • Needle marks may be infected, or infection introduced by dirty needles
Solvents (commonly inhaled) Glue, lighter fuel	• Nausea, vomiting, and headaches • Hallucinations • Possibly, unconsciousness • Rarely, cardiac arrest

INDUSTRIAL POISONS

Poisoning can occur in the workplace as a result of a leak, failure of a chemical plant, or a major accident; or in a public place following a road accident. Most cases of industrial poisoning involve poisonous gases. Spillage of corrosive chemicals can also result in burns. Factories using potentially dangerous chemicals or gases may keep oxygen equipment, and must display notices indicating the emergency procedures. Workers should be familiar with such advice.

See also:
Chemical Burns, *page 164.*
Hazardous Substances, *page 20.*
Inhalation of Fumes, *page 70.*
Unconsciousness, *page 110.*

TREATMENT

YOUR AIMS ARE:

- To remove the casualty from danger.
- To maintain an open airway.
- To arrange removal to hospital.

FOR INHALED GASES

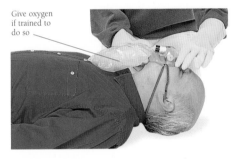

Give oxygen if trained to do so

1 If possible, remove the casualty from danger and into fresh air.
☎ *DIAL 999 OR 112 FOR AN AMBULANCE.* Administer oxygen if you have been trained in its use.

> **DO NOT** enter a gas-filled room unless you are authorised and are properly equipped to do so.

IF he is unconscious, open the airway, check breathing and pulse, and be ready to resuscitate if needed (*see pages 44–58*).

2 Place the casualty in the recovery position (*see page 48*).

FOR CHEMICALS ON THE SKIN

1 Flush away any residual chemical on the skin with plenty of cold water.

Make sure water drains *away* from casualty and yourself

> **DO NOT** contaminate yourself with the dangerous chemical or the rinsing water.

2 ☎ *DIAL 999 OR 112 FOR AN AMBULANCE.* Make sure that you give details of the chemical.

IF the casualty becomes unconscious, open the airway, check breathing and pulse, and be ready to resuscitate. Place her in the recovery position (*see page 48*).

ALCOHOL POISONING

Alcohol (chemical name, *ethanol*) is a drug that depresses the activity of the central nervous system. Prolonged intake can badly impair all physical and mental abilities, and deep unconsciousness may ensue.

Dangers of alcohol poisoning

♦ An unconscious casualty risks inhaling and choking on vomit.
♦ Alcohol dilates the blood vessels, so hypothermia may develop if the casualty is exposed to cold.
♦ A casualty with head injuries who smells of alcohol may be misdiagnosed and not receive appropriate treatment.

Recognition
There may be:

♦ A strong smell of alcohol.
♦ Unconsciousness: the casualty may be roused, but will quickly relapse.
♦ A flushed and moist face.
♦ Deep, noisy breathing.
♦ A full, bounding pulse.

In the later stages of unconsciousness:

♦ A dry, bloated appearance to the face.
♦ Shallow breathing.
♦ Dilated pupils that react poorly to light.
♦ A weak, rapid pulse.

See also:
Hypothermia, *page 170*
Drunkenness, *page 122*.
Unconsciousness, *page 110*.

TREATMENT

YOUR AIMS ARE:
■ To maintain an open airway.
■ To seek medical attention for the casualty if it is appropriate.

IF the casualty is unconscious, open the airway, check breathing and pulse, and be prepared to resuscitate if necessary (*see pages 44–58*). Place the casualty in the recovery position (*see page 48*).

IF in any doubt, ☎ *DIAL 999 OR 112 FOR AN AMBULANCE.*

2 Protect the casualty from cold, if possible; insulate him from the ground and cover him.

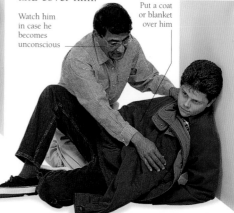

Shake and shout: "Can you hear me?" or "Open your eyes!"

Watch him in case he becomes unconscious

Put a coat or blanket over him

1 Check the casualty's level of consciousness. Gently shake his shoulders and speak to him loudly and clearly to see if he responds.

POISONOUS PLANTS

In the United Kingdom and Ireland, there are relatively few very poisonous plants which can cause serious illness if eaten. A number of other plants are mildly poisonous. Young children are most at risk, as they are attracted to brightly coloured berries and seeds, and are liable to eat them.

See also:
Unconsciousness, *page 110.*

TREATMENT

YOUR AIMS ARE:
■ To maintain the airway, breathing, and circulation.
■ To obtain medical aid.

DO NOT induce vomiting. It is often ineffective, and may cause the casualty further harm.

1 Check and, if necessary, clear the casualty's airway (*see page 47*).

IF the casualty is unconscious, check breathing and pulse, and be prepared to resuscitate if needed (*see pages 44–58*). Put the casualty in the recovery position (*see page 48*); he or she may vomit.

2 If you are concerned, call a doctor or ☎ *DIAL 999 OR 112 FOR AN AMBULANCE.*

3 Try to identify the plant, and which part has been eaten. Preserve pieces of the plant, and samples of any vomited material, to show to the doctor or to send with the casualty to hospital.

PLANTS THAT ARE POISONOUS IF SWALLOWED

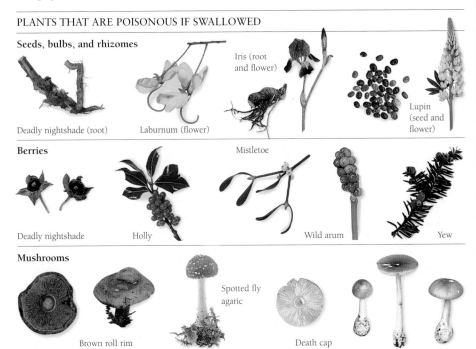

Seeds, bulbs, and rhizomes

Deadly nightshade (root)   Laburnum (flower)   Iris (root and flower)   Lupin (seed and flower)

Berries

Deadly nightshade   Holly   Mistletoe   Wild arum   Yew

Mushrooms

Brown roll rim   Spotted fly agaric   Death cap

FOOD POISONING

This may be caused by eating food that is contaminated by bacteria or by toxins produced by bacteria that were already in the food.

Types of food poisoning

Bacterial food poisoning is often caused by the *Salmonella* group of bacteria (associated with farm animals). Symptoms may appear rapidly or be delayed for a day or so.

Toxic food poisoning is frequently caused by toxins produced by the bacteria group of *Staphylococcus*. Symptoms usually develop rapidly, possibly within two to six hours of eating the affected food.

See also:
Shock, *page 78.*
Vomiting and Diarrhoea, *page 210.*

Recognition

There may be:

- Nausea and vomiting.
- Cramping abdominal pains.
- Diarrhoea (possibly bloodstained).
- Headache or fever.
- Features of shock.
- Collapse.

PREVENTING FOOD POISONING

- Ensure that frozen poultry and meat is fully defrosted before it is cooked.
- Cook meat, poultry, fish, and eggs thoroughly to kill harmful bacteria.
- Never keep food lukewarm for long periods; bacteria can multiply without obvious signs of spoilage.
- Wash hands before preparing food.
- Wear protective gloves or waterproof plasters if you have cuts on your hands.

TREATMENT

YOUR AIMS ARE:
- To encourage the casualty to rest.
- To seek medical advice or aid.
- To give the casualty plenty of clear fluids to drink.

1 Help the casualty to lie down and rest.

2 Call a doctor for advice.

Give clear fluids such as water or flat lemonade

Keep casualty warm and comfortable

3 Give the casualty plenty to drink, and a bowl to use if she vomits.

IF the casualty's condition worsens,
☎ *DIAL 999 OR 112 FOR AN AMBULANCE.*

BITES AND STINGS

14

M̲ost animals and insects do not usually attack unless injured or otherwise provoked, and common sense can prevent many bites and stings. You must always take sensible precautions before attempting, for example, to rescue a casualty from an angry dog or a swarm of bees. If you cannot cope alone, get help or call the emergency services.

Knowing when to seek medical attention

Although insect and marine stings can mar a picnic or seaside outing, they are often minor injuries, and first aid alone usually relieves any pain.

Animal (and human) bites, however, always require medical attention, because animals harbour germs in their mouths. Even if you have cleaned and dressed a bite wound satisfactorily, you must ensure that the casualty is protected from serious infections such as rabies and tetanus.

Snake bites carry the additional risk of poisoning. You must take care even when handling a dead animal; the venom of many creatures, particularly snakes, is just as active in death as in life.

FIRST-AID PRIORITIES

◆ Make sure that you are in no danger, then remove the casualty from further danger.

◆ Treat any visible wound or painful symptoms, and minimise the risk of further injury and infection.

◆ Obtain medical attention if necessary.

◆ Note the time and nature of the injury, and identify the attacking creature if possible. This enables medical personnel to deal with the injury itself and to anticipate possible complications, such as anaphylactic shock (*see page 81*).

ANIMAL BITES

Bites from sharp, pointed teeth cause deep puncture wounds that can carry germs far into the tissues. Human bites also crush the tissues. Hitting someone's teeth with a bare fist can produce a "bite" wound at the knuckles. Any bite that breaks the skin causes a wound very vulnerable to infection; it needs prompt first aid and medical attention.

See also:
Minor Wounds, *page 104.*
Severe External Bleeding, *page 88.*
Tetanus, *page 106.*

TREATMENT

YOUR AIMS ARE:
■ To control bleeding.
■ To minimise the risk of infection, both to the casualty and yourself.
■ To obtain medical attention.

FOR SERIOUS WOUNDS

1 Control bleeding by applying direct pressure and raising the injured part.

2 Cover the wound with a sterile dressing or a clean pad bandaged in place.

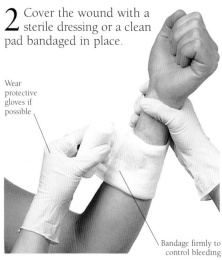

Wear protective gloves if possible

Bandage firmly to control bleeding

3 Arrange to take or send the casualty to hospital.

FOR SUPERFICIAL BITES

1 Wash the wound thoroughly with soap and warm water.

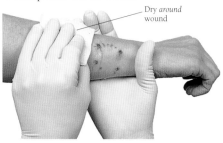

Dry *around* wound

2 Pat the wound dry with clean gauze swabs and cover with an adhesive dressing or a small sterile dressing.

3 Advise the casualty to see a doctor in case inoculation is needed.

POTENTIAL INFECTIONS

Rabies is a potentially fatal viral infection of the nervous system, spread in the saliva of infected animals. If bitten overseas, or by an animal that may have been smuggled into the UK or Ireland, the casualty must receive anti-rabies injections. The animal must be examined to confirm rabies. Seek the help of the police to secure a suspect animal.

There is probably only a small risk of hepatitis B or C viruses being transmitted through a human bite – and even less risk with the HIV (AIDS) virus. If you are concerned about the possibility of infection, seek medical advice.

INSECT STINGS

Bee, wasp, and hornet stings usually are painful rather than dangerous. An initial sharp pain is followed by mild swelling and soreness, which first aid can relieve. Some people are allergic to stings and can rapidly develop the serious condition of anaphylactic shock. Multiple stings can also be dangerous. Stings in the mouth or throat are serious, as the swelling they cause can obstruct the airway.

See also:
Anaphylactic Shock, *page 81.*
Breathing Difficulties, *page 72.*

TREATMENT

YOUR AIMS ARE:
- To relieve swelling and pain.
- To remove to hospital if necessary.

FOR A STING IN THE SKIN

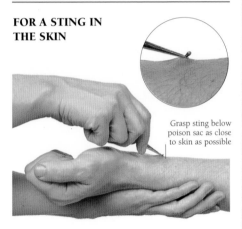

Grasp sting below poison sac as close to skin as possible

IF the casualty shows signs of anaphylactic shock, ☎ *DIAL 999 OR 112 FOR AN AMBULANCE.*

1 If the sting is still in the wound, pluck it out firmly with fine tweezers.

2 Apply a cold compress (*see page 221*) to relieve pain and minimise swelling. Advise the casualty to see his doctor if the pain and swelling persist.

FOR A STING IN THE MOUTH

1 Give the casualty ice to suck or cold water to sip, to minimise the swelling. ☎ *DIAL 999 OR 112 FOR AN AMBULANCE.* Reassure the casualty.

TICK BITES

Ticks are tiny, spider-like creatures found in grass or woodlands. They attach themselves to passing animals (including humans) and bite into the skin to suck blood. An unfed tick is very small and may not be noticed, particularly as its bite is painless, but when sucking blood, a tick swells to the size of a pea and can then easily be seen.

Ticks can carry disease and cause infection, so should be removed as soon as possible. Once removed, put the tick in a container; the casualty must take it with him or her to a doctor for analysis.

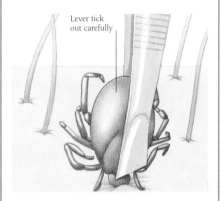

Lever tick out carefully

Removing a tick
Using fine-pointed tweezers, grasp the tick's head as close to the casualty's skin as possible. Use a slight to-and-fro action to lever, rather than pull, the head out. The mouthparts will be very firmly embedded in the skin; try to avoid breaking the tick and leaving the buried head behind.

INJURIES BY MARINE CREATURES

Sea creatures can cause injury in a number of ways. Painful stings can be caused by jellyfish and the related Portuguese man-of-war, corals, and sea anemones. Their venom is contained in special stinging cells (*nematocysts*) that stick to the victim's skin. The poison is released when each stinging cell ruptures.

If a spiny creature such as a sea urchin or weever fish is accidentally trodden on, its spines may puncture the skin and break off to become embedded in the sole of the foot.

A painful local reaction will usually develop, although serious general effects are rare.

Most marine species normally encountered in temperate regions are not very poisonous. In some parts of the world, particularly in tropical regions, severe poisoning can occur, and occasionally death results from a severe allergic reaction (anaphylactic shock), or paralysis of the chest muscles leads to drowning.

See also:
Anaphylactic Shock, *page 81.*

Portuguese man-of-war
This is actually a jellyfish-like, floating colony of creatures, with stinging tentacles that leave painful weals on the skin. The venom is rarely fatal, but multiple stings may cause problems.

Sea anemone
These small creatures are commonly encountered in rock pools. If touched or trodden on, venomous stinging cells on their tentacles, which surround the anemone's "mouth", may inflict great pain.

Weever fish
This fish, found around Ireland's coasts, lies buried in sand close to the shoreline, so it is easily trodden on. It has venomous spines that may puncture the skin, causing swelling and soreness.

TREATMENT FOR MARINE STINGS

YOUR AIMS ARE:
- To reassure the casualty.
- To inactivate stinging cells before they release their venom, and to neutralise any free venom.
- To relieve pain and discomfort.

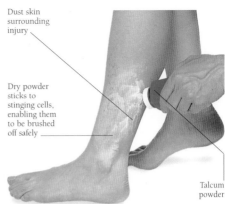

Dust skin surrounding injury

Dry powder sticks to stinging cells, enabling them to be brushed off safely

Talcum powder

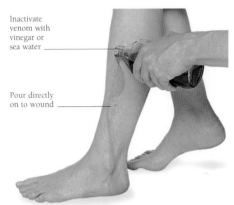

Inactivate venom with vinegar or sea water

Pour directly on to wound

1 Reassure the casualty and sit him or her down. Pour copious amounts of vinegar or sea water over the injury to incapacitate stinging cells that have not yet released venom. Alcohol may aggravate the injury and should not be used. Avoid rubbing sand on the affected area.

2 Dust a dry powder over the skin around the affected area to make any remaining stinging cells stick together. Meat tenderiser, used in barbecue cooking, is also good as it contains papain, which inactivates venom.

3 Gently brush off the powder with a clean, non-fluffy pad.

IF the injuries are severe, or there is a serious general reaction (*see page 81*), ☎ *DIAL 999 OR 112 FOR AN AMBULANCE.*

IF the casualty is having difficulty breathing, she may be in anaphylactic shock; treat as described on page 81.

TREATMENT FOR MARINE PUNCTURE WOUNDS

YOUR AIMS ARE:
- To inactivate the venom.
- To obtain medical aid.

1 Put the injured part in water as hot as the casualty can bear for at least 30 minutes. Top up the water as it cools, being careful not to scald the casualty.

2 Take or send the casualty to hospital, where spines remaining in the skin may have to be removed.

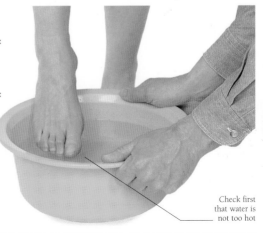

Check first that water is not too hot

SNAKE BITES

The only poisonous snake native to mainland Britain is the adder, and its bite is rarely fatal. However, more exotic snakes are kept as pets. While a snake bite is often not a serious injury, it can be very frightening. Reassurance is vital, for if the casualty keeps still and calm, the spread of venom may be delayed.

If you can, put the snake in a secure container (take care, as its venom is active whether it is dead or alive). Otherwise make a note of the snake's appearance; this may help the correct anti-venom to be given to the casualty. Notify the police if the snake remains at large.

Recognition

Signs and symptoms depend on the species

♦ A pair of puncture marks.
♦ Severe pain at the site of the bite.
♦ Redness and swelling around the bite.
♦ Nausea and vomiting.
♦ Laboured breathing; in extreme cases, respiration may stop altogether.
♦ Disturbed vision.
♦ Increased salivation and sweating.

TREATMENT

YOUR AIMS ARE:
■ To reassure the casualty.
■ To prevent the spread of venom through the body.
■ To arrange urgent removal of the casualty to hospital.

DO NOT apply a tourniquet, slash the wound with a knife, or suck out the venom.

1 Lay the casualty down. Tell her to keep calm and still.

2 Wash the wound well and pat dry with clean swabs.
☎ *DIAL 999 OR 112 FOR AN AMBULANCE.*

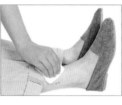

3 Lightly compress the limb above the wound with a roller bandage. Immobilise the injury (*see pages 130–31*).

IF she stops breathing, be ready to resuscitate (*see pages 44–58*) if needed.

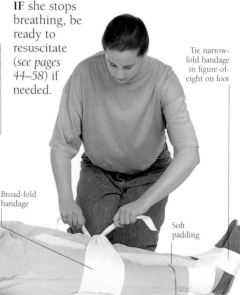

Tie narrow-fold bandage in figure-of-eight on foot

Keep heart above level of wounded part to contain venom locally

Broad-fold bandage

Soft padding

EMERGENCY CHILDBIRTH

15

A s a First Aider, there are two situations in which you may have to administer first aid to a pregnant woman: childbirth and miscarriage. Childbirth is a natural and often lengthy process, so if a woman goes into labour, there is no need to panic. Only very rarely is there no time to get the mother to hospital before the baby arrives. If this happens, you should not attempt to deliver the baby – this will happen naturally. Your role is to care for the baby, and comfort and listen to the wishes and advice of the mother, especially if she has experience of giving birth.

Miscarriage

Miscarriage, or *spontaneous abortion* of the foetus, is fairly common – about 20% of pregnancies end this way – and of these, 80% occur in the second or third month of pregnancy. The possibility of severe bleeding makes it potentially dangerous, so the woman must receive urgent medical attention and be treated with extreme sensitivity throughout this distressing experience. A foetus can also be lost through an induced abortion or as a result of an ectopic pregnancy (one that develops outside the womb or *uterus,* usually in the *fallopian tubes*).

CONTENTS

FIRST-AID PRIORITIES

Childbirth
◆ Be calm and reassure the mother.
◆ Seek expert help.
◆ Male First Aiders should seek a female chaperone.
◆ *Do not* try to delay childbirth.

Miscarriage
◆ Obtain medical assistance as soon as possible.

CHILDBIRTH

Most expectant mothers will be well prepared for what will happen during labour. However, a woman who goes into labour unexpectedly may become very anxious, and you will need to reassure her. If she is calm, she will be better able to remember any procedures she has been taught.

Most labours last for several hours and are straightforward, so there is usually plenty of time to arrange transport to hospital or to seek medical assistance. You should never try to delay a birth. Always allow a delivery to proceed without interference. The baby will be expelled naturally, so do not pull at the emerging head or shoulders.

Once the baby is delivered, wrap him or her in something warm to guard against hypothermia, then give the baby to the mother.

THE THREE STAGES OF LABOUR

	What happens	*Symptoms and Signs*
First stage Mucous plug 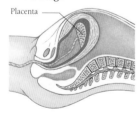	• Neck (*cervix*) of the womb (*uterus*) begins to enlarge (*dilate*); this can take 12–14 hours • Mucous plug, protecting the womb from infection, may be expelled • "Waters" (*amniotic fluid*) break as the need for protection ends	• Contractions, with an average interval of 10–20 minutes • Bloodstained discharge or "show", if the mucous plug is expelled • "Waters" flow out in a trickle or a rush, depending on the position of the baby
Second stage Cervix	• This stage takes up to two hours, and begins when the cervix is fully dilated • Baby descends from the womb towards the vaginal entrance • Baby is in close contact with the muscle of the womb • Vagina stretches to allow the baby to be expelled • The baby is delivered	• Mother experiences an involuntary urge to push • Pressure on the muscle of the womb stimulates stronger, more frequent, contractions • Stinging or burning sensation may occur in the vagina as it is stretched • Head emerges and the baby is pushed out rapidly
Third stage Placenta	• Afterbirth (*placenta and umbilical cord*) is naturally expelled, about 10–30 minutes after the baby is born • Womb should contract, closing down the area to which the placenta is attached and stopping the bleeding	• Mild contractions before the afterbirth is expelled • Some bleeding occurs once the afterbirth is delivered • More severe bleeding can occur if the womb does not contract sufficiently (*post-partum* or after-delivery *haemorrhage*). For treatment, see page 201.

THE START OF LABOUR

The first stage of labour begins when the neck (*cervix*) of the womb opens and begins to enlarge, or *dilate* (*see opposite*). The mother will be experiencing contractions, which are waves of intense pain that peak and then fade away. You will need to give her a great deal of reassurance and make her comfortable.

THE PREGNANCY RECORD

Each woman is issued with a special folder containing her pregnancy record. Check the folder for information, or any complications, so that you can alert the medical services. The mother may be able to interpret some of the medical abbreviations for you.

WHAT YOU SHOULD DO

YOUR AIM IS:
■ To obtain medical aid and arrange removal to hospital.

DO NOT let her have a bath if her waters have broken, as this can cause infection.

1 Summon a midwife or doctor. ☎ *DIAL 999 OR 112 FOR AN AMBULANCE,* if necessary, giving any information from her pregnancy record.

2 Allow the mother to assume the most comfortable position for her. Massaging her lower back can help to relieve pain.

Use heel of your hand to rub lower back

WHAT YOU WILL NEED FOR THE DELIVERY

Ensure that the area is warm, but never place a cot next to an open or electric fire. If possible, gather together a few essentials:

◆ an improvised cot (a box or drawer lined with soft material);
◆ disposable gloves;
◆ plastic bags;
◆ sanitary towels;
◆ handkerchiefs to wear as face masks;
◆ a bowl of hot water for washing;
◆ newspapers or a plastic sheet;
◆ clean, warm towels and a blanket.

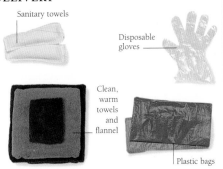

Sanitary towels

Disposable gloves

Clean, warm towels and flannel

Plastic bags

THE DELIVERY

In the second stage, the baby will be delivered. This begins when the cervix is fully dilated (*see page 198*) and lasts until the baby arrives, which could take as little as an hour. You need to prepare a comfortable and clean environment (*see right*) in preparation for the delivery.

The number of people present should be kept to a minimum, but do not exclude anyone whom the mother wishes to be present. You may want to enlist the help of a female friend or relative.

The delivery will happen naturally. However, it will be your responsibility to ensure the comfort and protection of the baby once he or she is born.

PREVENTING INFECTION

It is extremely important to pay strict attention to hygiene when preparing for, and during, the delivery.
 ◆ Keep anyone with a sore throat, cold, or septic spots on the hands well away.
 ◆ Wear a face mask. You can improvise one from a clean handkerchief or a folded triangular bandage.
 ◆ Remove your jacket, if any; roll up your sleeves. If possible, wear a plastic apron.
 ◆ Wash your hands and scrub your nails thoroughly for about five minutes. Wear disposable gloves, if available.
 ◆ After delivery, wash your hands again.

WHAT YOU SHOULD DO

YOUR AIMS ARE:
- To ensure the mother is comfortable.
- To prevent cross-infection.
- To care for the baby.

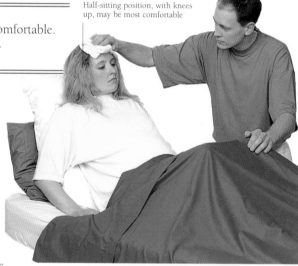
Half-sitting position, with knees up, may be most comfortable

1 Cover the bed, sofa, or floor with plastic sheeting, newspaper, or towels for warmth and to absorb mess. Help the woman into a comfortable position. Make sure that her back and shoulders are well supported.

2 Make sure that the ambulance is on its way, and any important details have been passed on, such as the expected delivery date, any medical needs, or the name of the hospital.

3 Check that the mother has removed any clothing that might interfere with the birth; cover her if she prefers.

DO NOT allow the mother to drink. If she is thirsty, moisten her lips with water.

4 Once the widest part of the baby's head is visible, make sure that the mother stops pushing and starts panting.

IF there is membrane covering the baby's face, tear it away so that he can breathe.

5 The baby's head and shoulders will soon appear. Allow the baby to be expelled naturally; this happens quickly.

> **DO NOT** pull on the baby's head.
>
> **DO NOT** pull on the baby's shoulders.

IF the umbilical cord is wrapped around the baby's neck, you should first check that it is loose, then very carefully pull it over the head to protect the baby from strangulation.

6 Lift the baby away from the birth canal. Newborn babies are very slippery, and need to be handled carefully. Gently pass him to the mother, and lay him on her stomach.

> **DO NOT** pull on or cut the umbilical cord.

7 The baby should start to cry at this point; if this does not happen, then immediately carry out the ABC of resuscitation (*see pages 54–8*).

> **DO NOT** smack the baby.

8 Wrap the baby in a clean cloth or blanket, and give him to the mother. When lying the baby down, keep him on his side with his head low down, so that any fluid or mucus can drain easily from his nose and mouth.

DELIVERY OF THE AFTERBIRTH

In the third stage, the baby will have been delivered, but the mother will still need your assistance while she delivers the afterbirth (the placenta and cord).

She will still be having mild contractions until it is expelled. The cord, which may continue to pulsate, should be left uncut until help arrives.

WHAT YOU SHOULD DO

YOUR AIMS ARE:
- To support the mother while she is delivering the afterbirth.
- To preserve the afterbirth.

1 Encourage the mother while she is delivering the afterbirth.

> **DO NOT** pull on the umbilical cord.
>
> **DO NOT** cut the umbilical cord.

2 Keep the afterbirth intact, preferably in a plastic bag, until a midwife examines it and cuts the cord. Even a small piece of the afterbirth left inside the mother can be dangerous.

3 Provide warm water, clean towels, and sanitary pads to clean the mother. She may prefer to do it herself.

Comfort and massage the mother until help arrives

4 It is normal for the mother to bleed slightly. Gently massaging her abdomen, just below the navel, helps the womb to contract and stops the bleeding.

IF bleeding is severe, treat her for shock (*see page 78*); tell the emergency services that she has a life-threatening condition.

MISCARRIAGE

A miscarriage is the loss of the foetus or embryo at any time before the 24th week of pregnancy. Some pregnant women experience a "threatened miscarriage" with slight vaginal bleeding. Miscarriages carry the danger of severe bleeding and of shock. Any woman who is, or appears to be, miscarrying must be seen by a doctor.

Remember that the woman may be frightened and very distressed at this time. Although your efforts may be rejected, offer her as much help as you can without being intrusive.

A woman who suspects that she is miscarrying may be reluctant to confide in a stranger, particularly if that person is a man.

Recognition

◆ Cramp-like pains in the lower abdomen or pelvic area.
◆ Signs of shock.
◆ Vaginal bleeding, possibly sudden and profuse.
◆ Passage of the foetus and other products of conception.

See also:
Shock, *page 78.*
Vaginal Bleeding, *page 103.*

WHAT YOU SHOULD DO

YOUR AIMS ARE:
■ To reassure and comfort the woman.
■ To obtain medical help.

1 Reassure the woman. Help her into the most comfortable position.

2 Find a sanitary pad or clean towel for the woman to use.

3 Monitor and *record* breathing and pulse every ten minutes.

4 Keep any expelled material and pass it to the medical services. Keep it out of the woman's sight, if possible.

IF the bleeding or pain is only slight, call a doctor.

Prop knees up with cushion or blanket to ease strain on abdomen

IF the bleeding or pain is severe,
☎ *DIAL 999 OR 112 FOR AN AMBULANCE.* Treat the woman for shock.

OTHER CAUSES OF SEVERE BLEEDING

Symptoms that are similar to natural, or spontaneous, miscarriage can be caused by other events such as a heavy period, induced abortion, or ectopic pregnancy. In an ectopic pregnancy, the fertilised egg does not develop as it should in the womb (*uterus*), but in the *fallopian tube* or even in the abdominal cavity. This is a life-threatening condition which occurs in about one in every 300 pregnancies. The symptoms will usually include severe abdominal pain and vaginal bleeding.

MISCELLANEOUS CONDITIONS 16

The boundary between first aid and home medicine is often blurred. Many everyday conditions (for example, headaches, cramp, or a raised temperature) develop quickly and need prompt treatment. While some of the common ailments described in this chapter are not included in formal first-aid training, they will nevertheless benefit from sensible first-aid measures. Common sense and good preparation can also help to prevent and treat illness while travelling overseas.

The use of medicines

This chapter describes the use of paracetamol and other tablets to relieve fever and pain; however, giving medication is not strictly within the scope of first aid. Always consult a doctor or pharmacist before administering any medication. Whenever a medicine is used, the manufacturer's recommendations on correct dosage should be carefully followed. Some first aid organisations may have protocols for the use of medicines which should be strictly followed by their personnel. More guidance is given on this subject on page 39.

When to seek medical aid

An apparently minor complaint may be the start of a serious illness. If you are in any doubt about your ability to deal with any condition, you should always consult a doctor, even if it is only by telephone.

CONTENTS

FIRST-AID PRIORITIES

♦ Make the casualty as comfortable as possible.

♦ If simple measures fail to provide relief within an hour or so, seek medical advice.

FEVER

A sustained body temperature above the normal level of 37°C (98.6°F) is known as fever. It is usually caused by a bacterial or viral infection, and may be associated with influenza, measles, chicken pox, meningitis, earache, sore throat, or local infections, such as an abscess.

When to call a doctor

A moderate fever is not harmful, but a temperature of above 40°C (104°F) can be dangerous, and may trigger fits in babies and young children. Call a doctor, even if only for advice, if in doubt about the casualty's condition.

Recognition

♦ Raised under-the-tongue temperature.

In the early stages:

♦ Pallor.
♦ A "chilled" feeling – goose pimples, shivering, and chattering teeth.

As the fever advances:

♦ Hot, flushed skin, and sweating.
♦ Headache.
♦ Generalised "aches and pains".
♦ Higher temperature.

See also:
Heatstroke, *page 174.*
Convulsions in Young Children, *page 118.*

TREATMENT

YOUR AIMS ARE:

■ To make the casualty comfortable.
■ To bring down the fever.
■ To seek medical aid if necessary.

1 Make the casualty comfortable in cool surroundings, preferably in bed with a light cover. Allow her to rest.

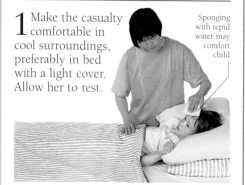
Sponging with tepid water may comfort child

2 Give the casualty frequent small drinks of clear fluid such as water.

3 An adult may take two paracetamol tablets. Give a child the recommended dose of paracetamol syrup (*not* aspirin).

IF you are worried about the casualty's condition, call a doctor.

BACTERIAL MENINGITIS

This is a very serious condition which must be treated promptly, so early recognition can be crucial. Meningitis can be difficult to recognise because many symptoms are similar to those of less serious conditions such as 'flu. If in any doubt, the casualty should be seen by a doctor immediately. Symptoms can develop rapidly, often within a few hours. They may include:

♦ fever;
♦ vomiting or loss of appetite;
♦ headache (in babies, the sign is slight tenseness of the soft parts of the skull, or *fontanelles*);
♦ sensitivity to light;
♦ stiffness in the neck;
♦ convulsions;
♦ a change for the worse in a child who has recently had an infection;
♦ a rash of red or purple blood spots (*purpuric rash*).

A simple way of confirming purpuric rash is to press the side of a glass lightly against the rash. If the rash disappears under pressure, it is not a purpuric rash.

HEADACHE

A headache may accompany any illness, particularly a feverish ailment such as 'flu, but it may be the most prominent symptom of a serious condition, such as meningitis (*see opposite*) or stroke. Mild "poisoning" caused by a stuffy or fume-filled atmosphere, or by excess alcohol or any other drug, can induce a headache in an otherwise healthy person.

Headaches may develop for no apparent reason, but can often be traced to tiredness, nervous tension, stress or emotional upset, or undue heat or cold. Headaches can range from constant low-grade discomfort to "blinding" pain that is completely incapacitating (*see box, below*).

When to call a doctor

Always seek urgent advice if the pain:
- develops very suddenly;
- is severe and incapacitating;
- is recurrent or persistent;
- is accompanied by loss of strength or sensation, or impaired consciousness;
- is accompanied by a stiff neck;
- follows a head injury.

TREATMENT

YOUR AIMS ARE:
- To relieve the pain.
- To seek medical aid if necessary.

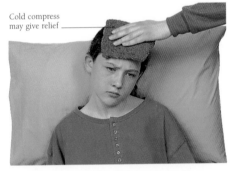

Cold compress may give relief

1 Help the casualty to sit or lie down comfortably in a quiet place. If possible, remedy any likely cause of the headache, such as loud noise, bright light, or lack of fresh air.

2 An adult may take two paracetamol tablets or her own painkillers. Give a child the recommended dose of paracetamol syrup (*not* aspirin).

IF in doubt or if the pain does not ease within two hours, call a doctor.

MIGRAINE

Many people are prone to these severe, "sickening" headaches. They can be triggered by a variety of causes, such as allergy, stress, or tiredness. Migraine sufferers usually recognise an attack and know best how to deal with it. They may carry special medicines with them.

Migraines usually follow a pattern
- There may be a warning period with disturbance of vision, in the form of flickering lights and/or a "blind patch".
- An intense throbbing headache may develop, sometimes just on one side.
- There may be discomfort in the upper abdomen, nausea, and vomiting.
- The casualty will not be able to tolerate any bright light or loud noise.

What you can do

Treatment for migraine is the same as for any severe headache. Help the casualty to take any special medication he or she may have been prescribed (such as tablets or nasal sprays) and provide some towels and a container in case he or she vomits. The casualty will often recover from an attack after lying down or sleeping for a few hours in a quiet, dark room.

EARACHE

An infection of the middle ear is the most common cause of earache, particularly in children. It often accompanies a cold, tonsillitis, or 'flu. Occasionally, pressure builds up in the middle ear causing the ear-drum to rupture. This allows pus and other matter to be discharged from the outer ear which may bring a temporary relief from pain. Earache can also be caused by an infection (*see page 179*), a boil, or a foreign body lodged in the ear canal, or be the result of another condition such as an abscess in a nearby tooth.

All common types of earache may be accompanied by partial or total hearing loss that is usually temporary.

TREATMENT

YOUR AIMS ARE:
- To relieve pain.
- To obtain medical aid if necessary.

FOR THROBBING EARACHE

IF there is a discharge, fever, or marked hearing loss, call a doctor immediately.

1 An adult may take two paracetamol tablets or her own painkillers. Give a child the recommended dose of paracetamol syrup (*not* aspirin).

2 Give the casualty a source of heat (such as a hot-water bottle wrapped in a towel) to hold against the affected ear. Let her sit up if lying flat makes the pain worse.

3 Advise the casualty to see her doctor. If you are worried about the casualty's condition (particularly if it is a child), call a doctor immediately.

PRESSURE-CHANGE EARACHE

Many people are prone to pressure-change earache on aeroplane journeys. It may help to chew gum or suck a sweet. (Remember that chewing gum or boiled sweets should never be given to young children as they may choke.)

Blowing air through nose equalises pressure in ears

Hold nose, close mouth, and blow

What you can do

Tell the casualty to swallow with her mouth wide open. If this fails to make the ears "pop", tell the casualty to close her mouth, hold her nose tightly closed, and "blow" her nose.

If nothing helps, reassure the casualty that the pain will go away when the pressure in the middle ear equalises (for example, when the aeroplane lands).

TOOTHACHE

Persistent toothache is usually caused by a decayed tooth and can be made worse by hot or cold food or drinks. Throbbing toothache indicates an infection; there may be some swelling of the gums in the painful area and bad breath. What appears to be "toothache" can be caused by conditions affecting the facial nerves such as sinusitis or an ear infection.

TREATMENT

YOUR AIMS ARE:
- To relieve pain.
- To ensure the casualty sees a dentist.

1 An adult may take two paracetamol tablets or her own painkillers. Give a child the recommended dose of paracetamol syrup (*not* aspirin).

2 Make the casualty comfortable. If lying down makes the pain worse, prop her up with pillows.

3 There are two methods for helping the casualty: either give him or her a hot-water bottle wrapped in a towel to hold to the affected side of the face,

Tell casualty to hold plug against affected tooth

or a rolled-up piece of cotton wool soaked in water for the casualty to hold against the affected tooth. The cotton wool will plug the cavity.

4 Arrange an early appointment for the casualty with her dentist.

SORE THROAT

The most common cause of a sore throat is the inflammation of the tissues at the back of the mouth. Coughs and colds caused by viruses often start with a sore throat, which usually passes within a day or two. Sometimes the tonsils at the back of the throat become infected with bacteria or a virus. The tonsils and surrounding tissues redden and white spots of pus or ulcers can be seen clearly. Swallowing is often difficult, and the glands under the angle of the jaw can become enlarged and sore.

TREATMENT

YOUR AIMS ARE:
- To relieve pain.
- To obtain medical aid if necessary.

1 Give the casualty plenty of fluids to drink, to ease the pain and to stop the throat becoming dry.

2 An adult may take two paracetamol tablets or his or her own painkillers. Give a child the recommended dose of paracetamol syrup (*not* aspirin).

IF you suspect tonsillitis, advise the casualty to make an appointment to see a doctor as soon as possible.

ABDOMINAL PAIN

Pain in the abdomen often has a relatively trivial cause, but can indicate serious disease, such as perforation or obstruction of the intestine.

Intestinal distension or obstruction causes pain that comes and goes in "waves" (*colic*). This often makes the sufferer double up in agony and can be accompanied by vomiting.

A perforated intestine or leakage of its contents into the abdominal cavity causes inflammation of the cavity lining (*peritonitis*). This potentially life-threatening condition causes sudden, intense pain, made worse by movement or abdominal pressure.

See also:
Food Poisoning, *page 190.*

TREATMENT

YOUR AIMS ARE:
- To relieve pain and discomfort.
- To obtain medical aid if necessary.

Put child on her side if she is vomiting

1 Make the casualty comfortable, and prop her up if breathing is difficult. Give her a container to use if vomiting.

DO NOT give the casualty any medicines or anything to eat or drink.

2 Give the casualty a covered hot-water bottle to place against the abdomen.

IF the pain is severe, or does not ease within 30 minutes, call a doctor.

WINDING

A blow to the upper abdomen may stun a local nerve junction, causing a temporary breathing problem. Sit the casualty down; loosen clothing at the chest or waist. Recovery should be rapid.

APPENDICITIS

An acutely inflamed appendix (known as *appendicitis*) is common especially in children. Symptoms include severe pain, usually in the lower right abdomen, loss of appetite, nausea, vomiting, bad breath, and fever. If the appendix bursts peritonitis will develop. Treatment includes surgical removal of the appendix.

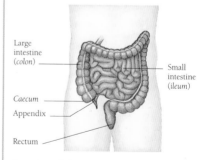

Large intestine (*colon*)

Small intestine (*ileum*)

Caecum

Appendix

Rectum

Location of the appendix
The appendix is a short tube attached to the lower end of the large intestine (caecum). It has no known function in humans. Inflammation usually occurs when the tube becomes blocked or ulcerated.

HERNIA

A hernia (rupture) is a protrusion of parts of the abdominal contents (often a small loop of intestine) through a weak part of the muscular wall. It may result from coughing or heavy exertion. The swelling may disappear if the casualty lies down. If it is painful, and especially if it occurs with vomiting and abdominal pain, the hernia is "strangulated" and needs urgent surgical attention.

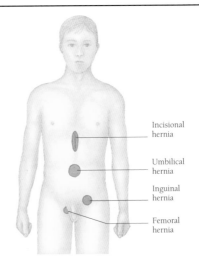

Incisional hernia

Umbilical hernia

Inguinal hernia

Femoral hernia

Common sites of hernia
Hernias may occur in the groin, at the navel, or through a scar.

Recognition

◆ Bulge or swelling in abdominal wall.
◆ Pain in abdomen or groin.
◆ Vomiting.

TREATMENT

YOUR AIMS ARE:
■ To reassure the casualty and relieve discomfort.
■ To obtain medical aid.

FOR A PAINLESS HERNIA

Reassure the casualty. Without causing him or her needless alarm, tell the casualty to arrange to see his or her own doctor about the condition as soon as possible.

> **DO NOT** attempt to push in the swelling or allow the casualty to do so.

FOR A PAINFUL HERNIA

1 Support the casualty in the position he finds most comfortable, by propping him up with cushions or pillows.

Casualty with abdominal pain may prefer to bend his knees

Use a folded pillow or rolled-up jacket as support

2 Call a doctor or, if the pain is severe,
☎ *DIAL 999 OR 112 FOR AN AMBULANCE.*

VOMITING AND DIARRHOEA

The causes of vomiting and diarrhoea are most likely to be food poisoning, contaminated water, allergy (*see page 213*), or unusual or exotic foods. Vomiting may, of course, occur without diarrhoea, and vice versa.

When both occur together there is a serious risk of dehydration, especially in infants and the elderly. Abdominal pains may also occur.

See also:
Food Poisoning, *page 190.*

TREATMENT

YOUR AIM IS:
- To restore lost fluid and salts.

1 Reassure the casualty while he or she is being sick. Afterwards, give the casualty a warm damp cloth with which to wash him- or herself.

2 Give the casualty lots of bland fluids to sip slowly and often. If the appetite returns, give him only bland, starchy or sugary food for the first 24 hours.

IF you are worried about the casualty's condition, particularly if it is persistent, call a doctor.

SUITABLE DRINKS

Water is sufficient in most cases, but still "isotonic" glucose drinks are ideal, if available. Alternatively, add salt (1 teaspoonful per litre) and sugar (4 or 5 teaspoonfuls per litre) to either water or diluted orange juice, which is a useful source of potassium.

VERTIGO

A disturbance in the ear canal (*see page 179*) can cause an abnormal sensation of movement: the casualty feels as if he or she is revolving in space and feels "giddy". This is vertigo, a fairly common complaint that often starts in middle age. It has many causes, including temporary conditions, such as ear infections, and psychological disorders, such as fear of open spaces (*agoraphobia*). Very occasionally, vertigo indicates a more serious condition, such as hardening of the arteries (*athero-sclerosis*), Ménière's disease (an inner ear disorder) or multiple sclerosis.

TREATMENT

YOUR AIMS ARE:
- To relieve pain.
- To obtain medical aid if necessary.

1 Place the casualty in a comfortable position and note any change in his or her condition.

2 If the casualty has special medication prescribed for this condition, he or she may need help to take it.

3 Call a doctor if the casualty is very distressed or requests medical help. Stay with the casualty until the doctor arrives, noting any changes in the casualty's condition in the meantime.

CRAMP

This is a sudden, involuntary, and painful muscle spasm. It commonly occurs during sleep, but can also happen after strenuous exercise, when it is caused by chemicals building up in the muscle, or by excessive loss of salt and fluid from the body through profuse sweating. Cramp is often relieved by stretching and massaging the affected muscle.

See also:
Heat Exhaustion, *page 173.*

TREATMENT

YOUR AIM IS:
■ To relieve both spasm and pain.

FOR CRAMP IN THE FOOT

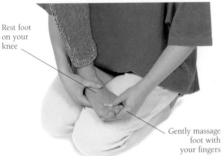

Rest foot on your knee

Gently massage foot with your fingers

Help the casualty to stand with her weight on the front of her foot. When the first spasm has passed, massage the foot.

FOR CRAMP IN THE CALF

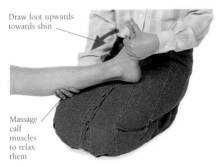

Draw foot upwards towards shin

Massage calf muscles to relax them

Straighten the casualty's knee, and draw her foot firmly and steadily upwards towards the shin. Massage the muscles.

FOR CRAMP IN THE THIGH

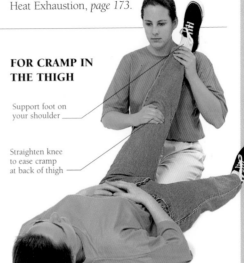

Support foot on your shoulder

Straighten knee to ease cramp at back of thigh

For cramp in the back of the thigh, straighten the casualty's knee by raising the leg. Bend the knee for cramp in the front of the thigh. In each case, massage the affected muscle firmly with your fingers until the pain eases.

STITCH

This common condition is usually associated with exercise, when pain is felt in the muscles of the trunk and the sides of the chest. The probable cause is the accumulation of waste products such as lactic acid in the muscles. The pain can be similar to that of angina (*see page 82*), but it is usually sharper.

If a casualty is suffering from a stitch, sit him or her down and be reassuring; the pain will usually ease quickly.

HYSTERIA

This is rather a vague term, which is often incorrectly used. True hysteria is a subconscious condition, caused by psychological stress, that manifests itself as some physical complaint, such as blindness.

We are more likely to apply the term "hysterical" to someone who is "over-reacting", possibly at the scene of an accident or on learning that a relative has died or been killed. People with this type of hysteria need to be handled firmly and positively.

Recognition
There may be:

◆ Attention-seeking behaviour, such as shouting or rolling on the ground, that is usually made worse by the presence of an audience.
◆ Hyperventilation, which may induce spasm in the wrists and hands.
◆ Marked tremor or "paralysis"; the casualty is apparently unable to move.

See also:
Hyperventilation, *page 72.*

Look after casualty's belongings

Do not question or contradict him

TREATMENT

YOUR AIM IS:
■ To help the casualty to calm down and regain self-control.

1 Escort the casualty to a quiet place, away from onlookers. Be firm and positive and do not over-sympathise.

2 Stay with the casualty quietly until he has recovered. Advise him to consult his doctor.

DO NOT throw any water over the casualty's face.

DO NOT slap the casualty's face.

DO NOT use force to restrain the casualty.

PANIC ATTACK

Some people occasionally display anxiety out of proportion to the stress they are actually experiencing. Attacks can be unpredictable with symptoms developing suddenly. Although they are distressing, panic attacks are harmless and last only a few minutes. Signs of an attack include:
◆ tension producing headaches, backache, and pressure in the chest;
◆ nervous overactivity, palpitations, trembling, sweating, and difficulty in swallowing;
◆ hyperventilation (*see page 72*).

What you can do

Treat as for hysteria. It is very important that the casualty sees a doctor, so that the cause of the attack can be treated.

HICCUPS

These short, repeated, noisy intakes of air are caused by involuntary contractions of the diaphragm, working against a partially closed windpipe. Hiccups are common and usually last only a few minutes. Short attacks are simply a nuisance, but if an attack is prolonged it may become worrying, tiring, and painful.

TREATMENT

YOUR AIM IS:
■ To increase temporarily carbon dioxide levels in the blood.

Try any or all of the following methods
◆ Tell the casualty to sit quietly and hold his breath for as long as possible.
◆ Make him take long drinks from the "wrong" side of a cup or glass.
◆ Place a paper (*not* plastic) bag over the nose and mouth and get the casualty to re-breathe his expired air for a minute to lower the level of oxygen in his blood.

Expired air has higher levels of carbon dioxide

IF the hiccups persist for more than a few hours, call a doctor for advice.

ALLERGY

In the same way that the body makes antibodies to combat germs, it may also make antibodies to other substances – pollen, foods, chemicals, drugs – that are regularly touched, inhaled, or swallowed. These could result in an allergy – an adverse reaction, caused by a hypersensitivity to some substance that is not generally recognised to be harmful. Allergies cause problems in one of three ways, but reactions can overlap.

◆ Respiratory allergies may result in asthma (*see page 73*) or in hay fever.
◆ Intestinal allergies may produce abdominal pain (*see page 208*), vomiting, and diarrhoea (*see page 210*).
◆ Skin allergies may take the form of "nettle rash" (*urticaria*) or dermatitis.
◆ Rarely, a generalised allergic reaction (*anaphylactic shock*) occurs that needs urgent medical attention.

See also:
Anaphylactic shock, *page 81.*

TREATMENT

YOUR AIM IS:
■ To treat any symptoms.
■ To obtain medical aid if necessary.

1 Treat any symptoms, for example, vomiting or an itchy rash.

2 Advise the casualty to see his or her doctor. Call a doctor if in doubt.

ILLNESS AND OVERSEAS TRAVEL

With the increase in travel, many people are now at risk from diseases that are not commonly encountered in their own country. A hot climate brings problems of its own, such as heat exhaustion and sunburn, to those who are unused to it.

The value of good preparation

When planning any foreign travel, obtain as much information as you can about the health problems of the area you are visiting. Many conditions can be avoided by common-sense measures (see below), and some can be prevented by vaccination (which is normally available from your doctor) before travelling.

See also:
Bites and Stings, *pages 191–6.*
Effects of Extreme Heat, *page 173–4.*
Rabies, *page 192.*
Sunburn, *page 166.*
Vomiting and Diarrhoea, *page 210.*

COMMON AILMENTS ENCOUNTERED OVERSEAS

Condition	Cause and features	Prevention
Malaria	The most common disease in the world, malaria affects around 200 million people every year. It is transmitted by a mosquito bite and is prevalent in almost all tropical and sub-tropical areas. In the early stages, malaria resembles 'flu, with fever and headache.	In affected areas, wear enveloping clothing, use insect repellent and mosquito nets, and take anti-malarial tablets which must be started before travel and continued on return. Anyone developing a fever in, or on return from, an infected area should be seen by a doctor.
Prickly heat	This is a highly irritating, prickly red rash caused by inflamed sweat glands. The rash particularly affects areas that are not well-aerated. Sufferers are more than usually liable to get heatstroke.	Maintain good personal hygiene and wear clean, loose clothing made of natural fibres. Sufferers should spend as much time as possible in cool conditions, and should avoid exercise in the heat.
Fungal infections	Conditions similar to "athlete's foot" are common in warm climates and can be more than usually painful and incapacitating. These fungal infections commonly affect the groin ("dhobi itch"), between the toes, and the armpits, causing great discomfort.	Maintain good personal hygiene and wear clean, loose clothing made of natural fibres. Use plenty of medicated talcum powder. If the infection is severe, specific medical treatment may be required.
Swimmer's ear	Swimmer's ear is an infective inflammation of the ear and external ear canal (see page 179). It can be very troublesome and difficult to cure.	Wear well-fitting ear plugs and take care to dry the ears thoroughly after swimming.

DRESSINGS AND BANDAGES

17

Applying dressings and bandages is an important part of good first-aid practice. Wounds usually require a dressing, and almost all injuries will benefit from the support that bandages can give.

Using first-aid materials

The materials that you need to equip a useful first-aid kit, and how to use them, are shown in this chapter. The dressing or bandage that you choose, and the technique for applying it, will depend upon the injury and materials that are available to you. Always use sterile first-aid equipment if it is available. However, if it is not, you can improvise using clean, everyday articles.

The following pages demonstrate the techniques required to apply each type of dressing and bandage; more detailed information about when to use each one is given on the pages dealing with specific injuries. If you wish to increase your proficiency in bandaging, it is well worth attending an approved first-aid course.

DRESSINGS ARE USED TO:

- Help control bleeding.
- Cover a wound and protect it, thereby reducing the risk of infection.

BANDAGES ARE USED TO:

- Maintain direct pressure over a dressing to control bleeding.
- Hold dressings, splints, and compresses in place.
- Limit swelling.
- Provide support to an injured limb or joint.
- Restrict movement.

CONTENTS

215

FIRST-AID MATERIALS

The materials necessary for first-aid are usually kept together in a first-aid kit or some other suitable container. First-aid kits should be kept in the workplace, at sports and leisure facilities, in your home and car.

The contents of a kit for a workplace or leisure centre must conform to legal requirements; they should also be clearly marked and readily accessible. The contents of this standard kit should form the basis of your first-aid kit at home, although you may wish to add to it.

Any first-aid kit must be kept in a dry atmosphere, and checked and replenished regularly, so that the items you need are always ready to use.

DRESSINGS

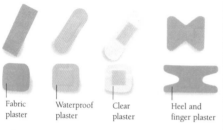

Fabric plaster

Waterproof plaster

Clear plaster

Heel and finger plaster

Adhesive dressings or plasters
Use for minor wounds. The waterproof types are the best choice for wounds on the hands.

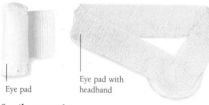

Eye pad

Eye pad with headband

Sterile eye pads
Any injury to the eye needs the protection of a sterile covering.

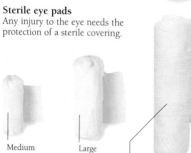

Medium dressing

Large dressing

Extra-large dressing

Sterile dressings
These are easy to apply, so are ideal in an emergency. They come in a range of sizes, and are sealed in a protective wrapping.

BANDAGES

Elasticated roller bandage

Conforming roller bandage

Crêpe conforming roller bandage

Crêpe roller bandage

Open-weave roller bandage

Self-adhesive roller bandage

Roller bandages
Use these to give support to joints, secure dressings, restrict movement, maintain pressure on a dressing, or limit swelling.

Folded cloth triangular bandage

Folded paper triangular bandage

Triangular bandages
Made of cloth or strong paper, these can be used as bandages and slings. If they are sterile and individually wrapped, they may be used as dressings for large wounds and burns.

Tubular grip for limbs

Finger gauze

Finger applicator

Tubular bandages
Use these specially shaped bandages on joints and digits.

Basic materials for a first-aid kit

- Easily identifiable watertight box;
- 20 adhesive dressings (plasters) in assorted sizes;
- six medium sterile dressings;
- two large sterile dressings;
- two extra-large sterile dressings;
- two sterile eye pads;
- six triangular bandages;
- six safety pins;
- disposable gloves.

Useful additions

- two crêpe roller bandages;
- scissors;
- tweezers;
- cotton wool;
- non-alcoholic wound cleansing wipes;
- adhesive tape;
- notepad, pencil, and tags;
- plastic face shield;
- for outdoor activities: blanket, survival bag, torch, and whistle.

OTHER USEFUL ITEMS

Adhesive tape
Use to fix bandages in place. Some people are allergic to the adhesive, so check before applying.

Safety pins

Clip

Pins and clips
Secure bandages or dressings with these.

Scissors
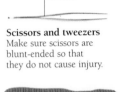
Tweezers

Scissors and tweezers
Make sure scissors are blunt-ended so that they do not cause injury.

Wound cleansing wipes
Clean skin around small wounds or your hands with these, if water and soap are not available.

Cotton wool
Never place this on a wound; use it as an absorbent outer layer, or as padding.

Disposable gloves
Wear gloves when dressing wounds or disposing of any waste materials.

Tags
Use to label casualties of major accidents.

Blanket, torch, and whistle
Add these to outdoor or camping first-aid kits. The blanket can protect a casualty from cold and a whistle will help rescuers locate you.

Gauze pads
Use as dressings, for extra padding, or as swabs.

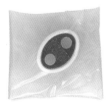

Plastic face shield
This can protect you when giving artificial ventilation.

Notepad and pencil
Use to record a casualty's details and your observations.

Survival bags
These keep a casualty warm and dry.

DRESSINGS

Dressings cover a wound, prevent infection from entering it, and help the blood-clotting process. Although they may stick to a wound, the benefits outweigh any discomfort caused on removal.

Use a pre-packed, sterile dressing where possible. If none is available, any clean, non-fluffy material can be used to improvise a dressing.

General rules for applying dressings

◆ The dressing pad should always extend well beyond the wound's edges.
◆ Place dressings directly on a wound.

Do not slide them on from the side, and replace any that slip out of place.
◆ If blood seeps through a dressing, do not remove it; instead, apply another dressing over the top.
◆ If there is only one sterile dressing, use this to cover the wound, and use other clean materials as top-dressings.

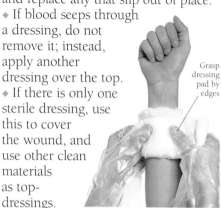

Grasp dressing pad by edges

PREVENTING CROSS-INFECTION

Follow the rules below to avoid passing infection to the casualty through an open wound, and to protect yourself.
◆ Wear disposable gloves, if available.
◆ Where possible, wash your hands thoroughly before dressing a wound.
◆ Cover cuts and grazes on your hands with waterproof dressings.
◆ Avoid touching the wound, or any part of the dressing that will come into contact with the wound.
◆ Try not to talk, sneeze, or cough over a wound while you are treating it.

When gloves are unavailable, use one of the following options.
◆ Ask the casualty to dress his or her own wound under your supervision.
◆ Enclose your hands in clean plastic bags.
◆ Dress the wound, but wash your hands very thoroughly afterwards.

Sharps container
Yellow containers for used needles are collected and disposed of safely by authorised waste collectors.

Dealing with waste

Clean up after treating a casualty as soon as possible. Always wear disposable gloves to perform these tasks.
◆ Use special chemical cleaner or a solution of bleach (one teaspoonful bleach to 0.5 litre or one pint water) to mop up bodily fluids from the floor, other surfaces, or first-aid equipment.
◆ Put sharp items such as needles or syringes in containers for disposal.
◆ Place all soiled dressings and materials, including gloves, in a suitably marked (yellow) plastic bag. Seal the bag and destroy it by incineration.

Bagging waste
Wear disposable gloves while you are disposing of waste, even if the bag is sealed.

STERILE DRESSINGS

Sterile dressings consist of a dressing pad attached to a roller bandage. The dressing pad is a piece of gauze or lint backed by a layer of cotton wool padding. Sterile dressings are sold singly in various sizes, and are sealed in protective wrappings. If the seal on a sterile dressing is broken, the dressing is no longer sterile.

METHOD

1 Remove the wrapping. Unwind the bandage's loose end, taking care not to drop the roll or touch the dressing pad.

> **DO NOT** bandage so tightly that the circulation is impaired.

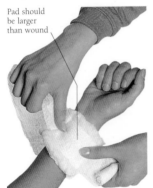

Pad should be larger than wound

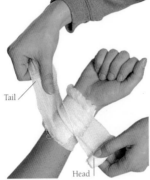

Tail

Head

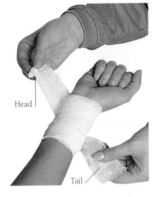

Head

Tail

2 Unfold the dressing pad, holding the bandage on each side of the pad. Put the pad directly on to the wound.

3 Wind the short end, or *tail*, of the bandage once around the limb and the dressing to secure the pad, then leave it hanging.

4 Wind the other end, or *head*, of the bandage around the limb to cover the whole pad, and leave the *tail* hanging free.

IF the dressing slips from place, remove it and apply a new dressing.

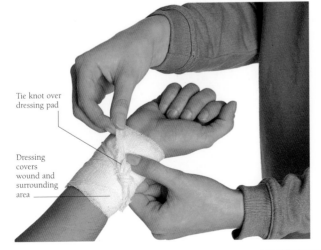

Tie knot over dressing pad

Dressing covers wound and surrounding area

5 To secure the bandage, tie the ends in a reef knot (*see page 230*), tied over the pad to exert firm pressure on the wound.

IF bleeding appears through the dressing, do not remove it. Apply another dressing on top.

6 Check the circulation to the extremity of the injured limb (*see page 223*). Loosen bandage if needed.

GAUZE DRESSINGS

If a sterile dressing is not available, use a gauze pad. Made from layers of gauze, it forms a soft covering for wounds. Cover the gauze with cotton wool to absorb blood or discharge. Secure the dressing with adhesive tape or a roller bandage if pressure is needed. Do not fully encircle a limb or digit with tape as it can impede circulation. If the casualty is allergic to adhesive tape, use a roller bandage.

METHOD

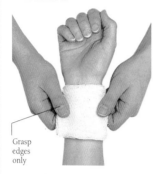

Grasp edges only

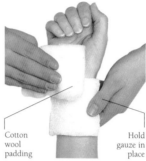

Cotton wool padding

Hold gauze in place

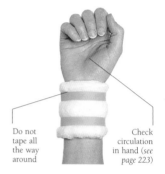

Do not tape all the way around

Check circulation in hand (see page 223)

1 Holding the gauze pad by the edges, place it directly on to the wound.

2 Add a layer of cotton wool padding on top of the gauze dressing.

3 Secure with adhesive tape or with a roller bandage (see page 224).

IMPROVISED DRESSINGS

If a prepared dressing is not available, you can improvise with any clean material. Do not use fluffy materials as the fibres may stick to and contaminate the wound. Freshly laundered cloths are best, but paper tissue could be used.

METHOD

Inner surface is less likely to be soiled

Clean tea-towel

Scarf makes good bandage

1 Hold the material by the edges only. Open it out and refold so that the inner surface is outermost.

2 Place the pad of material directly on to the wound. If necessary, cover with more material.

3 Secure the pad with a bandage or a clean cloth strip. Tie the ends in a reef knot (see page 230).

220

Adhesive Dressings

These dressings, or plasters, are useful for small wounds. They consist of a gauze or cellulose pad with an adhesive backing. Plasters come in various sizes (some are specially shaped for fingertips, heels, and elbows), often wrapped singly in sterile packs. Check the casualty is not allergic to adhesive dressings before use. Food handlers must apply waterproof plasters, usually blue, to wounds on their hands.

METHOD

1 Dry the surrounding area. Remove the wrapping and hold the dressing, pad-side down, by its protective strips.

2 Peel back, but do not remove, the protective strips. Without touching the pad, place it on to the wound.

3 Carefully pull away the protective strips. Press the ends and edges down.

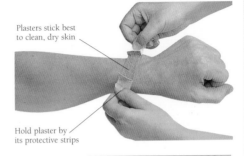

Plasters stick best to clean, dry skin

Hold plaster by its protective strips

Cold Compresses

Cooling an injury such as a bruise or sprain can reduce swelling and pain, although it will not alter the severity of the underlying injury. You can use an ice pack or cold compress, or place the injured part under cold running water or in a basin of cold water. A pack of frozen vegetables can also be used, but wrap it in a cloth before applying it to the skin.

APPLYING A COLD PAD

Wring pad out lightly

1 Soak a flannel or towel in very cold water. Wring it out lightly and place the cold, damp pad firmly over the injury and surrounding area.

2 Re-soak the pad in cold water every 3–5 minutes to keep it cold. Cool the injury for at least 20 minutes.

APPLYING AN ICE PACK

Press firmly

1 Partly fill a plastic bag with small ice cubes or crushed ice. Seal and wrap in a bandage or a cloth.

2 Hold the ice pack firmly in place over the injury.

3 Cool the injury for 10–15 minutes only, replacing the ice as necessary.

BANDAGES

Bandages have a number of purposes: they are used to hold dressings in position over wounds, to control bleeding, to support and immobilise injuries, and to reduce swelling. There are three main types of bandage:

◆ *roller bandages*, which secure dressings and can give support to injured limbs;

◆ *tubular bandages*, which can secure dressings on fingers or toes or support injured joints;

◆ *triangular bandages*, which are usually made of cloth; they are used as slings or large dressings, to secure dressings, and to immobilise limbs.

In an emergency, you may have to improvise bandages from everyday items (*see pages 220 and 234*).

GENERAL RULES FOR BANDAGING

Before applying bandages

◆ Reassure the casualty and explain clearly what you are going to do.

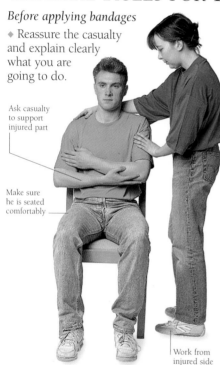

Ask casualty to support injured part

Make sure he is seated comfortably

Work from injured side

◆ Make the casualty comfortable, in a suitable position, sitting or lying.

◆ Keep the injured part supported. The casualty or an assistant may do this.

◆ Always work in front of the casualty, and from the injured side where possible.

When applying bandages

Use natural hollows of body

◆ If the casualty is lying down, pass the bandages under the body's natural hollows at the ankles, knees, waist, and neck. Then slide the bandages into position by easing them back and forth under the body. To bandage the head or upper torso, pull a bandage through the hollow under the neck, and slide into place.

◆ Apply bandages firmly, but not so tightly as to impede circulation to the extremity (*see opposite*).

◆ Leave fingers and toes on a bandaged limb exposed, if possible, so that you can check the circulation afterwards.

◆ Use reef knots to tie bandages. Ensure that the knots do not cause discomfort and do not tie the knot over a bony area. Tuck loose ends under a knot if possible.

◆ Regularly check the circulation to the extremity of a bandaged limb (*see opposite*). Loosen the bandages if necessary.

When bandaging to immobilise a limb

◆ Place some soft, bulky padding, such as towels, folded clothing, or cotton wool, between an arm and the body, or between the legs so that the bandaging does not displace any broken bones.
◆ Bandage around the limb at intervals, avoiding the injury as much as possible.
◆ Tie the knots on the uninjured side towards the upper part of the body. If both sides are injured, tie knots in the middle of the body or where there is least chance of causing further damage.

After applying bandages

◆ Check the circulation in a bandaged limb every ten minutes (*see below*).

IMMOBILISING A LEG WITH BANDAGES

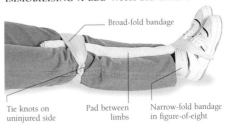

Broad-fold bandage

Tie knots on uninjured side

Pad between limbs

Narrow-fold bandage in figure-of-eight

CHECKING THE CIRCULATION

You must check the circulation in a hand or foot immediately after bandaging a limb or using a sling, and again every ten minutes until medical aid arrives.

Rechecking the circulation is vital because limbs swell following an injury, and a bandage can quickly become too tight and impede the circulation. The symptoms will change, as first the veins in the limb, and then the arteries supplying the limb, become impeded.

Recognition of impaired circulation
Initially, there may be:

◆ A swollen and congested limb.
◆ Blue skin with prominent veins.
◆ A feeling of painful distension.

Later, there may be:

◆ Pale, waxy skin and cold numbness.
◆ Tingling, followed by deep pain.
◆ Inability to move fingers or toes.

METHOD

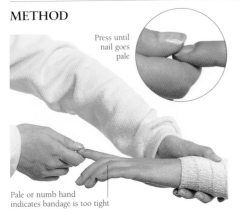

Press until nail goes pale

Pale or numb hand indicates bandage is too tight

Undo turns until warmth and colour return to hand

1 Press one of the nails (*see inset*), or the skin of the hand or foot, until it is pale. If, on releasing the pressure, the colour does not return, or returns slowly, the bandage may be too tight.

2 Loosen tight bandages by unrolling just enough turns for warmth and colour to return to the extremity. The casualty may feel a tingling sensation. Re-apply the bandage as necessary.

223

ROLLER BANDAGES

These are made of cotton, gauze, or linen, and are applied in spiral turns. There are three principal types:

♦ *open-weave bandages*, which are used to hold light dressings in place; because of their loose weave, they allow good ventilation, but cannot be used to exert pressure on the wound or to give support to joints;

♦ *conforming bandages*, which mould to the body shape, are used to secure dressings and lightly support injuries;

♦ *crêpe bandages*, which are used to give firm support to joints.

SECURING ROLLER BANDAGES

There are several ways to fasten a roller bandage; specialised clips, safety pins, or adhesive tape may all be found in first-aid kits. If you do not have any of these, a simple tuck should keep the *tail* of the bandage neatly in place.

Adhesive tape

The ends of bandages can be stuck down with small strips of adhesive tape.

Bandage clips

These are sometimes supplied with elasticated and crêpe roller bandages.

CHOOSING THE CORRECT SIZE OF BANDAGE

Before applying a roller bandage, make sure that it is tightly rolled and of a suitable width – Finger 2.5 cm (1 in), Hand 5 cm (2 in), Arm 7.5–10 cm (3–4 in), Leg 10–15 cm (4–6 in).

MAKING A RING PAD (TO PROTECT AROUND A WOUND)

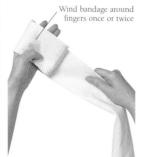

Wind bandage around fingers once or twice

1 Make a narrow bandage and place it across the fingers of one hand. Wind one end around your fingers to make a loop.

Work your way around the loop

2 Bring the other end of the bandage through the loop and wind it once around the loop. Pull it tight and begin working around the loop.

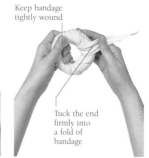

Keep bandage tightly wound

Tuck the end firmly into a fold of bandage

3 Continue passing the end through, until the whole of the bandage is used up, making a firm ring. Tuck in the end.

APPLYING A ROLLER BANDAGE

Follow these general rules when you are applying a roller bandage.

♦ When the bandage is partly unrolled, the roll is called the "head", and the unrolled part, the "tail". Keep the *head* of the bandage uppermost when bandaging.

♦ Position yourself towards the front of the casualty at the injured side.

♦ While you are working, support the injured part in the position in which it will remain after bandaging.

♦ Check the circulation (*see page 223*) beyond a bandage, especially when using conforming and crêpe bandages; these mould to the shape of the limb, and may become tighter if the limb swells.

METHOD

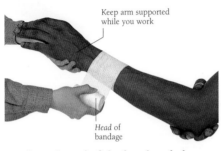

Keep arm supported while you work

Head of bandage

1 Place the *tail* of the bandage below the injury and, working from the inside of the limb outwards, make two straight turns with the *head* of the bandage to anchor it in place.

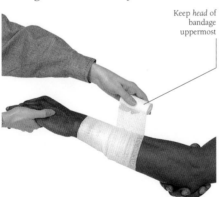

Keep *head* of bandage uppermost

2 Make a series of spiralling turns, winding from the inside to the outside of the limb and working up the limb. Make sure that each turn covers between a half and two-thirds of the previous layer of bandaging.

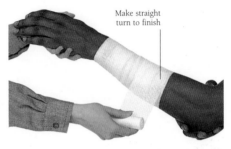

Make straight turn to finish

3 Finish off with one straight turn, and secure the end (*see opposite*).

IF the bandage is too short, apply another one in the same way to extend it.

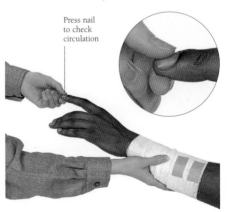

Press nail to check circulation

4 Regularly check the circulation to the extremity of the injured limb (*see page 223*).

IF the bandage is too tight, partially undo it, and re-apply it more loosely.

Elbow and Knee Bandage

Roller bandages can be used on elbows and knees to hold dressings in place or to support soft tissue injuries, such as strains or sprains. They are not effective for this purpose if applied with the standard spiralling turns, so use the method shown below for elbows and knees. Always make sure that you bandage sufficiently far on either side of the injured joint to exert an even pressure.

METHOD

1 Support the injured arm in a comfortable position, with the joint partly flexed if possible.

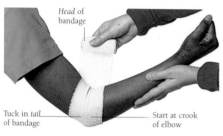

Head of bandage

Tuck in *tail* of bandage

Start at crook of elbow

2 Place the *tail* of the bandage on the inside of the elbow. Pass the bandage under and around to the outside of the elbow one-and-a-half times, so that the bandage is fixed, covering the elbow joint.

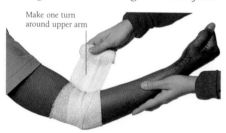

Make one turn around upper arm

3 Pass the bandage around the elbow joint to the inner side of the upper arm. Make a diagonal turn around the upper arm, covering the upper half of the bandage from the first turn.

4 Take the bandage from the inner side of the upper arm to just below the elbow joint. Make one diagonal turn around the forearm, to cover the lower half of the bandage from the first straight turn.

Make alternate turns above and below elbow

5 Continue to bandage diagonally above and below the joint in a figure-of-eight, steadily extending the bandaging by covering approximately two-thirds of the previous layer each time.

DO NOT bandage so tightly that the circulation is impeded.

Secure end with safety pin

6 Make two straight turns to finish off, and secure the end (*see page 224*).

7 Check the circulation to the fingers or the toes every ten minutes (*see page 223*). This is particularly important with this type of bandaging.

IF the bandage is too tight, undo it until the blood supply to the hand or foot returns. Re-apply the bandage less tightly.

Hand and Foot Bandage

A roller bandage may be used to hold dressings in place on the hand or foot, or to provide support to wrists or ankles that have been sprained or strained. Support bandaging should extend well beyond the joint to provide pressure over the injured area. The method shown below for bandaging a hand can be used on a foot, substituting the big toe as the thumb and leaving the heel unbandaged.

METHOD

Support casualty's hand

1 Place the *tail* of the bandage on the inside of the wrist, by the base of the thumb. Make two straight turns over and around the wrist.

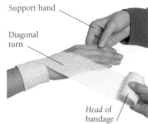

Support hand

Diagonal turn

Head of bandage

2 From the thumb side of the wrist, take the bandage diagonally across the back of the hand, so that the top edge touches the nail of the little finger.

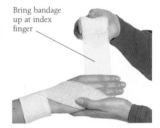

Bring bandage up at index finger

3 Take the bandage under and across the fingers so that the upper edge of the bandage touches the base of the nail of the index finger.

4 Take the bandage diagonally across the back of the hand to the outer side of the wrist, then around the wrist and up.

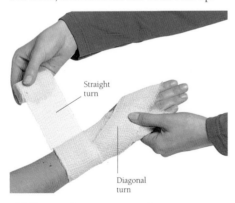

Straight turn

Diagonal turn

On a bandaged foot, check the circulation in the toes.

5 Repeat the sequence of turns, covering two-thirds of the bandage from the previous turn each time. Leave the thumb free. When the hand is covered, make two straight turns around the wrist.

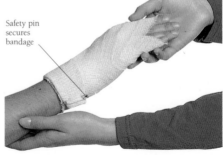

Safety pin secures bandage

6 Secure the bandage with either a safety pin or clip (see page 224). Regularly check the circulation in the fingers (see page 223). Loosen the bandage if necessary.

TUBULAR GAUZE

This is a tubular bandage made from a roll of seamless gauze, which is used to support joints such as the elbow or ankle. A small tubular gauze can be applied to a finger or toe with a special applicator, supplied with each roll. A tubular gauze is useful for holding light dressings in place, but it cannot exert enough pressure to control the bleeding from a wound.

METHOD

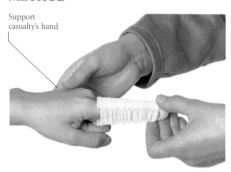

Support casualty's hand

1 Cut a piece of tubular gauze two-and-a-half times the length of the injured finger. Push the whole length on to the applicator. Gently slide the applicator over the casualty's finger.

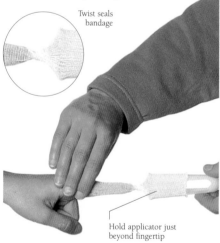

Twist seals bandage

Hold applicator just beyond fingertip

2 Holding the end of the gauze on the finger, pull the applicator slightly beyond the fingertip to leave a gauze layer on the finger. Twist the applicator twice.

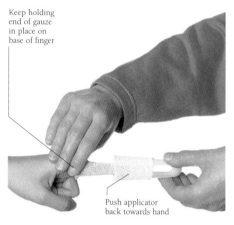

Keep holding end of gauze in place on base of finger

Push applicator back towards hand

3 While still holding the gauze firmly at the base of the finger, gently push the applicator back over the finger until the finger is covered with the second layer of gauze tubular bandage. Remove the applicator from the finger.

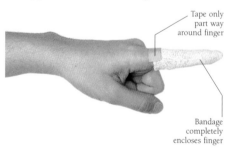

Tape only part way around finger

Bandage completely encloses finger

4 Secure the tubular bandage at the base of the finger with adhesive tape. Do not encircle the finger with tape, as this may impede circulation. Regularly check the circulation to the finger (see page 223). Re-apply the tape if needed.

TRIANGULAR BANDAGES

Sold in sterile packs, these bandages can also be made by cutting or folding a square metre of sturdy fabric (such as linen or calico) diagonally in half. They can be used:

♦ folded into broad-fold bandages (*see below, right*) to immobilise and support limbs and secure splints and bulky dressings;

♦ folded into narrow-fold bandages (*see below*), to immobilise feet and ankles, and hold dressings in place;

♦ straight from a pack and folded into a pad to form a sterile improvised dressing pad;

♦ open, as slings to support an injured limb, or to hold a hand, foot, or scalp dressing in position.

OPEN TRIANGULAR BANDAGE

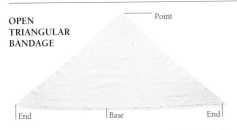

Point

End   Base   End

MAKING A BROAD-FOLD BANDAGE

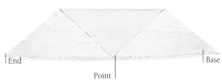

End   Base

Point

1 Open out a triangular bandage and lay it flat on a clean surface. Fold it horizontally so that the *point* touches the centre of the *base*.

2 Fold the triangular bandage in half again in the same direction. This completes the broad-fold bandage.

MAKING A NARROW-FOLD BANDAGE

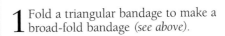

1 Fold a triangular bandage to make a broad-fold bandage (*see above*).

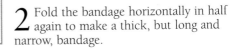

2 Fold the bandage horizontally in half again to make a thick, but long and narrow, bandage.

STORING A TRIANGULAR BANDAGE

Store triangular bandages in their packs, or in the way shown below so that, in an emergency, they are either ready-folded for use or can simply be shaken open.

1 Start with a narrow-fold bandage (*see right*). Bring the two ends of the bandage into the centre.

2 Keep folding the ends into the centre until a convenient size is reached. Keep the bandage in a dry place.

REEF KNOTS

When tying a bandage, always use a reef knot. It lies flat so is more comfortable for the casualty; it is secure and will not slip, but is easy to untie. Avoid tying the knot around or over the injury itself as this may cause discomfort.

TYING A REEF KNOT

1 Pass the left end (*dark*) over and under the right.

2 Bring both ends up again.

3 Pass the right end (*dark*) over and under the left.

4 Pull the ends firmly to tighten; tuck in ends.

UNTYING A KNOT

1 Pull one end and one piece of bandage apart.

2 Hold the knot; pull the end through it and out.

HAND AND FOOT COVER BANDAGE

An open triangular bandage on a hand or foot will not exert enough pressure to control bleeding, but is useful for holding a dressing in place. This method for bandaging a hand can also be applied to a foot; tie the ends around the ankle.

METHOD

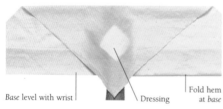

Base level with wrist | Dressing | Fold hem at *base*

1 Lay the bandage flat and place the casualty's hand on it, fingers towards the *point*. Place the dressing on the wound. Fold the *point* of the bandage over the hand, bringing it to the forearm.

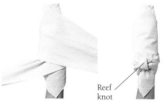

Reef knot

2 Pass the ends around the wrist in opposite directions. Tie a reef knot over the *point* and pull the *point* gently to tighten the bandage over the dressing. Fold the *point* over the knot and tuck it in.

SCALP BANDAGE

An open triangular bandage may be used to hold a dressing in position on the top of a casualty's head, although it cannot provide enough pressure to control profuse bleeding. A dressing on a bleeding scalp wound should be held in position with a roller bandage (see pages 90 and 224). If possible, sit the casualty down because this makes it easier to apply the scalp bandage.

METHOD

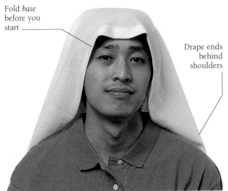

Fold *base* before you start

Drape ends behind shoulders

1 Fold a hem along the *base* of the bandage. Place the bandage on the casualty's head with the centre of the *base* just above his eyebrows. Let the *point* hang down at the back of his head.

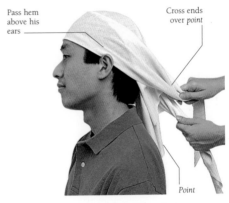

Pass hem above his ears

Cross ends over *point*

Point

2 Bring the two ends around the casualty's head, with the hem just above his ears, to the back of his head. Cross the two ends at the nape of his neck over the *point* of the bandage.

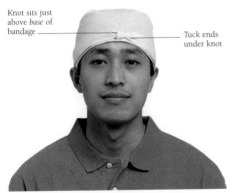

Knot sits just above *base* of bandage

Tuck ends under knot

3 Bring the two ends of the bandage around to the front of the casualty's head. Use a reef knot (see opposite) to tie the ends together, at the centre of the casualty's forehead and close to the *base* of the bandage.

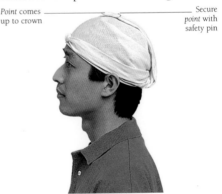

Point comes up to crown

Secure *point* with safety pin

4 Steadying his head with one hand, draw the *point* down to tighten the bandage; take the *point* up towards the top of his head; secure with a safety pin. If you have no pin, fold the *point* over the crossed ends at the back and tuck in.

SLINGS

Slings are used to support the arm of a casualty who is sitting or is able to walk. There are two types of sling:
* *arm sling*, which supports the arm with the forearm horizontal or slightly raised, used for an injured upper arm, wrist, or forearm, or a simple rib fracture;

* *elevation sling*, which supports the upper limb with the hand in a well-raised position. It is used for some fractures, to help control bleeding from wounds in the forearm, to reduce swelling in burn injuries, and for complicated rib fractures.

APPLYING AN ARM SLING

1 Support the injured arm so its hand is above the uninjured elbow. Pass one end of the bandage through at the injured elbow and pull to the opposite shoulder. Spread the bandage out so the *base* is level with her little finger nail.

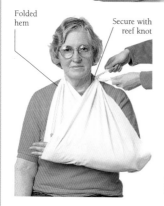

Pull *point* beyond elbow

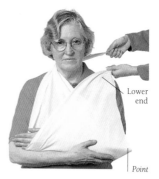

Take end around back of neck

Lower end

Point

2 Bring the lower end of the bandage up over her forearm to meet the other end at her shoulder.

IF you do not have a safety pin, twist the *point* until the sling fits her elbow snugly, then tuck it into the sling at the back of her arm.

Folded hem

Secure with reef knot

Pin at front of elbow

3 Tie a reef knot (*see page 230*) at the hollow over her collar bone on the injured side. Tuck both ends of the bandage under the knot to pad it.

4 Fold the *point* forward at her elbow. Tuck any loose bandage underneath it, and secure the *point* to the front of the bandage with a safety pin.

5 Regularly check the circulation in her exposed fingers (*see page 223*). If necessary, undo the sling and loosen any underlying bandages.

APPLYING AN ELEVATION SLING

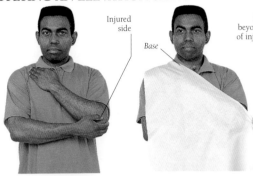

Injured side

Base

Point well beyond elbow of injured side

Leave thumb showing

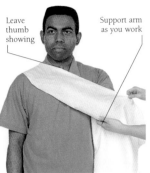

Support arm as you work

1 Ask the casualty to support the injured arm across his chest, with his fingertips touching the opposite shoulder.

2 Drape one end of a triangular bandage over his shoulder on the uninjured side, with the *point* on his injured side.

3 Ask the casualty to release his arm. Tuck the *base* of the bandage under his hand and forearm and behind his elbow.

Bring ends up to shoulder

Watch thumb for signs of impaired circulation

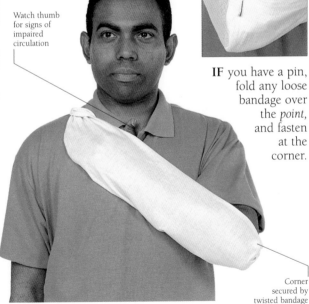

IF you have a pin, fold any loose bandage over the *point*, and fasten at the corner.

4 Bring the lower end up diagonally across his back to meet the other end at his shoulder.

Corner secured by twisted bandage

5 Tie the ends in a reef knot (*see page 230*) at the hollow above his collar bone. Tuck the ends under the knot to pad it.

6 Twist the *point* until the bandage fits snugly around his elbow. Tuck the *point* into the sling at his elbow to secure it.

7 Regularly check the circulation in his fingers (*see page 223*). If necessary, undo the sling and loosen any bandages.

IMPROVISED SLINGS

You can improvise a sling (*see pages 232–3*) with a square of cloth. Make sure it is sturdy and large enough to support the arm. You can also improvise slings from items of clothing, or adjust the casualty's clothes to support an injured arm.

METHODS

Jacket

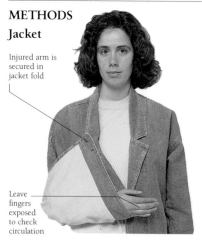

Injured arm is secured in jacket fold

Leave fingers exposed to check circulation

◆ Undo the jacket, and turn the hem up and over the injured arm. Pin the hem to the jacket breast with a large safety pin.

Button-up jacket

Jacket button supports wrist

◆ Undo a button of a jacket, coat, or waistcoat and place the hand of the injured arm inside the fastening.

Long-sleeved shirt

Pin must be sturdy enough to take weight of arm

◆ If the casualty is wearing long sleeves, pin the cuff of the sleeve of the injured arm to the opposite breast of her shirt or jacket, as shown above. For an improvised elevation sling, pin the sleeve further up at her shoulder to raise her arm.

Short-sleeved shirt

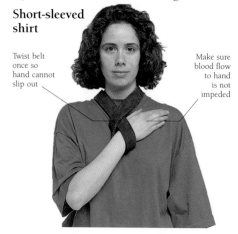

Twist belt once so hand cannot slip out

Make sure blood flow to hand is not impeded

◆ Use a belt, tie, or a pair of braces or tights to make a "collar-and-cuff" support.

> **DO NOT** use this method if you suspect that the forearm is broken.

Handling and Transport 18

When moving a casualty, it is important to be aware of the dangers to yourself and to the casualty. Incorrect handling and transport methods could aggravate the casualty's condition, and cause you to injure yourself. You should not move a casualty unless you have received comprehensive training, or the casualty is in imminent danger and it is safe for you to approach him or her.

Safety guidelines and training

This chapter demonstrates the safe methods of moving or handling a casualty, including advice on how to use the different types of stretcher, when it is necessary to transport the casualty. However, it is no substitute to full instruction and training which can *only* be given on a practical first-aid training course. The regular or professional First Aider may also consult ambulance-aid training manuals for information. Manual handling courses are available from Irish Red Cross Society's handling instructors.

HANDLING AND TRANSPORT RULES

◆ Move a casualty only if it is absolutely necessary, and you are not putting yourself in danger.

◆ Always explain to a casualty what is happening, so that he or she can co-operate as much as possible.

◆ Do not attempt to move a casualty by yourself if help is available. Ensure that helpers understand what they need to do, so that they can co-operate fully.

◆ When more than one person is moving a casualty, always appoint someone to give verbal commands.

◆ Always use the correct lifting technique (*see overleaf*) to avoid injuring your back when lifting or carrying a casualty.

MANUAL MOVES

You can be at risk of injury when making a manual move, so it is important to plan each step before you begin. The method you choose to remove a casualty from immediate danger will depend on the situation, the casualty's condition, and whether there is any help available (*see below*).

If there are several helpers, it is important to appoint a team leader to co-ordinate the manoeuvre. Once this has been decided, consider and discuss the risks involved as a team.

◆ *The task:* is it really necessary? Can the casualty move himself? Is it possible to get help? Is there any equipment available?

◆ *The load:* how heavy is the casualty? What are his injuries and will the move aggravate them?

◆ *The environment:* have you made enough space for your move? What sort of ground will you be crossing? Do you have everything you need?

◆ *The handlers:* are you and any team members properly trained?

LIFTS AND CARRIES FOR ONE AND TWO FIRST AIDERS

Condition of casualty	One First Aider	Two First Aiders
Conscious, able to walk	• Human crutch method	• Human crutch method
Conscious, unable to walk	• Piggyback or cradle method (light-weight casualties only) • Drag method (may aggravate shoulder, head, or neck injuries)	• Two-handed seat • Fore-and-aft carry (not for casualties with arm, shoulder, or rib injuries)
Unconscious	• Cradle method (light-weight casualties only) • Drag method (*see above*)	• Fore-and-aft carry (*see above*)

LIFTING SAFELY

If you lift and lower a casualty correctly, you are less likely to harm the casualty or yourself. Always use your strongest muscles (those at the thigh, hip, and shoulder) and follow these rules:

◆ think before you lift;
◆ stand as close as possible to the casualty or lifting aid;
◆ bend at the hip;
◆ keep your back straight, but not rigid;
◆ use your legs to provide the power that you need for the lift;
◆ move smoothly, holding the casualty or the lifting aid as close to you as possible.

Keep back straight

Bend at hip

Place feet hip distance apart, both firmly on the ground

Keep weight close to body

Grip with whole hand

CARRIES FOR ONE FIRST AIDER

If no help is available, encourage a casualty to walk with a little help from you or a walking aid. If you are by yourself, you should only attempt to move a casualty in an emergency, when the casualty is in real danger. Only use the cradle and piggyback methods for lightweight casualties, such as children.

HUMAN CRUTCH METHOD

IF possible, give the casualty a walking aid for extra support.

1 Stand on the casualty's injured or weaker side. Pass his arm around your neck, and grasp his hand or wrist with your hand.

2 Pass your other arm around his waist. Grasp his clothes to support him.

3 Move off with your inside foot. Take small steps, and walk at the casualty's pace. Reassure the casualty throughout.

Ask him not to drag on your neck

DRAG METHOD

1 Crouch behind the casualty, help her to sit up, and cross her arms over her chest.

DO NOT use this method if there are shoulder, head, or neck injuries.

Grasp her wrists firmly

Keep back straight

2 Pass your arms under the casualty's armpits and grasp her wrists. Carefully pull her backwards and squat walk.

IF she is wearing a jacket, unbutton it and pull it up under her head. Grasp the jacket under the shoulders, and pull her backwards.

CRADLE METHOD

1 Squat beside the casualty. Pass one of your arms around the casualty's trunk, above the waist.

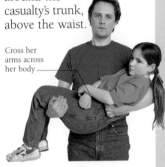

Cross her arms across her body

2 Pass your other arm under her thighs. Stand, hugging her towards you.

PIGGYBACK METHOD

1 Crouch in front of the casualty, with your back to her. Ask her to put her arms over your shoulders, and, if possible, grasp her own hands.

She must be able to hold on

Grip her thighs

2 Grasp the casualty's thighs and rise slowly, keeping your back straight.

CARRIES FOR TWO FIRST AIDERS

It is easier to control a move with two First Aiders. However, such a carry must still be undertaken with extreme caution, and only in an emergency. Use the two-handed seat to move conscious casualties. Only use the fore-and-aft carry to move a casualty on to a stretcher or a carry chair (see opposite).

THE TWO-HANDED SEAT

Squat down

1 Squat facing each other on either side of the casualty. Cross arms behind her back and grasp her waistband.

2 Pass your other hands under the casualty's knees, and grasp each other's wrists. Bring your linked arms up to the middle of the casualty's thighs.

Prepare to lift in unison

Keep back straight

3 Move in close to the casualty. Keeping your backs straight, rise slowly, and move off together.

THE FORE-AND-AFT CARRY

DO NOT use this method if the arms, shoulders, or ribs are injured.

1 Sit the casualty up and put her arms across her chest.

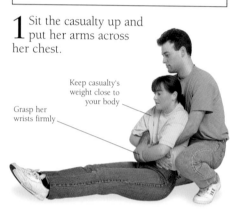

Keep casualty's weight close to your body

Grasp her wrists firmly

2 Squat behind the casualty. Slide your arms under her armpits and firmly grasp her wrists.

Squat beside her and grasp her thighs

3 Ask your partner to squat beside the casualty and pass his arms under her thighs, taking hold of her legs.

4 Working together, keeping your backs straight, rise slowly, and move off.

MOVES USING EQUIPMENT

You should obtain proper and adequate training before attempting to move a casualty using specialist equipment. The information given in this section will familiarise you with the type of aids available, and give you a basic guide to their use. Full instruction on how to use such equipment is given on first-aid training courses and laid out in ambulance-aid training manuals.

You should not attempt to improvise moving aids, or to lift patients in equipment not designed for lifting, such as wheelchairs, except in an emergency.

CARRY CHAIRS

These chairs are kept in many schools, shops, and workplaces, and are used for moving casualties along passages and up or down stairs. A carry chair should be carried; wheel it only if you have to move the casualty on your own. Test any carry chair before use to ensure that it will support the casualty's weight. As with all mobile aids, using a carry chair is not without dangers, and the safety guidelines (*see below and overleaf*) should always be followed.

BEFORE MOVING THE CASUALTY

1 Unfold the chair, following the maker's instructions, if available. Test the chair by pushing down on the seat, to check that it can support the casualty's weight.

Unfold and test chair

Strap around casualty's arms and body

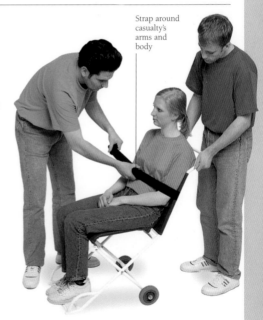

2 Ensure that the canvas seat and back are not showing signs of wear and tear, the wheels move freely, the safety strap is secure, and that there are no signs of any other damage.

3 Sit the casualty in the chair. Secure the safety strap over the casualty's arms, and put her feet on the footbar. One person should always support the back of the chair to stop it tipping back.

MOVING A CASUALTY

ALONG SMOOTH GROUND ON YOUR OWN

1 Reassure the casualty and explain what is going to happen. Make sure that she is strapped in properly.

2 Tip the chair back gently. Push it forwards carefully, ensuring that you maintain a steady speed.

3 Make sure you take corners widely to prevent the chair from overbalancing.

> **DO NOT** pull the chair. This could cause both the chair and the casualty to fall forwards on to you.

IF you come across any immovable objects, treat them as steps and alter your method accordingly (*see below*).

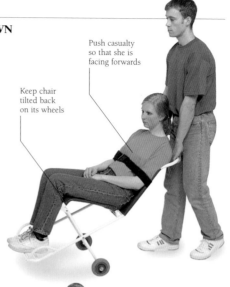

Push casualty so that she is facing forwards

Keep chair tilted back on its wheels

DOWN STEPS WITH HELP

1 Standing behind the chair, face it towards the top of the steps. Your partner should stand a few steps down, facing the front of the chair.

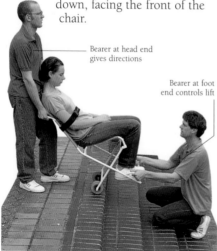

Bearer at head end gives directions

Bearer at foot end controls lift

Keep back straight

2 Tip the chair back; push it forwards so that the wheels are on the edge of the steps. Ask your partner to squat down and grasp the handles on the footrest.

3 Your partner at the foot end controls the lift. When he commands, you should both pick up the chair, with your partner straightening his legs as he lifts.

4 Although your partner controls the pace, you will need to direct him.

IF you need a rest in mid-lift, use a landing rather than the steps.

IF going up steps, reverse the procedure.

STRETCHERS

These are used to carry casualties (*see page 248*) to an ambulance or to shelter. The robust standard stretcher is found at many sports grounds, schools, and workplaces. Orthopaedic stretchers (*see page 244*) may be used when you suspect a spinal injury, when a rigid collar and back board have been applied. Special training is needed in these techniques.

General rules for stretchers

◆ Always test stretchers regularly for wear and tear, and make sure that they can support a casualty's weight.
◆ When loading a stretcher, explain to the casualty what is happening.
◆ Always ensure that an unconscious casualty, or a casualty who needs to be transported any distance, is securely strapped on to the stretcher.

STANDARD STRETCHERS

The Furley stretcher and the Utila folding stretcher are standard first-aid stretchers. The Furley stretcher consists of a canvas or plastic sheet attached to two carrying poles with feet underneath. Hinged cross bars, or traverses, keep the stretcher open. The Utila is similar to the Furley, but is lighter and more compact when folded.

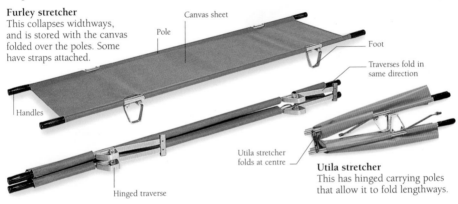

Furley stretcher
This collapses widthways, and is stored with the canvas folded over the poles. Some have straps attached.

Canvas sheet

Pole

Foot

Traverses fold in same direction

Handles

Utila stretcher folds at centre

Utila stretcher
This has hinged carrying poles that allow it to fold lengthways.

Hinged traverse

SPECIALIST STRETCHERS

There are two types of stretchers that are commonly used only by trained personnel. The stretcher trolley, also known as a "trolley cot", is usually carried in an ambulance. It is fully adjustable, from a flat to a chair-like position, to suit the casualty. The second type of specialist stretcher is the rescue stretcher. It is designed for moving casualties from places that are difficult to access, such as cliffs, and must only be used by trained rescue personnel.

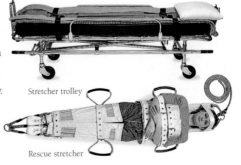

Stretcher trolley

Rescue stretcher

OPENING A FURLEY STRETCHER

Unfold canvas and pull poles apart

Outward-facing traverse

Hold stretcher upright

Press down with sole of your foot to lock open traverse

1 Place the stretcher on its side, undo any straps, and pull it open.

2 Push the outward-facing traverse open with the sole of your foot.

3 Stand the stretcher on its end, and press the other traverse open.

IF both traverses are inward-facing, open both with the stretcher upright.

CLOSING A FURLEY STRETCHER

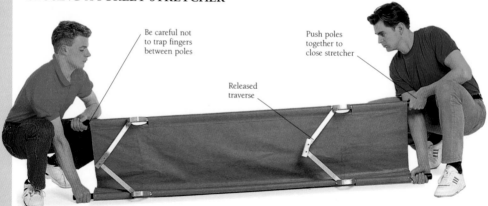

Be careful not to trap fingers between poles

Push poles together to close stretcher

Released traverse

1 Release both traverses. To do this, place the stretcher on its side. Press the sole of your foot against the hinge of each traverse until it releases.

2 Bring the two poles together, making sure that the canvas is clear of them. Fold the canvas neatly over the poles, securing it with straps, if there are any.

CANVAS-AND-POLES STRETCHER

This is used as a stretcher or to load a casualty on to an ambulance trolley. A strong canvas sheet supports the casualty. Poles are inserted to move the stretcher. Spreader bars either end ensure it is rigid.

See also:
Loading a Stretcher, *page 247.*

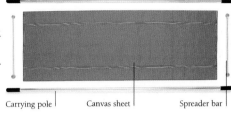

Carrying pole | Canvas sheet | Spreader bar

METHOD

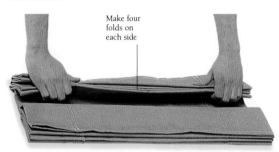

Make four folds on each side

1 Concertina-fold the top and bottom ends of the canvas in towards the centre.

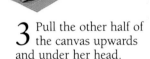

Hold centre down and pull top end to head

3 Pull the other half of the canvas upwards and under her head.

4 Slide the poles through the sleeves at the sides of the canvas.

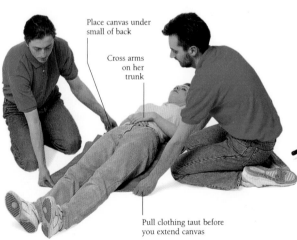

Place canvas under small of back

Cross arms on her trunk

Pull clothing taut before you extend canvas

2 With one person working on each side of the casualty, gently lift up her hips no more than 2.5 cm (1 in). Push the folded canvas through the hollow at the small of the casualty's back. Together, pull the bottom part of the canvas down to the casualty's feet.

5 Fit the spreader bars over the ends of the poles for rigidity.

Put spreader bar in place

ORTHOPAEDIC STRETCHER

This "scoop" stretcher is used to lift a casualty who must be moved in the position in which he or she is found, such as a casualty with suspected spinal injuries (*see page 143*). The stretcher splits lengthways into two halves, which are placed on either side of the casualty, then reassembled. It must not be used to carry a casualty over any distance.

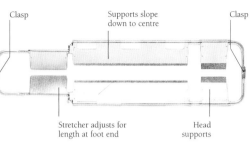

Clasp

Supports slope down to centre

Clasp

Stretcher adjusts for length at foot end

Head supports

METHOD

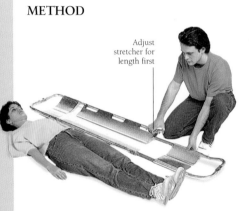

Adjust stretcher for length first

1 Place the stretcher alongside the casualty. Adjust it so that it is slightly longer than the casualty at either end.

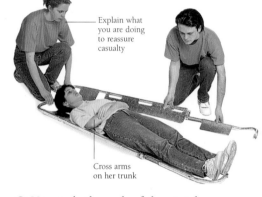

Explain what you are doing to reassure casualty

Cross arms on her trunk

2 Uncouple the ends of the stretcher, and ease one half, and then the other, under each side of the casualty.

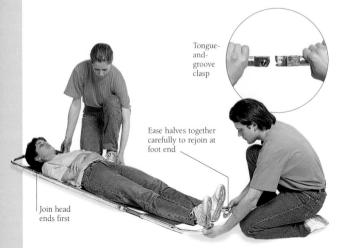

Tongue-and-groove clasp

Ease halves together carefully to rejoin at foot end

Join head ends first

3 Rejoin the stretcher at the head end, while your helper holds the two halves at the foot end firmly in line.

4 Join the foot ends firmly. Your helper should apply a gentle traction at the casualty's waist to avoid catching the skin between the blades.

5 Lifting from the ends only, carefully place the scoop on to a stretcher. Undo the scoop and ease it away.

PREPARING A STRETCHER

Blanketing a stretcher will help to keep the casualty warm, and will protect him or her against any bumps and jolts. One blanket will suffice (*see below*), although two are better (*see overleaf*).

A canvas carrying sheet may be placed beneath the casualty, so that he or she can be more easily transferred to another stretcher or to a stretcher trolley (*see page 241*), if necessary.

USING ONE BLANKET

1 Place the open blanket diagonally over the stretcher so that the corners overhang at the sides, top, and bottom.

2 Lay the casualty in the centre of the stretcher (*see page 247*). Explain what you are going to do. Bring the foot overhang over her feet, and tuck it around her ankles.

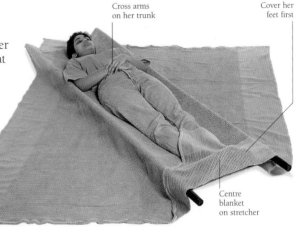

Cross arms on her trunk

Cover her feet first

Centre blanket on stretcher

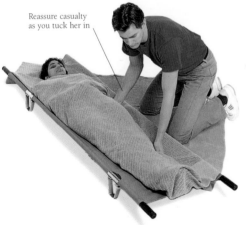

Reassure casualty as you tuck her in

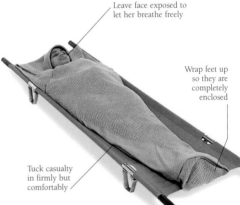

Leave face exposed to let her breathe freely

Wrap feet up so they are completely enclosed

Tuck casualty in firmly but comfortably

3 Bring one side of the blanket over the casualty, and tuck it in securely underneath her body.

4 Fold the other side of the blanket over and tuck it in. You may wish to reassure the casualty as you do this.

5 Tuck the overhang at the head end around the casualty's head and neck, leaving her face exposed.

IF the casualty is unconscious, or you need to transport her over any distance, ensure that she is strapped in securely.

PREPARING A STRETCHER USING TWO BLANKETS

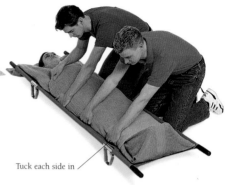

1 Place the first blanket widthways across the stretcher so that one side of the blanket covers the handles at the head end. Centre the blanket on the stretcher.

Tuck each side in

4 Bring one side of the blanket over and tuck it in. Repeat with the other side.

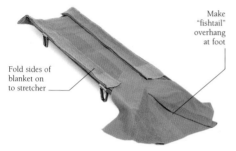

Make "fishtail" overhang at foot

Fold sides of blanket on to stretcher

2 Fold the second blanket lengthways into three, and lay it along the stretcher, leaving a two-foot overhang at the foot end. Open out the edges of this overhang diagonally. Concertina-fold the edges of the first blanket on to the sides of the stretcher.

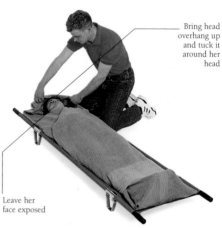

Bring head overhang up and tuck it around her head

Leave her face exposed

5 Tuck the overhang at the head end around the casualty's head and neck.

Place casualty's arms on her trunk

Cover her feet first

3 Place the casualty on the stretcher (*see opposite*). Bring the "fishtailed" overhang up over the casualty's feet, and tuck it in around her legs.

MAKING A BLANKET ROLL

Prepare a stretcher for storage with two blankets, and roll them up, starting at the foot end. Always make sure that the roll is stored in a dry place.

LOADING A STRETCHER

The standard way to load a stretcher is to use a canvas-and-poles stretcher (*see page 243*), if available. If not, you can use the blanket lift (*see below*). Once the casualty has been lifted, she can be lowered on to a stretcher placed either at her feet, or beneath her. If you do not have a blanket, or if there are fewer than four bearers available, use the fore-and-aft carry (*see page 238*). You must not lift a casualty whom you suspect has a spinal injury (*see box, below*).

BLANKET LIFT

> **DO NOT** lift a casualty whom you suspect has a fractured spine. If an immediate risk to life outweighs the danger of movement, use the "log-roll" technique (*see page 145*).

Place roll up against her back

Support casualty

1 Roll a blanket lengthways to half its width, and place it alongside the casualty. Turn the casualty on to her side and place the roll against her back.

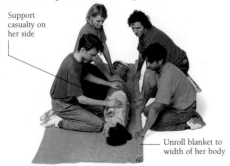

Support casualty on her side

Unroll blanket to width of her body

2 Turn the casualty back over the blanket roll and on to her other side. Unroll enough of the blanket to lay the casualty down flat on it.

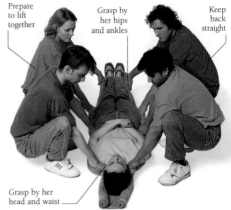

Prepare to lift together

Grasp by her hips and ankles

Keep back straight

Grasp by her head and waist

3 Tightly roll the open blanket on both sides to meet the casualty's body; the rolls act as handles for the bearers.

4 Two bearers squat on either side of the casualty, at her trunk and legs, and grasp the rolls firmly.

5 On command, all four bearers lift the casualty by leaning back and straightening their knees.

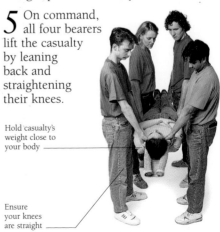

Hold casualty's weight close to your body

Ensure your knees are straight

CARRYING A STRETCHER

On the rare occasions when it is necessary to transport a casualty any distance on a stretcher, follow the technique described below. The most experienced First Aider should assume leadership and co-ordinate the actions of the other bearers, giving commands for each movement.

As a general rule, always carry a stretcher with the casualty's feet first, except in the following circumstances:

◆ when carrying a casualty with serious limb injuries, or a casualty with hypothermia, *down* stairs or down an incline, such as a hillside.

◆ when carrying a casualty with a stroke (*see page 119*) or cerebral compression (*see page 115*). He or she should not be carried with the head lower than the feet.

More advanced techniques for carrying can be found in standard manuals on ambulance aid.

METHOD

1 One bearer stands at each of the four handles.

IF there are only three bearers, two stand at the head and one at the feet.

2 Each bearer squats and grasps a handle firmly. On command, all bearers rise together and stand holding the stretcher level.

3 On a further command, the bearers move off, each on the foot next to the stretcher. They take short steps, keeping the stretcher close to their bodies.

4 To lower the casualty, the bearers stop on command. On a further command, they squat, and lower the stretcher until it rests gently on the ground.

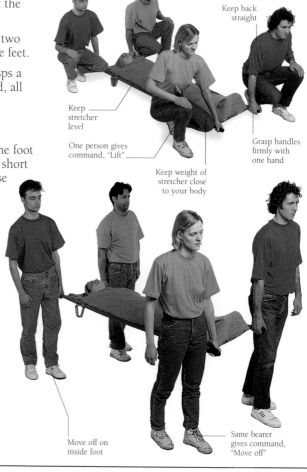

Keep back straight

Keep stretcher level

One person gives command, "Lift"

Grasp handles firmly with one hand

Keep weight of stretcher close to your body

Move off on inside foot

Same bearer gives command, "Move off"

LOADING AMBULANCES

This is carried out by a trained ambulance crew. Only assist if you are asked to do so. You may be asked to support the foot end of the trolley. Do not overlift, because this could throw other bearers off balance.

RESCUE BY HELICOPTER

Rescue helicopters are used for sea and mountain evacuation; smaller helicopter ambulances are increasingly being used in less remote locations. When a helicopter is landing, ground activities are usually co-ordinated by a member of the emergency services. Your main aims as a First Aider are to care for the casualty and control bystanders. However, you should be aware of the standard ground-safety precautions while the helicopter is landing, and the guidelines that you should follow to ensure your own safety once it is on the ground. The complete procedure is detailed below.

SAFETY PROCEDURES

1 Limit crowd access to a circle of 100 metres diameter, and keep animals under control.

2 Extinguish any cigarettes within 50 metres of the landing area, and remove loose articles, such as broken branches, helmets, or first-aid equipment.

IF possible, ask someone to hold up a piece of light material, such as a bandage, to act as a windsock for the crew.

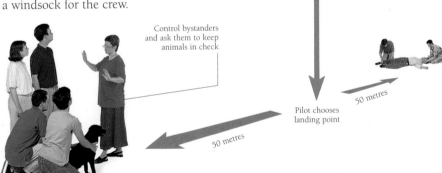

Control bystanders and ask them to keep animals in check

Pilot chooses landing point

50 metres

50 metres

3 As the helicopter is landing, kneel at the ten o'clock position to its nose, well clear of the rotor blade.

DO NOT move as the helicopter lands.

4 Once the helicopter has landed, wait for a crewman to meet you.

DO NOT approach the helicopter before being asked to do so by the rescue crew.
DO NOT touch winch lines until they reach the ground; they carry a static electrical charge until earthed.

IF asked to approach, lower your head and walk to the door indicated.

REGULATIONS AND LEGISLATION

First aid may be practised in any situation where accidents or illnesses have occurred. In many instances, the first person on the scene is a volunteer who wants to help, rather than someone who is medically trained. That person may or may not have knowledge of first-aid procedures and treatments. However, in some circumstances the provision of first aid and first-aid responsibilities are defined by statutes. In the Republic of Ireland, these apply to the workplace and to mass gatherings.

FIRST AID AT WORK

The Safety, Health and Welfare at Work (General Application) Regulations, 1993 (S. I. No. 44 of 1993) place a general duty on employers to make first-aid provision for employees in case of injury or illness at the workplace.

Employers have a duty to provide first-aid equipment at all places of work where working conditions require it. Depending on the size and/or specific hazards of the undertaking or establishment, occupational first aiders must also be provided.

Necessary external contacts must be made as regards first-aid and emergency medical care. Information must be provided to employees and/or safety representatives as regards first-aid facilities and arrangements in place.

Occupational first-aiders are required to be trained and certified as competent at least once every three years by a recognised occupational first-aid instructor.

Recording first aid administered at work

Following an incident, the following details should be noted:
- full name and address of the casualty;
- casualty's occupation;
- date when entry made;
- date and time of accident;
- place and circumstances of accident (describe the work process being performed by the casualty at the time);
- details of injury and treatment given;
- signature of person making the entry.

FIRST AID AT MASS GATHERINGS

The Hamilton Report was published in 1990 following the Hillsborough football ground disaster. This report made many recommendations and stated that there should be a standard approach to the provision of medical and First-Aid facilities at sport's stadiums and at other events where large numbers of people gather for recreational activity.

The Report's recommendations included:
- at least one trained First Aider per 2,500 people;
- at least one approved and designated first-aid room;
- at least two doctors at any event, one of whom should be Site Medical Officer;
- one fully-equipped ambulance, at any event with an expected crowd of 5,000;
- medical staff should have recognisable identification, access to public address systems, and secure communication lines.

The responsibility for providing the necessary level of first aid facilities rests with the promoter of the event.

DUTY OF CARE

Providing First Aiders practise their skills in accordance with proper accepted first-aid practice, it is unlikely that a civil action for alleged negligence in the application of first aid would succeed. By legal definition, correct first-aid practice is that which is approved by the Voluntary Aid Societies and the Irish Red Cross Society for publication in the manual, where this is used in the training of the First Aider.

EMERGENCY FIRST AID

19

This section has been designed to help you administer effective first aid instantaneously for conditions that are life-threatening or very serious. It is positioned at the back of the *Manual* for quick access in an emergency, and is also provided as a separate booklet for you to carry with you at all times.

Read the quick-reference action plan on pages 252–3, which will help you to establish your priorities and guide you through the correct course of action for dealing with a conscious or an unconscious casualty.

HOW TO USE THIS SECTION

Recognition lists help you to make quick diagnosis

Precaution boxes help you to decide on best course of action

Action summaries enable you to give quick and effective treatment

Cross-references refer you to relevant chapters in book

Bullet points allow you to access information quickly

Photographs show you how to treat casualty step-by-step

CONTENTS

ACTION IN AN EMERGENCY

1 ASSESS THE SITUATION

Are there any risks to **you** or the **casualty**?

YES →

- Put your safety first.
- If possible, remove the danger from the casualty.
- If not possible, remove the casualty from danger.
- When it is safe:

- Move on to **step 4** and carry out the resuscitation sequence **for one minute**, before calling an ambulance.

NO ↓

2 ASSESS THE CASUALTY

Is the casualty visibly conscious? If he has collapsed, does he respond to shaking of the shoulders?

NO →

3 ASSESS THE CONDITION

Is the condition due to **injury**, **drowning**, or is the casualty an **infant**?

YES → **ARE YOU ALONE?**

YES ↑

NO ↓

ARE YOU ALONE? **NO** →

YES ↓

- Call an ambulance immediately.
- Move on to **step 4** and carry out the resuscitation sequence.

NO ↓

- Ask a helper to call an ambulance, and to pass on details of the casualty's condition.
- Move on to **step 4** and carry out the resuscitation sequence.

YES ↓

- Treat the casualty and call for an ambulance if necessary.

TREATMENTS FOR OTHER CONDITIONS

4 OPEN THE AIRWAY; CHECK BREATHING

Gently tilt the casualty's head well back and check for breathing (*see page 254*).

Is the casualty breathing?

NO

YES → ◆ Place the casualty in the recovery position (*see page 256*).

5 BREATHE FOR THE CASUALTY

ADULT: Give **two** breaths of mouth-to-mouth ventilation (*see page 258*).

CHILD/BABY: Give **five** ventilations (*see page 259*).

Has breathing returned?

NO

YES →

6 CHECK FOR CIRCULATION

Feel for a pulse for **ten** seconds and look for signs of recovery (*see page 260*).

Is there a pulse or any sign of circulation?

NO

YES → ◆ Continue with ventilations (*see step 5*).
◆ Check the pulse and look for signs of recovery after every minute.

7 COMMENCE CPR

ADULT: Alternate **15** chest compressions with **two** ventilations (*see page 260*); repeat as needed.

CHILD/BABY: Give **five** compressions to **one** ventilation (*see page 261*).

253

ASSESS THE CASUALTY

ADULT

1 CHECK RESPONSE

▶ Ask a question, such as "What's happened?", loudly and clearly or give a command: "Open your eyes".
▶ Gently shake the casualty's shoulders.
▶ **IF there is no response**, call for help, then proceed to step 2.
▶ **IF the casualty is conscious**, treat as necessary (*see pages 262–79*).

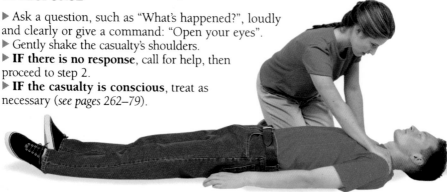

2 OPEN AIRWAY

▶ Place two fingers under the casualty's chin and your other hand on his forehead, and tilt his head well back.

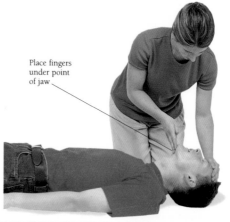

Place fingers under point of jaw

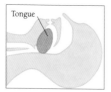

Tongue

Closed airway

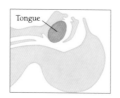

Tongue

Open airway

3 CHECK BREATHING

▶ Check his breathing for up to five seconds, by looking for chest movement, listening for sounds of breathing, and feeling for breath on your cheek.
IF breathing is absent, breathe for the casualty (*see page 258*).
IF breathing is present, place the casualty in the recovery position (*see page 256*).

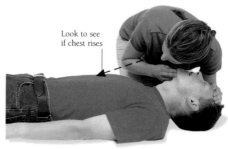

Look to see if chest rises

BABY OR CHILD (AGED 0–8)

1 CHECK RESPONSE

▶ Try to stimulate a baby by talking to her or tapping the sole of her foot.
▶ Try to stimulate a child by talking to her or gently shaking her.

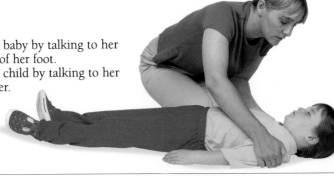

2 OPEN AIRWAY

▶ Place one finger under a baby's chin and tilt head only very slightly.
▶ Place two fingers under a child's chin and one hand on her forehead, and gently tilt her head back.

For baby

3 CHECK BREATHING

▶ Check the casualty's breathing for up to five seconds by looking for chest movement, listening for breathing sounds, and feeling for breath on your cheek.
IF breathing is absent, breathe for the casualty (*see page 259*).
IF breathing is present, place the casualty in the recovery position (*see page 257*).

For baby

Look to see if chest rises

THE RECOVERY POSITION

1 OPEN AIRWAY AND STRAIGHTEN LIMBS

▶ Place two fingers under the casualty's chin and one hand on his forehead, and gently tilt his head well back.
▶ Straighten his limbs.
▶ Tuck the hand nearest to you, arm straight and palm upwards, under his thigh.

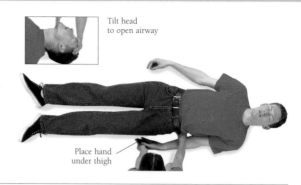

Tilt head to open airway

Place hand under thigh

2 POSITION FAR ARM, HAND, AND KNEE

▶ Bring the furthest arm from you across the casualty's chest.
▶ Place his hand, palm outwards, against his cheek.
▶ Using your other hand, pull up the casualty's far leg, just above the knee.

3 ROLL CASUALTY TOWARDS YOU

▶ Keeping the casualty's hand pressed against his cheek, pull on the far leg and roll him towards you, until he is lying on his side.

4 STEADY CASUALTY'S BODY

▶ Use your knees for support to prevent the casualty from rolling too far forwards.
▶ Bend the casualty's upper leg at the knee so that it is at a right angle to his body.

5 MAKE ANY NECESSARY ADJUSTMENTS

▶ Ensure that the casualty's head is tilted well back to keep his airway open (*see inset*).
▶ Check that the casualty's lower arm is free, and lying alongside his back, with his palm facing uppermost.

Tilt head to open airway

BABY (UNDER ONE)

▶ Cradle the baby in your arms with his head tilted downwards to prevent him from choking on his tongue or inhaling vomit.

CHILD (AGED 1–8)

▶ Place the child in the recovery position to prevent her from choking on her tongue or inhaling vomit. The procedure for placing her in this position is the same as for an adult (*see opposite*).

Tilt head to open airway

PRECAUTION

IF you suspect back or neck injuries, modify the recovery position as follows:
◆ ensure that the head and neck are supported at all times;
◆ place the arm furthest from you over the casualty's chest, not under his cheek (*see step 2*).

Keep casualty's head and trunk aligned throughout turn

257

BREATHE FOR THE CASUALTY

1 REMOVE ANY OBVIOUS OBSTRUCTION

▶ Place the casualty flat on his back.
▶ Check his mouth and, using one finger, remove any *obvious* obstruction.

Sweep finger around mouth to hook out obstruction

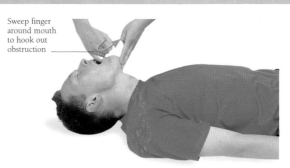

2 OPEN AIRWAY

▶ Place two fingers under the casualty's chin and one hand on his forehead, and gently tilt the head well back.

3 PINCH CASUALTY'S NOSE

▶ Use your thumb and index finger to pinch the casualty's nose firmly.
▶ Make sure that his nostrils are tightly closed to prevent air from escaping.

4 GIVE MOUTH-TO-MOUTH VENTILATION

▶ Take a full breath. Place your lips around the casualty's lips and make a good seal.
▶ Blow into the mouth until the chest rises. Take about two seconds for full inflation.

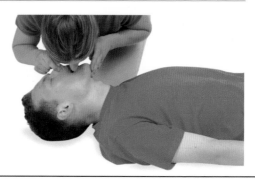

5 REPEAT BREATH AND ASSESS CASUALTY

▶ Keeping your hands in the same position, remove your lips and allow the chest to fall fully.
▶ Repeat mouth-to-mouth ventilation once more.
▶ Check the pulse and look for signs of recovery (*see page 260*).
IF the pulse is absent, commence Cardio-pulmonary Resuscitation (known as CPR, *see page 260*).
IF the pulse is present, continue with mouth-to-mouth ventilation. Re-check the pulse and look for other signs of recovery after every ten breaths.
IF breathing returns, place the casualty in the recovery position (*see page 256*).

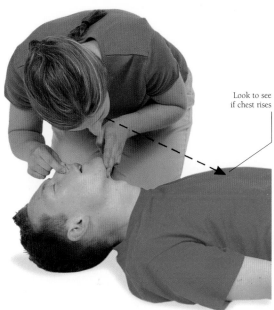

Look to see
if chest rises

FOR A BABY (UNDER ONE) OR A CHILD (AGED 1–8)

GIVE MOUTH-TO-MOUTH VENTILATION FOR ONE MINUTE

▶ Carefully remove any *obvious* obstruction from the mouth.
▶ Seal your lips tightly around the mouth and nose for a baby, or just the mouth for a child.
▶ Breathe into the lungs until the chest rises.
▶ Give two breaths.
▶ Check the pulse (*see page 261*) and look for other signs of recovery.
IF the pulse is absent, commence Cardio-pulmonary Resuscitation (CPR, *see page 261*).
IF the pulse is present, continue artificial ventilation for one minute and then call an ambulance.

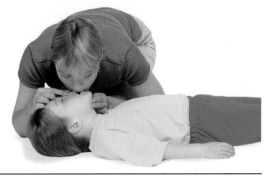

COMMENCE CPR

ADULT

1 CHECK CASUALTY FOR CIRCULATION

▶ Check the casualty's carotid pulse for ten seconds.

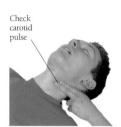

Check carotid pulse

▶ **IF you cannot find the pulse**, begin CPR immediately.

2 POSITION HANDS FOR CHEST COMPRESSIONS

▶ Place the middle finger of your lower hand over the point where the lowermost ribs meet the breastbone.

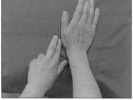

Slide heel of hand down

▶ Place your index finger above it on the breastbone.
▶ Place the heel of your other hand on the breastbone; slide it down to meet your index finger.
▶ Place the heel of your first hand on top of the other hand, and interlock your fingers.

Interlock fingers

3 GIVE CHEST COMPRESSIONS AND MOUTH-TO-MOUTH

▶ Lean well over the casualty with your arms straight.
▶ Press down vertically on the breastbone and depress it by approximately 4–5 cm (1½–2 in).
▶ Complete 15 chest compressions, aiming for about 100 per minute.
▶ Give two breaths of mouth-to-mouth ventilation (*see page 258*).
▶ Continue alternating 15 chest compressions with two breaths of mouth-to-mouth ventilation.

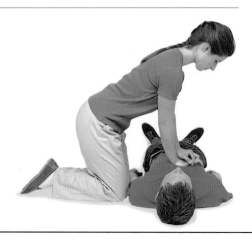

BABY (UNDER ONE)

1 ASSESS BABY FOR CIRCULATION

▶ Check the pulse for ten seconds: use two fingers to feel for a pulse on the inside of the baby's upper arm.
▶ **IF you cannot find a pulse** and there are no other signs of recovery, begin chest compressions.

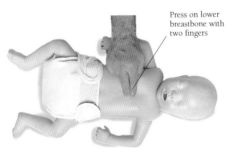

Press on lower breastbone with two fingers

2 GIVE CHEST COMPRESSIONS AND MOUTH-TO-MOUTH

▶ Place the tips of two fingers one finger's breadth below the nipple line.
▶ Press down at this point to a depth of 1.25–2.5cm (½–1in). Do this five times at a rate of at least 100 chest compressions per minute.
▶ Give one gentle breath of mouth-to-mouth ventilation (*see page 259*). Alternate five compressions with one ventilation for one minute before calling an ambulance; continue while waiting for help.

CHILD (AGED 1–8)

▶ **IF the child is nine years** or over, treat as for an adult (*see opposite*).

1 ASSESS CHILD FOR CIRCULATION

▶ Check the pulse for ten seconds: use two fingers to feel in the hollow between the windpipe and the large muscle on either side of the neck.
IF you cannot find a pulse and there are no other signs of recovery, begin chest compressions.

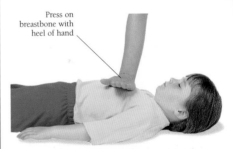

Press on breastbone with heel of hand

2 GIVE CHEST COMPRESSIONS AND MOUTH-TO-MOUTH

▶ Position your hand as you would for an adult (*see opposite*), but use the heel of one hand only.
▶ Press down 2.5–3.75cm (1–1½in). Do this five times at a rate of about 100 chest compressions per minute.
▶ Give one breath of mouth-to-mouth ventilation (*see page 259*). Alternate five compressions with one ventilation for one minute before calling an ambulance; continue while waiting for help.

ASTHMA ATTACK

SEE ALSO: PAGES 59–74

RECOGNITION

- ◆ Difficulty in breathing

There may be:

- ◆ Wheezing
- ◆ Difficulty in speaking
- ◆ Grey-blue skin
- ◆ Dry, tickly cough

PRECAUTIONS

■ **DO NOT** lay the casualty down.

■ **DO NOT** use a preventer inhaler.

■ **IF** the casualty falls unconscious, be prepared to resuscitate if necessary (*see pages 252–61*).

■ **IF** the inhaler has no effect after 5–10 minutes, ☎ DIAL 999 OR 112 FOR AN AMBULANCE. Ask the casualty to use her inhaler every 5–10 minutes. Monitor and *record* breathing and pulse every ten minutes.

ACTION

MAKE CASUALTY COMFORTABLE

LET CASUALTY USE INHALER

ENCOURAGE CASUALTY TO BREATHE SLOWLY

1 MAKE CASUALTY COMFORTABLE

▶ Keep calm and reassure the casualty.
▶ Help her into a position which she finds most comfortable; sitting slightly forwards is usually best.
▶ Tell her to try to take slow, deep breaths.

2 LET CASUALTY USE INHALER

▶ Help the casualty to find her *reliever* inhaler (it is usually blue).
▶ Allow the casualty to use the inhaler; it should take effect within minutes.

3 ENCOURAGE CASUALTY TO BREATHE SLOWLY

▶ If the attack eases within 5–10 minutes, encourage the casualty to take another dose from her inhaler and to breathe slowly and deeply.
▶ Tell the casualty to inform her doctor of the attack if it is severe or if it is her first attack.

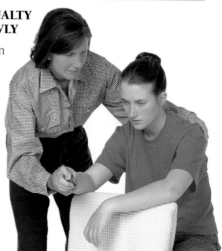

CHOKING: ADULT

SEE ALSO:
PAGES 59–74

RECOGNITION

- ◆ Difficulty in speaking and breathing

There may be:

- ◆ Congested face and neck initially
- ◆ Distress

Later:

- ◆ Grey-blue skin

PRECAUTIONS

- ■ **IF** the casualty becomes unconscious, be prepared to resuscitate if necessary (*see pages 252–60*).

ACTION

HOLD CASUALTY
FROM BEHIND

GIVE UP TO FIVE
ABDOMINAL
THRUSTS

REPEAT ENTIRE
SEQUENCE UNTIL
OBSTRUCTION
CLEARS OR
CASUALTY IS
UNCONSCIOUS

CALL AN
AMBULANCE

1 HOLD CASUALTY FROM BEHIND

▶ Stand behind the casualty.
▶ Put your arms around him; put one fist, thumb inwards, above his navel and below the lower tip of his breastbone.

2 GIVE UP TO FIVE ABDOMINAL THRUSTS

▶ Link your hands and pull sharply inwards and upwards up to five times.

Place thumb
side of fist
against
abdomen

3 REPEAT ENTIRE SEQUENCE

▶ Continue abdominal thrusts (*see steps 1–2*) until the obstruction clears or the casualty becomes unconscious.
▶ If unsuccessful,
☎ *DIAL 999 FOR 112 FOR AN AMBULANCE*

Maintain hand
position
between navel
and breastbone

263

CHOKING: CHILD

SEE ALSO:
PAGES 59–74

RECOGNITION

◆ Difficulty in speaking and breathing
◆ Flushed face and neck
◆ Distress

Later:
◆ Grey-blue skin

PRECAUTIONS

■ **DO NOT** feel blindly down the throat.

■ **IF** the child becomes unconscious, be ready to resuscitate if necessary (*see* pages 252–61).

ACTION

GIVE
ABDOMINAL
THRUSTS

CHECK MOUTH

CONTINUE
ABDOMINAL
THRUSTS

CHECK MOUTH

CALL
AMBULANCE
AFTER ONE
MINUTE, THEN
REPEAT
ENTIRE
SEQUENCE

1 GIVE ABDOMINAL THRUSTS

▶ Stand or kneel behind the child.
▶ Make a fist and place it against his abdomen, midway between his navel and the lower tip of his breastbone.
▶ Grasp your fist with your other hand and press into the chest with a sharp inward thrust, at a rate of about one every three seconds.
▶ Check child's mouth to see if the obstruction has cleared.

Thumb side of fist against abdomen

2 CONTINUE ABDOMINAL THRUSTS

▶ Continue with the abdominal thrusts for one minute or until the obstruction clears or the casualty becomes unconscious. Check mouth to see if foreign object has cleared.

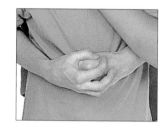

3 ☎ DIAL 999 OR 112 FOR AN AMBULANCE

▶ If the obstruction has not cleared after giving abdominal thrusts for one minute, call for help. Repeat the cycle of abdominal thrusts until the ambulance arrives.

CHOKING: BABY

SEE ALSO:
PAGES 59–74

RECOGNITION

- ◆ Difficulty in breathing
- ◆ Flushed face and neck
- ◆ Strange noises or no sound

Later:

- ◆ Grey-blue skin

PRECAUTIONS

- ■ **DO NOT** feel blindly down the throat.

- ■ **DO NOT** use abdominal thrusts on a baby.

- ■ **IF** at any stage the baby becomes unconscious, begin resuscitation (see pages 252–61).

ACTION

GIVE FIVE
BACK SLAPS

CHECK BABY'S
MOUTH

GIVE FIVE
CHEST THRUSTS

CHECK MOUTH

↓

CALL
AMBULANCE
THEN REPEAT
ENTIRE
SEQUENCE

1 GIVE FIVE BACK SLAPS

- ▶ Lay the baby face down along your forearm.
- ▶ Give five sharp slaps on his back.
- ▶ Turn the baby face up on your arm or lap with head lower than trunk.

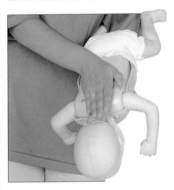

2 CHECK BABY'S MOUTH

- ▶ Use one finger to remove any *obvious* obstruction, without touching the baby's throat.
- ▶ If back slaps have failed, proceed to next step.

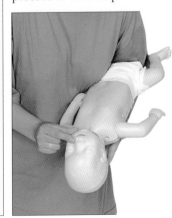

3 GIVE FIVE CHEST THRUSTS

- ▶ Place two fingertips on the lower half of the baby's breastbone, one finger's breadth below the nipples.
- ▶ Give five sharp thrusts into the chest.
- ▶ Check his mouth again.

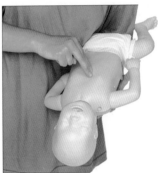

4 REPEAT ENTIRE SEQUENCE

- ▶ Repeat steps 1–3 three times.
- ▶ If the obstruction has not cleared, or the baby becomes unconscious, take the baby with you to ☎ **DIAL 999 OR 112 FOR AMBULANCE**.
- ▶ If baby is conscious, repeat steps 1–3 until help arrives.

HEART ATTACK

SEE ALSO:
PAGES 75–84

RECOGNITION

There may be:

◆ Vice-like chest pain, spreading to left arm

◆ Breathlessness

◆ Discomfort, like indigestion

◆ Sudden faintness

◆ A sense of impending doom

◆ Ashen skin

◆ Blueness at lips

◆ A rapid, then weakening, pulse

◆ Sudden collapse

PRECAUTIONS

■ **DO NOT** give any fluids.

■ **IF** the casualty becomes unconscious, be prepared to resuscitate if necessary (*see pages 252–60*).

ACTION

MAKE CASUALTY
COMFORTABLE

⬇

CALL
AMBULANCE

⬇

MONITOR
BREATHING AND
PULSE

⬇

GIVE CASUALTY
ASPIRIN

1 MAKE CASUALTY COMFORTABLE

▶ Help the casualty into a half-sitting position.

▶ Support his head, shoulders, and knees.

▶ If the casualty has tablets or a puffer aerosol for angina, let him administer it himself. Help him if necessary.

▶ Reassure casualty.

2 ☎ DIAL 999 OR 112 FOR AN AMBULANCE

▶ Tell the controller that you suspect a heart attack.

▶ Call the casualty's doctor also, if he asks you to do so.

3 MONITOR BREATHING AND PULSE

▶ Encourage the casualty to rest and keep any bystanders at a distance.

▶ Monitor and *record* the casualty's breathing and pulse constantly.

4 GIVE CASUALTY ASPIRIN

▶ Give the casualty one tablet of aspirin, if available.

▶ Tell him to *chew* it slowly.

SEVERE BLEEDING

SEE ALSO:
PAGES 85–106

PRECAUTIONS

■ **DO NOT** apply a tourniquet.

■ **IF** there is an embedded object in the wound, apply pressure on either side of the wound, and pad around it before bandaging.

■ **IF** possible, wear gloves to protect against infection.

■ **IF** the casualty becomes unconscious, place her in the recovery position, and be ready to resuscitate if needed (*see pages 252–61*).

ACTION

APPLY PRESSURE
TO WOUND

RAISE AND
SUPPORT
INJURED PART

BANDAGE
WOUND

CALL
AMBULANCE

TREAT FOR
SHOCK AND
MONITOR
CASUALTY

1 APPLY PRESSURE TO WOUND

▶ Remove or cut the casualty's clothing to expose wound.
▶ If a sterile dressing or pad is *immediately* available, cover the wound.
▶ Apply direct pressure over the wound with your fingers or palm of your hand.

2 RAISE AND SUPPORT INJURED PART

▶ Make sure the injured part is raised.
▶ Lay the casualty down.
▶ Handle the injured part gently if you suspect the injury involves a fracture.

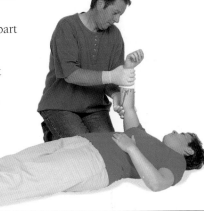

3 BANDAGE WOUND

▶ Apply a sterile dressing over any original pad, and bandage firmly in place.
▶ Bandage another pad on top if blood seeps through.
▶ Check the circulation beyond the bandage at intervals; loosen it if needed.

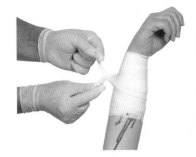

4 ☎ DIAL 999 OR 112 FOR AN AMBULANCE

▶ Give details of the site of the injury and the extent of the bleeding when you telephone.

5 TREAT FOR SHOCK AND MONITOR CASUALTY

▶ Treat for shock (*see page 268*).
▶ Monitor and *record* breathing, pulse, and level of response.

SHOCK

SEE ALSO:
PAGES 75–84

RECOGNITION

- ◆ A rapid pulse
- ◆ Grey-blue skin, especially on lips
- ◆ Sweating and cold, clammy skin

Later:

- ◆ Weakness and giddiness
- ◆ Nausea or thirst
- ◆ Rapid, shallow breathing
- ◆ A weak pulse

Eventually:

- ◆ Restlessness
- ◆ Gasping for air
- ◆ Unconsciousness
- ◆ Cardiac arrest

PRECAUTIONS

- ■ **DO NOT** leave the casualty alone, except to call an ambulance.

- ■ **DO NOT** let the casualty eat, move, smoke, or drink.

ACTION

LAY CASUALTY DOWN

⬇

LOOSEN TIGHT CLOTHING

⬇

CALL AMBULANCE

⬇

MONITOR BREATHING AND PULSE

1 LAY CASUALTY DOWN

▶ Use a blanket to protect him from the cold ground.
▶ Raise and support his legs as high as possible.
▶ Treat any cause of shock, such as bleeding.

2 LOOSEN TIGHT CLOTHING

▶ Undo anything that constricts his neck, chest, and waist.

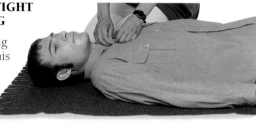

3 ☎ *DIAL 999 OR 112 FOR AN AMBULANCE*

▶ Give details of the cause of shock, if known.

4 MONITOR BREATHING AND PULSE

▶ Monitor and *record* breathing, pulse, and level of response every ten minutes.
▶ Be prepared to resuscitate if necessary (*see pages 252–61*).

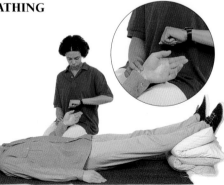

EYE INJURY

SEE ALSO:
PAGES 98 and 165–6

RECOGNITION

◆ Intense pain in the affected eye

There may also be:

◆ A visible wound

◆ A bloodshot eye if wound is not visible

◆ Partial or total loss of vision

◆ Leakage of blood or clear fluid from the injured eye

PRECAUTIONS

■ **DO NOT** touch the eye or any contact lens, or allow the casualty to rub the eye.

■ **IF** it will take some time to obtain medical aid, bandage an eye pad in place over the injured eye.

ACTION

SUPPORT CASUALTY'S HEAD

⬇

GIVE EYE DRESSING TO CASUALTY

⬇

TAKE OR SEND CASUALTY TO HOSPITAL

1 SUPPORT CASUALTY'S HEAD

▶ Lay casualty down, holding her head in a comfortable position. Keep it as still as possible.

▶ Tell the casualty to keep her "good" eye still, as movement of the uninjured eye may damage the injured eye further.

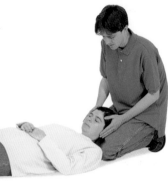

2 GIVE EYE DRESSING TO CASUALTY

▶ Give the casualty a sterile dressing or clean pad, and ask her to hold it over the injured eye and to keep her uninjured eye closed.

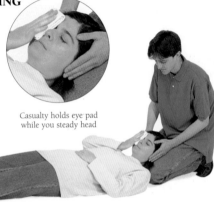

Casualty holds eye pad while you steady head

3 TAKE OR SEND CASUALTY TO HOSPITAL

▶ Call an ambulance if you cannot transport the casualty lying down.

Provide support for casualty's head

UNCONSCIOUSNESS

SEE ALSO:
PAGES 107–22

PRECAUTIONS

- **DO NOT** leave the casualty alone, except to call an ambulance.

- **DO NOT** give anything by mouth.

- Monitor and *record* breathing, pulse, and response every ten minutes.

- **IF** necessary, be prepared to resuscitate (*see pages 252–61*).

ACTION

ASSESS CASUALTY'S RESPONSE

CALL AMBULANCE

OPEN AIRWAY; CHECK BREATHING AND PULSE

EXAMINE AND TREAT CASUALTY

PLACE CASUALTY IN RECOVERY POSITION

1 ASSESS RESPONSE
☎ *DIAL 999 OR 112 FOR AMBULANCE*

▶ Gently shake the casualty's shoulders. Question the casualty, speaking loudly and clearly.
▶ *Record* her level of response.
▶ Call for help.

2 OPEN AIRWAY; CHECK BREATHING AND PULSE

▶ Place two fingers under the casualty's chin and one hand on her forehead: tilt her head back.
▶ Check breathing and pulse (*see pages 254 and 260*).

3 EXAMINE AND TREAT CASUALTY

▶ Examine the casualty.
▶ Control bleeding (*see page 267*).
▶ Support suspected fractures (*see page 274*).
▶ Treat any other life-threatening conditions.

4 PLACE CASUALTY IN RECOVERY POSITION

▶ Take extra care if you suspect spinal injury (*see page 257*).

HEAD INJURY

SEE ALSO:
PAGES 90 and 113–5

PRECAUTIONS

■ **IF** possible, wear gloves to protect against infection.

■ **IF** the casualty becomes unconscious, place in recovery position *(see page 256)*, and resuscitate if necessary *(see pages 252–61)*.

■ **IF** the casualty is unconscious for three minutes, ☎ DIAL 999 OR 112 FOR AN AMBULANCE.

■ **IF** the bleeding does not stop, reapply pressure on the wound, and add another pad on top of the first.

ACTION

CONTROL
BLEEDING

⬇

SECURE
DRESSING WITH
BANDAGE

⬇

LAY CASUALTY
DOWN

⬇

TAKE OR SEND
CASUALTY TO
HOSPITAL

1 CONTROL BLEEDING

▶ Replace any displaced skin flaps.
▶ Place a sterile dressing or clean pad over the wound and apply firm, direct pressure.

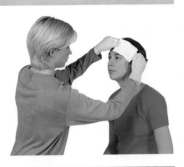

2 SECURE DRESSING WITH BANDAGE

▶ Secure the dressing over the wound with a roller bandage.

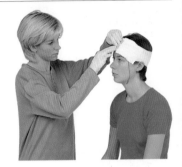

3 LAY CASUALTY DOWN

▶ Ensure her head and shoulders are slightly raised.
▶ Make sure that she is comfortable.

4 TAKE OR SEND CASUALTY TO HOSPITAL

▶ Call an ambulance if you cannot transport the casualty lying down.

CONVULSIONS: ADULT

SEE ALSO:
PAGES 107–22

RECOGNITION

- ◆ Unconsciousness
- ◆ Rigidity
- ◆ Breathing may cease
- ◆ Convulsive movements
- ◆ Muscles relax
- ◆ Casualty regains consciousness

PRECAUTIONS

■ **DO NOT** restrain the casualty forcibly.

■ **IF** the casualty is unconscious for more than ten minutes, is having repeated fits, or it is her first fit, ☎ DIAL 999 OR 112 FOR AN AMBULANCE. Note the time and duration of the fit.

ACTION

SUPPORT CASUALTY

⬇

PROTECT CASUALTY

⬇

LOOSEN CASUALTY'S CLOTHING

⬇

PLACE CASUALTY IN RECOVERY POSITION

1 SUPPORT CASUALTY

▶ Try to ease her fall.
▶ Talk to her calmly and reassuringly.

2 PROTECT CASUALTY

▶ Clear away any surrounding objects to prevent injury to the casualty.
▶ Ask bystanders to keep clear.

3 LOOSEN CASUALTY'S CLOTHING

▶ Undo tight clothing around the casualty's neck.
▶ Protect the casualty's head, if possible, with soft material, until the convulsions cease.

4 PLACE CASUALTY IN RECOVERY POSITION

▶ Place the casualty in the recovery position (*see page 256*).
▶ Stay until the casualty is fully recovered.

CONVULSIONS: CHILD

SEE ALSO:
PAGES 107–22

RECOGNITION

◆ Fever
◆ Violent muscle twitching

There may be:

◆ Twitching of the face
◆ Breath-holding
◆ Drooling at the mouth
◆ Loss of, or impaired, consciousness

ACTION

COOL CHILD

⬇

PROTECT CHILD FROM INJURY

⬇

SPONGE WITH TEPID WATER

⬇

PUT CHILD IN RECOVERY POSITION

⬇

CALL AMBULANCE

1 COOL CHILD

▶ Remove her clothing.
▶ Ensure a good supply of cool air.

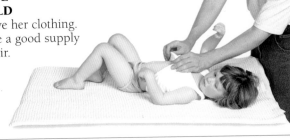

2 PROTECT CHILD FROM INJURY

▶ Clear away any nearby objects.
▶ Surround the child with soft padding.

3 SPONGE WITH TEPID WATER

▶ Start at her head and work down.

4 PUT CHILD IN RECOVERY POSITION

▶ Once the convulsions have ceased, put the child in the recovery position (*see page 257*).
▶ Keep her head tilted well back.

5 ☎ DIAL 999 OR 112 FOR AN AMBULANCE

BROKEN BONES

SEE ALSO:
PAGES 123–54

PRECAUTIONS

- **DO NOT** attempt to bandage if medical assistance is on its way.

- **DO NOT** attempt to move the injured limb unnecessarily.

- **DO NOT** allow a casualty with a suspected fracture to have anything to eat or drink.

ACTION

STEADY AND SUPPORT INJURED PART

PROTECT INJURY WITH PADDING

TAKE OR SEND CASUALTY TO HOSPITAL

1 STEADY AND SUPPORT INJURED PART

▶ Help the casualty to support the affected part above and below the injury in the most comfortable position.

2 PROTECT INJURY WITH PADDING

▶ Place padding, such as towels or cushions, around the affected part, and support it in position.

3 TAKE OR SEND CASUALTY TO HOSPITAL

▶ Call for an ambulance if you are unable to transport the casualty to hospital.

BACK INJURY

SEE ALSO: PAGES 142–48

RECOGNITION

◆ Pain in neck or back

◆ A step or twist in curve of spine

◆ Tenderness to touch on spine

There may be:

◆ Loss of control over movement of limbs

◆ Loss of, or abnormal, sensation

◆ Difficulty in breathing

PRECAUTIONS

■ **DO NOT** move the casualty unless she is in danger or she becomes unconscious.

■ **IF** the casualty becomes unconscious, put her into recovery position while keeping the head and neck aligned with the spine. Be ready to resuscitate if necessary (*see pages 252–61*).

ACTION

STEADY AND
SUPPORT HEAD

SUPPORT
CASUALTY'S NECK

CALL
AMBULANCE

1 STEADY AND SUPPORT HEAD

▶ Reassure casualty and tell her not to move.

▶ Keep the head, neck, and spine aligned by placing your hands over the casualty's ears to hold her head still.

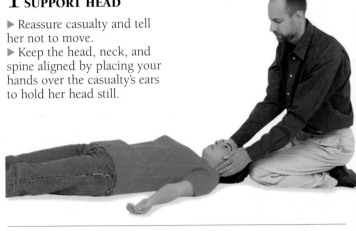

2 SUPPORT CASUALTY'S NECK

▶ If you suspect a neck or spinal injury, ask a helper to place rolled towels or other padding around the casualty's neck and shoulders.

▶ Keep holding her head *throughout*.

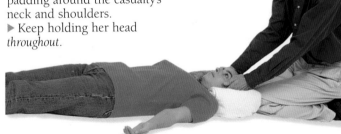

3 ☎ DIAL 999 OR 112 FOR AN AMBULANCE

▶ If possible, ask a helper to call an ambulance and to inform the controller that spinal injury is suspected.

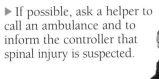

BURNS: TREATMENT

SEE ALSO:
PAGES 155–66

PRECAUTIONS

■ **DO NOT** apply lotions, ointment, or fat to a burn, or touch the injured area or burst any blisters.

■ **DO NOT** remove anything sticking to the burn.

■ **IF** the burn is to the face, do not cover it. Keep cooling with water until help arrives.

■ **IF** the burn is large or deep, treat the casualty for shock (*see page 268*). ☎ DIAL 999 OR 112 FOR AN AMBULANCE. Monitor and *record* breathing, pulse, and level of response every ten minutes.

■ **IF** the burn is chemical, rinse for at least 20 minutes.

ACTION

COOL BURN

REMOVE ANY CONSTRICTIONS

COVER BURN

TAKE OR SEND CASUALTY TO HOSPITAL

1 COOL BURN

▶ Make the casualty comfortable.
▶ Pour cold liquid on injury, or immerse in water for ten minutes.
▶ While cooling the burn, watch for signs of difficulty in breathing. Be ready to resuscitate if needed (*see pages 252–61*).

2 REMOVE ANY CONSTRICTIONS

▶ Carefully remove any clothing or jewellery from the affected area before the injury starts to swell.

3 COVER BURN

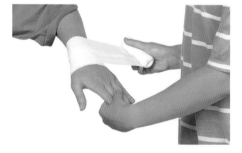

▶ Cover the burn and surrounding area with a sterile dressing, or a clean piece of material.
▶ Reassure the casualty.

4 TAKE OR SEND CASUALTY TO HOSPITAL

▶ Call an ambulance if you cannot transport the casualty to hospital.
▶ *Record* details of the casualty's injuries and any possible hazards.

BURNS: ACTION AND SAFETY

SEE ALSO:
PAGES 15–26

PRECAUTIONS

Fires

- **DO NOT** attempt to fight a fire unless it is safe and you have called the emergency services.

- **DO NOT** enter a burning building.

- **DO NOT** enter a smoke or fume-filled room.

PRECAUTIONS

Clothing on Fire

- **DO NOT** use flammable materials to try to smother flames.

- **DO NOT** let the casualty run about or go outdoors.

PRECAUTIONS

Electrical Injuries

- **DO NOT** go within 18 metres (20 yards) of live high-voltage electrical sources.

PRECAUTIONS

Chemical Spills

- **DO NOT** delay starting treatment by searching for antidote.

- **NEVER** attempt to neutralise acid or alkali burns.

FIRES

▶ ☎ *DIAL 999 OR 112 FOR THE EMERGENCY SERVICES*, and ask for the fire brigade.
▶ Remove the casualty from danger, if it is safe to do so.

CLOTHING ON FIRE

▶ Either:
◆ STOP, DROP, WRAP, and ROLL the casualty on the ground; or
◆ lay the casualty down, burning side upwards, and douse him with water.

ELECTRICAL INJURIES

▶ Stay clear of the casualty until:
◆ you have switched off a domestic current; or
◆ you have been officially informed that a high-voltage current has been switched off and isolated.

CHEMICAL SPILLS

▶ Protect yourself from corrosive chemicals.
▶ Make sure that any contaminated rinsing water drains away safely.
▶ Be aware of the dangers of toxic fumes.
▶ Seal the chemical container, if possible; ventilate the area.

SWALLOWED POISONS

SEE ALSO:
PAGES 183–90

PRECAUTIONS

- **DO NOT** attempt to induce vomiting.

- **IF** there is vomit in the mouth, lay the casualty on his side to allow any vomit to drain away safely.

- **IF** the casualty stops breathing, be prepared to resuscitate (*see pages 252–61*). When giving mouth-to-mouth ventilation, use a face shield to protect yourself.

- **IF** the casualty is conscious and the lips are burned, give the casualty frequent sips of cold water or milk, and seek medical advice immediately.

ACTION

CHECK AIRWAY
AND BREATHING

PLACE CASUALTY
IN RECOVERY
POSITION

CALL
AMBULANCE

FOR AN UNCONSCIOUS CASUALTY

1 CHECK AIRWAY AND BREATHING

▶ Check there is no foreign matter in the mouth (*see left*).
▶ Place two fingers under the casualty's chin and one hand on his forehead, and tilt the head well back.
▶ Check the airway and check breathing (*see pages 254 and 255*).

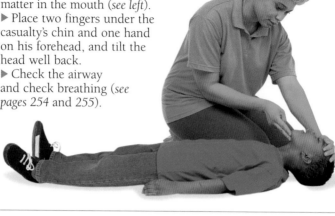

2 PLACE CASUALTY IN RECOVERY POSITION

▶ Ensure the airway remains open (*see pages 254 and 255*).

3 ☎ DIAL 999 OR 112 FOR AN AMBULANCE

▶ Give as much information as possible about the swallowed poison.
▶ Monitor and *record* breathing, pulse, and level of response every ten minutes until help arrives.

ALLERGIC REACTIONS

SEE ALSO:
PAGES 81 and 213

RECOGNITION

- ◆ Anxiety
- ◆ Red, blotchy skin
- ◆ Swelling of face and neck
- ◆ Puffiness around eyes
- ◆ Impaired breathing
- ◆ Rapid pulse

PRECAUTIONS

■ Check for an Epi-Pen or syringe of adrenaline. If necessary, assist the casualty to use it. It can save his life when given promptly.

■ **IF** the casualty becomes unconscious, place him in the recovery position (*see page 256*), and be ready to resuscitate, if necessary (*see pages 252–61*).

ACTION

CALL
AMBULANCE

▼

MAKE CASUALTY
COMFORTABLE

▼

MONITOR
CASUALTY

1 ☎ *DIAL 999 OR 112 FOR AN AMBULANCE*

▶ Pass on as much information about the cause of the allergy as possible.

2 MAKE CASUALTY COMFORTABLE

▶ A sitting position should help to relieve any breathing difficulties.

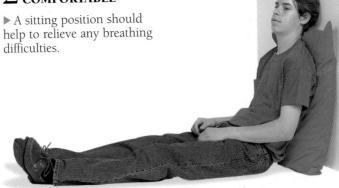

3 MONITOR CASUALTY

▶ Monitor and *record* breathing, pulse, and level of response every ten minutes until help arrives.

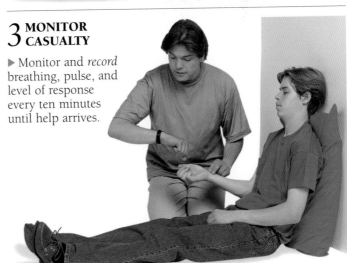

279

OBSERVATION CHART

The information from this chart will be very valuable when decisions are taken about further treatment:
- use a photocopy of it to record your observations while waiting for help;
- tick the appropriate boxes;
- update them at ten-minute intervals;
- send the completed chart, and any notes, with the casualty when he or she leaves your care.

DATE . . . . CASUALTY'S NAME . . . .

Time of observation (10-minute intervals)		10	20	30	40	50	60
Eyes Observe for reaction while testing other responses.	Open spontaneously						
	Open to speech						
	Open to painful stimulus						
	No response						
Movement Apply painful stimulus: pinch the ear lobe or skin on back of hand.	Obeys commands						
	Responds to painful stimulus						
	No response						
Speech When testing responses, speak clearly and directly, close to casualty's ear.	Responds sensibly to questions						
	Seems confused						
	Uses inappropriate words						
	Incomprehensible sounds						
	No response						
Pulse (beats per minute) Take pulse at wrist or at neck on adult (*page 260*); at inner arm on baby (*page 261*). Note rate, and whether beats are weak (**w**) or strong (**s**), regular (**reg**) or irregular (**irreg**).	Over 110						
	101-110						
	91-100						
	81-90						
	71-80						
	61-70						
	Below 61						
Breathing (breaths per minute) Note rate, and whether breathing is quiet (**q**) or noisy (**n**), easy (**e**) or difficult (**diff**).	Over 40						
	31-40						
	21-30						
	11-20						
	Below 11						

INDEX

ACKNOWLEDGMENTS

Authors of the 7th edition

St. John Ambulance
Dr Michael Webb *Medical Director (Association and Resources)*
Consultant Occupational Physician

St. Andrew's Ambulance Association
Mr Roy Scott *Chief Medical Officer*
Consultant Urologist, Royal Infirmary, Glasgow

British Red Cross
Sir Peter Beale *Chief Medical Adviser*
late Royal Army Medical Corps (retd)

Irish edition reviewed and amended by:
Dr Jane Rothwell, FRCSI., Dr John Dowling, FRCSI., DipSports Med,
Professor Gerard Bury *(Medical Advisory Committee, Irish Red Cross),*
Professor of General Practice UCD., Mr Frank Kelly, *First Aid Instructor*
(Training Committee, Irish Red Cross Society).
Editor Fergus Collins, Designer Chloë Steers.

Authors' acknowledgments
The medical authors wish to acknowledge the advice and help of many others, in particular: Anita
Eade, First Aid Training Manager, British Red Cross; Dr Tom Rogerson and Linda Allen from St. John
Ambulance; Dr Anthony Handley, Dr Douglas Chamberlain, and Dr David Zideman; Dr Virginia
Murray from the Medical Toxicology Unit, Guy's and St.Thomas's Hospital Trust; Mrs K. Jackson of
Enlighten; and the First Aid Training Officers Lyn Covey, Carol Lock, Kevin Noble, Terry Perkins,
John Perry, and Chris Pickin.

The publishers would like to thank the following for their kind permission to reproduce the photographs:
Bruce Coleman Ltd, Dr Freider Sauer. 194*br*; Natural Science Photo, Dave Fleetham, 194*l*; NHPA,
Laurie Campbell, 194*tr*; Shout Picture Company, 249*tr*.

The publishers would also like to thank:
Joanna Cameron and Halli Verrinder for the illustrations; Hilary Bird for the index; Pebbles for make-
up; Karen Sherriff Brown, Dan Fry, and Kirsty Young for additional make-up; Sarah Ashun and Andy
Crawford for additional photography; Andy Komoroski for the sets; Sarah Mackay, Fergus Muir, and
Helen Stallion for picture research; Vic Hayes Ltd, Blooming Marvellous, City Bridge Dental Practice,
and the British Red Cross for props; Shushana Jogia and Leisure Sport Ltd (Thorpe Park) for allowing
location photography; Ian Merrill for DTP work; Fergus Collins, Elaine Harries, Sarah Prest, Debbie
Voller, and Emily Wood for editorial assistance; Sue Callister, Evan Jones, Derek Lee, Annette O'Sullivan,
Julie Reid, Kate Scott, and Chloë Steers for design assistance; and all those who appeared as models.

THE IRISH RED CROSS SOCIETY

The Irish Red Cross cares for people in crisis
at home and abroad. It gives vital support during
both major emergencies and personal crises, and
provides comprehensive training in First Aid
and caring skills.
The Red Cross emblem is a symbol of protection
during armed conflict and its use is restricted
by law.

THE ORDER OF MALTA AMBULANCE CORPS

The Order of Malta Ambulance Corps is a
nationally based voluntary organisation, operating
in 90 communities throughout the Republic of
Ireland and Nothern Ireland.
The Order of Malta Ambulance Corps provides
training in occupational First Aid, basic First Aid,
and allied subjects. It also provides a First Aid
service at events throughout Ireland.